Intermediary NGOs

Kumarian Press Library of Management for Development
Selected Titles

Intermediary NGOs

The Supporting Link in Grassroots Development

Thomas F. Carroll

Kumarian Press

Intermediary NGOs: The Supporting Link in Grassroots Development

Published 1992 in the United States of America by Kumarian Press, Inc., 630 Oakwood Avenue, Suite 119, West Hartford, Connecticut 06110-1529 USA.

Cover design by Laura Augustine
Cover photographs by Miguel Sayago. Courtesy of the Inter-American Foundation.
Book design by Jenna Dixon
Typeset by Rosanne Pignone
Proofread by Sydney Landon Plum
Index prepared by Barbara DeGennaro

Printed in the United States of America by Thomson-Shore
Text printed with soy-based ink on recycled acid-free paper.

Library of Congress Cataloging-in-Publication Data

Carroll, Thomas F.
    Intermediary NGOs : the supporting link in grassroots development / Thomas F. Carroll.
        p.   cm. — (Kumarian Press library of management for development)
    Includes bibliographical references and index.
    ISBN 1-56549-010-X (cloth : alk. paper). — ISBN 1-56549-009-6 (pbk. : alk. paper)
    1. Economic development projects—Latin America. 2. Economic development projects—Latin America—Case studies. 3. Non-governmental organizations—Latin America. 4. Non-governmental organizations—Latin America—Case studies. I. Title. II. Series.
HC130.E44C37   1992
338.98—dc20   92-6424

96   95   94   93   92   5   4   3   2   1
First Printing 1992

Contents

Tables, Figures, and Boxes

Tables

Figures

Boxes

About the Author

Thomas F. Carroll is professor of economics and urban planning at George Washington University. During his four decades of involvement with development, he managed to combine scholarly pursuits with the practical concerns of international technical and financial assistance, especially in the planning and evaluation of poverty-oriented projects. He was a staff member of the Food and Agriculture Organization of the United Nations in Rome and a senior official of the Inter-American Development Bank (IDB) in Washington, D.C. He has written widely on land reform, cooperatives, rural development, and regional planning and has carried out numerous field assignments for the United Nations Development Programme, U.S. Agency for International Development, International Labor Office, Centro Internacional de Papa, International Service for National Agricultural Research, the World Bank, and other development agencies around the world. During 1986–87 he taught at the John F. Kennedy School of Government at Harvard University.

Foreword

Columbus discovered America 500 years ago, say the textbooks, although America was already there. Recently, the development establishment has "discovered" an intricate web of nongovernmental organizations (NGOs) that for many years have been quietly laboring in the field of poverty alleviation.

The NGOs have been discovered by a variety of colonizers. They are the darlings of some in the development community for whom state bureaucracies have grown insufferable. Other colonizers include ideologues of privatization who assume anything bearing a nongovernmental label is superior ipso facto. Many see NGOs as democratic counterweights to authoritarian regimes of left and right. Throughout the Americas, emerging (and amorphous) social movements are often led and stimulated by NGOs. From various corners of the world come enthusiasts who would like to see NGOs take over from resource-poor state agencies in the social sector. They argue that the delivery of goods and services works better through NGOs, which are more deeply rooted among the poor than are state bureaucracies or extension, or welfare service agencies.

Now that NGOs have been discovered, the expectations dumped upon this congeries of organizations are indeed remarkable. International development agencies have upped the volume of rhetorical and financial commitment to NGOs. The U.S. Congress has told the U.S. Agency for International Development to channel fixed portions of its budget through private voluntary organizations. European efforts at development cooperation increasingly use NGO channels. A great deal of this new attention is due to the lobbying efforts of international Northern-based NGOs, often called private voluntary organizations (PVOs) in the United States. However, the focus of attention is shifting to the hitherto much less visible Southern, developing-country-based NGOs, the subject of this volume.

Are NGOs cure-alls for the spiraling woes of the development world? Hardly. But, as this book will show, they do some things very well and with well-aimed support could do even more to help grassroots groups move from powerlessness and isolation to self-help and mobilization.

Despite the flurry of attention NGOs are receiving, little is know about this diverse group of organizations—who they are, how they work, and how one can assess their effectiveness. There is especially a lack of knowledge about national developmental NGOs that work directly with grassroots groups. To help fill the gap, the Inter-American Foundation (IAF) sponsored this study, which provides a typology for the universe of the important subset of NGOs in Latin America and the Caribbean, provides a set of criteria for assessing NGO performance, and applies these criteria to 30 well-regarded organizations. *Intermediary NGOs: The Supporting Link in Grassroots Development* is an in-depth, field-based analysis, in contrast to most other studies on this subject.

Carroll's distinction between NGOs that are more adept at service delivery and those intent on empowerment is significant. He contributes much to our understanding by separating and comparing and then interrelating the two main types of intermediaries he has identified: grassroots support organizations (GSOs) and membership support organizations (MSOs). He finds many paradoxes in the performance of these two types of organizations, but also some surprising linkages. The book's central theme revolves around the role of intermediary NGOs in grassroots capacity building.

Near the end, Carroll subjects the IAF and other donors to some ribbing. He reminds us that we all have some entrenched myths to overcome before we can truly help NGOs realize their full potential. The critique is done with tongue in cheek: It may be irreverent, as the author himself admits, but it is good-natured and, as is the entire book, very positive.

The book was written during a period of great ferment in Latin America, dominated by the redemocratization of many nations but also by a pervasive financial crisis. The role of NGOs and grassroots organizations is shifting. On the one hand, the new trends reduce the past confrontational attitudes and antagonisms between NGOs and the public sector. This will permit more fruitful collaboration of the kind advocated in this book. On the other hand, the economic crisis and a likely shrinkage of external funding might place increased and unrealistic demands on NGOs to provide social services to ease the states' burden. Whatever the specifics, the 1990s will see a much more complex and interesting public-private relationship, especially in the context of decentralization and the universal desire to strengthen local government. Carroll shows that even in times of unfriendly regimes, informal and pragmatic collaboration is often possible at the local and regional levels.

One final comment about the general validity of the book's findings: Throughout the research period I pressed Tom Carroll to come up with generalizable "propositions." He kept resisting, on the grounds of insufficient evidence and too great a diversity of situations. But I finally prevailed, at least to the extent that by drawing widely on the comparative literature and experience, the author has ventured beyond the realm of his cases. He has managed to formulate many hypothesis and conclusions that, however tentative, are valuable lessons for all of us who work in grass-roots development.

Charles Reilly
Inter-American Foundation

Acknowledgments

This work started out as a relatively straightforward exploration of the qualities of grassroots support organizations and ended with the discovery that sympathetic outside support can actually strengthen self-reliant organizational and local initiative. In the process of this study, I began to question some of the widely held beliefs about NGOs and to make irreverent comments about some of the common myths of grassroots development. Many colleagues helped me in this journey.

First, I wish to single out the contributions made by my two teammates, Denise Humphreys and Helga Baitenmann, who were responsible for much of the fieldwork and wrote the original case studies. I enjoyed their enthusiasm and dedication to what turned out to be a complex and at times difficult research process.

Comments on earlier drafts of the manuscript by Martin Scurrah, Charles Reilly, Gabriel Cámara, Anne Hornsby, and Denise Humphreys are gratefully acknowledged. Many of the dedicated staff members at the Inter-American Foundation shared their experiences with me. I also benefited from the critique of two anonymous reviewers chosen by the publisher.

Jack Montgomery, Norman Uphoff, Eric Shearer, Arthur Domike, and Anthony Bebbington, friendly but tough critics, read the entire completed manuscript and made many good suggestions for the final version.

Diane Bendahmane served as general editor and collaborated with me in preparing the manuscript for publication. Her keen eye and good sense made the book more coherent and more accessible to a wide readership. Regina Rippetoe and Sharon Hershey cheerfully and competently assisted with the final editorial tasks.

Finally, I dedicate this volume to an exceptional group of graduate students whose contributions helped me energize the long process of research and writing. As a teacher at George Washington University and at the John F. Kennedy School of Government, and as a member of the doctoral fellowship committee of the Inter-American Foundation, I was fortunate to interact with a number of young social scientists who, unlike most of their elders, have had the curiosity to read, the inspiration to react, and the generosity to share.

Introduction

Development Support Organizations—
A Special Kind of NGO

During the 1980s, nongovernmental organizations (NGOs) emerged as major actors on the international development scene. Specialists concerned with poverty alleviation and grassroots initiatives have tracked this evolution with growing interest and have contributed to its flowering with external funding. Yet it was not until the second part of the decade that the development community at large, both individual experts and financial agencies, "discovered" NGOs as a new institutional form of development resource.

Just how "mainstream" had this discovery become by mid-decade? In 1985, an evaluator for the World Bank stated in a staff working paper that private development organizations were superior to other aid agencies in implementing rural development in Latin America. He also suggested that these NGOs were an important and underutilized resource that should be mobilized to supplant the action of the state (Lacroix 1985). This was the conclusion of an engineer—neither a social scientist nor a rural development specialist—in a report for the mainstream development agency.

Like others working for development agencies, the Bank staffer had arrived independently at the same conclusion that a small band of aficionados had reached earlier: that the advantages of NGOs, such as flexibility, informality, commitment, and participatory style, outweighed their disadvantages and made them especially suited for the complex task of rural development projects aimed at alleviating poverty, in which physical capital is combined with human and organizational resources (Korten 1980; Paul 1982; Hellinger et al. 1983; Tendler 1982b, 1983a; Development Alternatives, Inc. 1985).

The engineer did not say—and perhaps did not realize—that his observation, as well as those that followed in the chorus of approval, referred to a special kind of NGO, not just any or every private or civic organization.

1

What he saw at work were indigenous intermediary NGOs that directly supported base groups, that is, local village or community organizations.

In the mid-1980s development scholars began to focus on the useful role of these intermediaries. Earlier, most of the scholarly work had centered on local or grassroots groups and how they related with government and on international, Northern NGOs. It was subsequently discovered that national ("indigenous") intermediary organizations could energize local groups and provide vertical mediating links between them and the higher reaches of the financial, technical, and political power structure (Leonard 1982a, 1982b; Gorman 1984; Esman and Uphoff 1984; Uphoff 1986; Van der Heijden 1985).

But the 1980s also ushered in a shift in the very nature of Southern NGOs. Back in the 1960s and early 1970s, most, including those operating in Latin America, worked in relief and welfare and often acted as affiliates or conduits for private voluntary organizations in the developed countries. The increased independence and direct involvement of these Southern NGOs in rural and urban development are now part of an emerging national civic mobilization and social activism in Latin America (Hirschman 1984; Padrón 1982; Ladim 1987). The Inter-American Foundation (IAF) has identified some 11,000 NGOs operating in Latin America and the Caribbean, and there are probably many more.

Working with indigenous NGOs is now becoming increasingly fashionable in international development circles, but for the IAF it is nothing new. During the first fifteen years of its operation, the IAF granted the bulk of its assistance to supra-local intermediary NGOs in Latin America. Over $150 million, or nearly 75 percent of all IAF commitments between 1972 and 1986, was granted to such institutions. This total includes over 1,000 separate grants, which represent an IAF clientele of between 500 and 600 national organizations (Carroll, Baitenmann, and Humphreys 1987). Many of these NGOs have histories that antedate discovery by international donors. Others are more recent manifestations of the impact of debt, adjustment, austerity, or frustration with government.

Although these organizations are enormously important for IAF operations, they are viewed with skepticism and have been generally downplayed in IAF rhetoric. What accounts for this paradox? Part of the answer may be pragmatic and part may be philosophical. Operational concerns have clearly favored working with intermediary organizations. They are able to formulate projects, mobilize resources to implement them, reach larger numbers of poor families, and work with unorganized populations. In repressive situations, intermediary organizations have represented the only way the IAF could hope to make an impact; working directly with base groups was either impractical or dangerous. Although intermediary organizations have served as useful conduits, they have never quite fit into the IAF's philosophical framework for bottom-up development. Because intermediaries are one or two steps removed from primary grassroots groups, they were often perceived as less genuine and regarded with suspicion as being merely temporary or convenient. Thus, the IAF's close relationship and extensive experience with intermediary organizations was publicly deemphasized. A few quality case studies have been carried out (Tendler, Hatch, and Grindle 1984, on the Fundación Nicaragüense de Desarrollo [FUNDE]; Diskin, Sanderson, and Thiesenhusen 1987, on the Fundación Mexicana de Desarrollo Rural [FMDR]), but aside from these, few attempts have been made to see what the IAF has learned about intermediaries.

In 1985, an ad hoc committee of IAF staff members proposed that a systematic effort be undertaken (a "learning exercise") to assess and communicate the IAF's experience with intermediary organizations. The committee concluded:

> Thinking about how to deal effectively with intermediate organizations is a critically important yet sadly neglected area of inquiry in our profession. The Foundation has an exceptionally rich and diverse body of experience on which it may draw and . . . the Foundation itself stands to profit from a systematic inquiry into its experience in this area (Inter-American Foundation 1985)

The roles that intermediary-type organizations play in the development of their own countries are currently viewed with international interest and approval, but they are poorly understood. The literature on NGOs is growing, but there is very little disaggregated treatment of the many different kinds of such organizations and no accepted methods or criteria for measuring their performance. There is a confusing proliferation of terminology and acronyms, yet intermediary-type NGOs do not even have a proper name. Furthermore, many donors share the IAF's ambivalence about intermediaries. Because they operate at a higher level than primary grassroots groups and are often not formally accountable to their clients, there is fear that they may siphon off money that would otherwise go directly to the poor. On the other hand, donors rely on them for invaluable services that the donors' staffs cannot perform.

It was in response to these gaps and controversies that the present study was undertaken. It was carried out by the author with the assistance of Denise Humphreys, who is currently regional project officer for Catholic Relief Services in La Paz, Bolivia, and Helga Baitenmann, who is studying for a doctorate in anthropology at the New School for Social Research in New York. IAF representatives served as advisers, sources of information, and critics.

Thirty organizations were examined for the study (summary information on them is presented in Table 2.1). To select the organizations, the team first established a working definition and a typology that was used to classify all IAF grants during the 1972–86 period. In each country the IAF portfolio was reviewed and the universe of organizations and their contextual situations were examined.

During 1987 by the research team visited fifteen of the selected organizations in Chile, Costa Rica, and Peru. These three countries provided sharply contrasting sociopolitical environments for the comparative examination of intermediary NGOs. They range from authoritarian, "free market" Chile, to the "yeoman democracy" of Costa Rica, to Peru's social turmoil of a "disappearing state" governed by alternating military and civilian regimes.

The in-depth assessments of these fifteen organizations resulted in lengthy case studies. Shorter versions were written up as profiles and appear as Part II of this volume. The text refers to these case studies frequently and in as much detail as space permits. However, a full understanding of the author's ideas depends on some familiarity with the profiles, which have the additional value of containing more insights about the inner workings of the organizations.

Data on the remaining fifteen organizations were obtained from inhouse reviews using interviews, evaluations, and reports in IAF files. For each organization, key sources of information were mid-term or final evaluations by independent researchers. Mini case studies of many of these organizations appear as sidebars, throughout the text. In addition, the author and Martin Scurrah directed a comprehensive survey of forty-two intermediary organizations in Peru that have received support from the IAF since 1975. Findings of this survey are also incorporated into some of the chapters. The full names and acronyms of the organizations discussed here can be found in the list of abbreviations at the back of the book.

It is probably fair to say that no other donor organization has more experience (in temporal and spatial terms) with intermediaries in Latin America than the IAF. This gives weight and substance to the study. However, the subject of the study goes beyond the IAF's experience. Evidence from many other sources and organizations is used. The book addresses issues of general interest. It is intended for the growing group of donor organizations that interact or hope to interact with intermediaries to improve the lives and prospects of the poor, for all development scholars and students of Latin American development, and for the NGO's themselves.

The book is divided into two main parts. The first contains an analysis of the performance of intermediary NGOs; the second part offers condensed versions of the case studies of the organizations that formed the main empirical basis for the study, with a brief contextual background for each country.

The heart of Part I is five chapters on performance characteristics: service delivery, poverty reach, participation, group capacity building, and wider impact. These are preceded by two background chapters that define and characterize the subset of NGOs being examined and explain the criteria used to evaluate their performance (including a review of the available literature relevant to intermediary NGOs). Part I ends with a discussion of the organizational attributes of strong performers and some recommendations for donors.

The three chapters of profiles, one for each country, that make up Part II begin with a description of the setting in which the NGOs operate. The profiles provide a thumbnail history of each organization but concentrate mainly on its performance characteristics and the challenges it has overcome. The volume also has an extensive bibliography.

I

Features and Performance of Intermediary NGOs

1

Tending the Grassroots: GSOs and MSOs

The overall purpose of this book is to examine the common or recurring organizational features and development strategies of intermediary-type nongovernmental organizations (NGOs) to ascertain which approaches and institutional configurations appear to be associated with good performance and to suggest how donor agencies can enhance these desirable elements.

The term *intermediary* is not felicitous in Latin America. Although intermediation is one of the key functions of certain NGOs, the term evokes a negative perception of their role (akin to "exploitative middlemen"), especially in Spanish or Portuguese. In addition, leaders and members of this important subgroup of NGOs object to being labeled intermediaries. Albert Hirschman, who reviewed a selection of Inter-American Foundation (IAF) projects in 1983, also dislikes the terms *intermediary, facilitator,* and *broker*. He suggests a substitute *organizations involved in social activism* (Hirschman 1984). His alternative vividly imparts the sense of social commitment that characterizes most of these organizations, but it does not convey anything about their relationship to the local level, which is their distinguishing characteristic. To rectify this situation, this book re-christens these NGOs as grassroots support organizations (GSOs) and membership support organizations (MSOs).

Terms and Definitions

GSOs and MSOs are two subsets of the broad spectrum of NGOs. The term NGO covers hundreds of types of organizations within civil society, ranging from political action committees to sports clubs. Only those NGOs with specific developmental purposes and main activities and that operate on a certain level are classed as GSOs or MSOs, as shown in Figure 1.1.

In general terms, GSOs and MSOs may be defined as developmental NGOs involved *directly* in grassroots work. Accordingly, research organizations or educational institutions without outreach or action features

Figure 1.1 Identification of GSOs and MSOs within the
Spectrum of NGOs

PURPOSES   Charity
                  Relief
                  Development

```
┌─────────────────────────────────────────────────────┐
│   Economic development                                │
│   Social development                                  │
│   Social business (business combined with             │
│       equity objectives)                              │
└─────────────────────────────────────────────────────┘
```

                  Political action
                  Advocacy of special interests

```
┌─────────────────────────────────────────────────────┐
│   Advocacy combined with service or                   │
│       assistance to the base                          │
└─────────────────────────────────────────────────────┘
```

MAIN ACTIVITY   Fraternal, social, recreational
                  Education

```
┌─────────────────────────────────────────────────────┐
│   Education combined with development services        │
│       or direct assistance                            │
│   Organizational assistance                           │
└─────────────────────────────────────────────────────┘
```

                  Research

```
┌─────────────────────────────────────────────────────┐
│   Research combined with development services         │
│       or direct assistance                            │
└─────────────────────────────────────────────────────┘
```

                  Lobbying

```
┌─────────────────────────────────────────────────────┐
│   Lobbying combined with development services         │
│       or direct assistance                            │
└─────────────────────────────────────────────────────┘
```

                  Networking

```
┌─────────────────────────────────────────────────────┐
│   Coordination, brokerage, representation             │
└─────────────────────────────────────────────────────┘
```

LEVEL   Local (single primary groups and communities)

```
┌─────────────────────────────────────────────────────┐
│   Locality (grouping of communities)                  │
│   Regional                                            │
│   National                                            │
└─────────────────────────────────────────────────────┘
```

                  International

GSOs and MSOs are within the boxes.

will be called GSOs or MSOs. The following paragraphs expand on these basic definitions.

> *GSO.* A GSO is a civic developmental entity that provides services allied support to local groups of disadvantaged rural or urban households and individuals. In its capacity as an intermediary institution, a GSO forges links between the beneficiaries and the often remote levels of government, donor, and financial institutions. It may also provide services indirectly to other organizations that support the poor or perform coordinating or networking functions.

> *MSO.* An MSO has similar attributes. It also provides service and linkages to local groups. However, an MSO represents and is accountable to its base membership, at least in principle. For example, a primary or base-level membership organization is a local cooperative or labor union. A regional association of such base groups is a secondary, or second-level, group. This is sometimes capped by a third-level national federation. It is these second- and third-level membership organizations that are referred to as MSOs here.

> *Primary grassroots organizations.* Both GSOs and MSOs are distinguished from primary grassroots organizations by scope, level, complexity, and function. A primary group is the smallest aggregation of individuals or households that regularly engage in some joint development activity as an expression of collective interest. GSOs and MSOs tend to serve, represent, and work with several primary groups. In other words, they operate on the next level above the primary grassroots organizations and seek to assist and support them.

Some of the words used in these definitions merit comment. The concept of *local* is sometimes ambiguous. Uphoff (1986) includes three types of collective action units under his definition of local institutions: (1) the group level (a self-identified set of persons having some common interest), (2) the community level (a relatively self-contained socioeconomic residential unit), and (3) the locality level (a set of communities having cooperative and commercial relations). This book considers only the first two, the group and the community, as local or primary. The third is already an aggregation of base groups and is therefore considered within the GSO/MSO category.

Unlike international NGOs based in developed countries, GSOs and MSOs are national in that they operate within the institutional framework of developing countries. However, sometimes the boundary is blurred, as when expatriates support GSOs or MSOs that operate under local legislation, have local staffs, and are financially and legally independent from their sponsoring or affiliated institutions.

Figure 1.2 delineates the continuum of public-private institutions. One of the first tasks in carrying out this study was to sort out the various types of entities working in grassroots development programs. The two extremes—government line agencies and private, profit-making firms—are excluded from consideration here, although in many parts of the world, state or business organizations also have a role in grassroots programs. The GSOs and MSOs examined here fall in the middle area, or the civil sector, in the figure. This sector has been defined as "neither private in the sense of the market, nor public, in the sense of the state" (Wolfe 1991).

The expression *development oriented* when used to define GSOs and MSOs, is meant to provide a contrast to charity or relief, which were the traditional functions of private and religious agencies and continue to be important in the world of international private voluntary organizations. Charity and relief stress distribution without reciprocity; development aid stresses some contribution from the recipient and aims at growth and capacity building, resulting in an eventually self-sustainable process. In development aid, capacity building is central, as it is in this book. The word *support* is meant to convey a sympathetic form of assistance close to the concept of *tending*, which implies not simply giving but a mutually respectful reciprocity between the supporter and the supported.

GSOs may be distinguished from MSOs on the basis of ownership and control. A GSO is a promotional and service organization whose beneficiaries are not members; an MSO is a federation, union, or association of primary groups in which the members are stakeholders. GSOs are sometimes called "outsiders" and MSOs "insiders."

Outsiders, or GSOs, are primarily facilitator organizations whose management is made up of professional middle- or upper-class individuals or, generally, individuals whose social status is not the same as that of the beneficiaries with whom they work. GSOs are not controlled by or accountable to these beneficiaries, although some beneficiaries may function as board members or advisers.

Insiders, or MSOs, are more typically extensions of the base groups themselves. Their leaders come from the same social classes as the

Figure 1.2   The Public-Private Organizational Continuum

Public Sector ⟶		Civil Sector ⟵		Private Sector
Line agencies (public administration)	Public-Private entities	Civic organizations	Nonprofit "businesses"	For-profit commercial, manufacturing, and service organizations
	Parastatals	NGOs GSOs		
Elected or appointed entities		MSOs		

members, and accountability mechanisms such as elected representation are built in. GSOs independently advocate and lobby for social causes, and MSOs practice representational advocacy on behalf of specific constituencies.

The distinction between a GSO and an MSO is less sharp in practice than in theory. In later chapters, some of the differences in their operational styles are discussed. As will be seen, the two types interact and sometimes even overlap in practice.

During the study, controversy surfaced, both within the IAF and in the field, about whether cooperatives and other membership associations should be included in a study of intermediary organizations. Membership control is qualitatively significant, especially in terms of accountability, and institutions created by the local groups themselves have greater claims to continuity and legitimacy. However, second- and third-level membership organizations operating as MSOs serve as intermediaries between donors or governments and their base units and constituencies. They thus work above the grassroots level, even though they are upward extensions of grassroots organizations and, at least in principle, represent and are accountable to their base membership.

Typology: The ABCs of GSOs and MSOs

The universe of GSOs and MSOs is highly varied and complex. For analytical and comparative purposes, a classification system based on four characteristics has been developed: (1) scope and level of operation, (2) clientele, (3) functions, and (4) inspiration/affiliation.

Concerning the first classifying characteristic, GSOs and MSOs can be national or regional or, as shown in Figure 1.1, can encompass a multi-communal space, called a locality. Most of the organizations included in this study operate at the level of a specific region or are multiregional. Even those that have a national charter and operate out of the capital city do not cover the whole country but rather operate projects in various locations. MSOs tend to be organized by multiple levels; co-ops or labor unions have their regional associations and frequently a national federation.

The second classification is by clientele. GSOs and MSOs work in either rural or urban areas, although some have both village and town beneficiaries. A fair number of GSOs serve distinct social groups, ethnic communities, women, children, and landless workers. Their clientele can consist of individuals or more or less organized groups.

Turning now to function, some GSOs and MSOs are narrowly focused and specialized. More typically, however, they are mixed but clustered around a central purpose. For GSOs, three functional clusters predominate: productive and income-generating activities, social services, and networking. Most GSOs in the sample are involved in agricultural

Table 1.1   Inspiration/Affiliation of GSOs and MSOs

Categories	Examples
Church inspired	CIDE CAPS
Business inspired (national development foundations)	FMDR FUNDE
Government-promoted civic collaboration	CACH PURISCAL
Cooperative inspired	CAMPOCOOP HORTICOOP
Professional/technical service (development catalyst)	CET INDES PROTERRA
Public service contracting	FDN
Ethnic advocacy and representation	APCOB USEMI FUNCOL
"Greens" (environment)	ANAI
Academic affiliation	FDN FIDENE
Land-reform beneficiary association	CENTRAL CAMPOCOOP

See Table 2.1 for a comprehensive list of the organizations in the study sample.
See the list of abbreviations for the organizations' full names.

production. Significant sets of GSOs focus on education, health, handicrafts, and microenterprise. For MSOs, the two principal functions are providing technical and representational services and operating central facilities for members. The functional classification is represented in Figure 1.3.

The inspiration/affiliation of a GSO or MSO is generally related to its origins, dominant philosophy, and operational style. MSOs are frequently inspired by cooperative or labor union movements. GSOs may trace their origin to and affiliation with the Catholic church (or other religious groups), business interests, the academic community, or certain government initiatives. Table 1.1 gives the inspiration/affiliation of a number of organizations in the sample.

The way this typology works can be illustrated by some of the cases in the sample. Centro de Investigación y Promoción del Campesino

(CIPCA), a Peruvian GSO, is affiliated with the Catholic Church through its Jesuit leadership. It is regional in scope, working in the Department of Piura in northern Peru, with headquarters in the provincial capital. CIPCA has a predominantly rural clientele made up of peasant cooperatives and small farmers. It started out as an educational institution but is now more diversified with health and agricultural technology components (see the profile in Chapter 11).

Confederación Nacional de Cooperativas Campesinas (CAMPOCOOP) is a Chilean cooperative federation, an MSO assisting land-reform cooperatives. It is a national organization but works through regional affiliates that are the main operating entities. CAMPOCOOP offers a range of agricultural services, including credit and marketing and legal assistance. It has a genuine campesino leadership (see the profile in Chapter 13).

Fundação de Integração Desenvolvimento e Educação do Noroeste do Estado (FIDENE), a GSO in southern Brazil, drew its inspiration from the popular education movement and is now affiliated with a provincial university. It is regional in scope, working throughout Rio Grande de Sul. FIDENE has a mixed clientele, with a very strong influence among rural unions. The organization has gradually moved into more agricultural productive activities but also works on urban employment-related projects (see the description in Box 5.1).

The Fundación Mexicana de Desarrollo Rural (FMDR) is typical of a business-inspired GSO, one of a number of so-called national development foundations. It is national in scope but works only in certain states. Its clientele is primarily small commercial farmers, and its main service is production credit.

Fundación para las Comunidades Colombianas (FUNCOL) is a Colombian GSO inspired by advocates of Indian cultures (*Indigenistas*), and is one of the foremost legal-aid sources for native groups. It is national in scope but works in fourteen departments. In addition to its main legal function, it also has a health program (see the description in Box 3.2).

It should be pointed out that the GSOs and MSOs discussed in this book are not "voluntary organizations" as that term is often used (Alliband 1983; Brown and Korten 1989). Although their board members or directors usually donate their time, management and operating staffs are compensated and most get regular salaries. Hence these organizations can be more properly thought of as nonprofit rather than voluntary.[1]

Brief Review of the Relevant Literature

There are no analytical and comparative studies that focus on intermediary-type organizations, although a few studies covering general institutional development in the context of servicing the poor are indirectly and

Figure 1.3   Intermediary Organizations Classified by Function

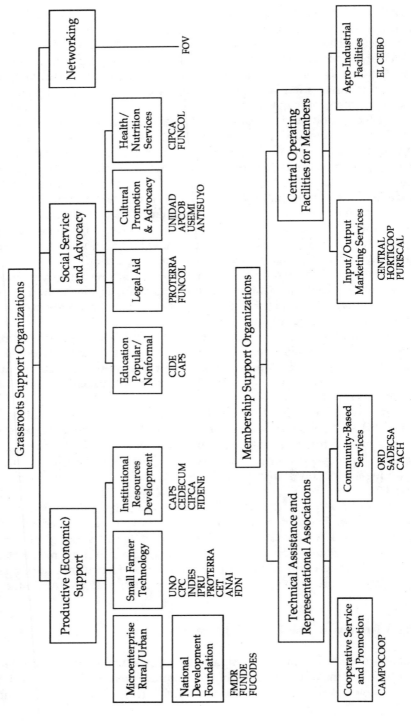

See Table 2.1 for a comprehensive list of the organizations in the study sample. See the list of abbreviations for the organizations' full names.

fragmentarily relevant. Most of these date from the early 1980s and reflect a renewed interest in development management and institutional development supported by the U.S. Agency for International Development (USAID), the World Bank, and some of the major private foundations.

Perhaps most notable is the work of the Cornell group. Esman and Uphoff's (1984) pioneering study of local organizations in rural development systematically reviews public and private groups, including membership-based organizations such as cooperatives. In analyzing structural factors, the study isolates variables having to do with size, vertical and horizontal linkages, membership roles, and the public-private continuum on which various intermediary organizations are located. It also applies quantitative estimates of organizational performance, based on a set of cases collected from secondary sources.

Uphoff's *Local Institutional Development* (1986) is a massive and useful review of a much wider range of organizations, categorized according to various functions: (1) natural resource management, (2) infrastructure, (3) primary health care, (4) agriculture, and (5) nonagricultural enterprise. As mentioned above, Uphoff's "local" levels can be made up of a group, a community, or a locality. Groups on this level are also known as grassroots or base-level organizations. Although the term *intermediary* is occasionally used to denote both public and private service or support institutions, Uphoff reserves the term *intermediation* for one of four alternative ways of decentralization. Intermediation, as Uphoff defines it, refers to the role of membership organizations (like cooperatives and other farmer organizations) in providing services that might otherwise be undertaken by government agencies or local government bodies. Other entities involved in decentralization are government agencies, philanthropic or private voluntary organizations that channel resources to the local level "where the state allows," and private enterprises that provide services through "marketization." Uphoff's overall analysis of strategies for supporting local institutional development is relevant and useful to this examination of supra-local support organizations. Indeed, a fair number of Uphoff's case summaries, which take up about one-third of his book, include support of local development efforts by organizations that fall into the intermediary group.

The work of David Leonard and what has been known as the Berkeley group is also of interest, particularly a paper by Stephen Peterson (1982) that deals very intelligently with the functions, incentives, linkages to government, and sequences of special-interest organizations. One of Peterson's relevant and controversial points is that vertically integrated interest organizations with a single function are much more conducive to local group formation and effective service delivery than those that assume multiple tasks and promote horizontal integration. He writes, "The institutional blueprint for intermediate organizations in inegalitarian settings . . . should entail the vertical extension of single functions and the establishment of brokerage roles that facilitate vertical cooperation." (This conclusion appears to be based on a limited empirical basis. The Cornell group's more systematic data and analysis [Esman and Uphoff 1984] gave rise to alternative conclusions.) In another paper in the Berkeley series, Leonard (1982a) stresses the "exclusive" nature of many support organizations for the poor in contrast to government service organizations, which are almost always "inclusive." He also elaborates a set of conclusions about assistance linkages and control linkages. He cites Esman and Montgomery (1980) in support of the proposition that "the need for the center (both government and donors) to provide assistance beyond simply finances to intermediate and local organizations is the great decentralization lesson of our generation" (Leonard 1982b, p. 36). This assistance by intermediaries (such as accounting by secondary co-ops) is seen as beneficial not only for the intrinsic value of the service but also to permit the primary groups to be more informal and therefore more accessible to control by their poorer members.

Samuel Paul (1982) dissects six successful national programs, each carried out by a large service organization, most of which are linked to the public sector but also display features of self-management. He looks especially at structural characteristics, autonomy, decentralization, and what he calls the strategic management process. He concludes that strategic management is complementary to the roles played by political commitment and resources in program performance. Especially relevant were the following critical interventions: (1) focusing initially on a single goal or service, (2) diversifying goals sequentially, (3) phasing program implementation properly, (4) confirming organizational autonomy, (5) using network structures, (6) using sample information with fast feedback systems, and (7) selecting and training staff in a flexible manner. Surprisingly, Paul found no consistent explanatory value in different patterns of participation or of motivation of beneficiaries.

David Korten's work (1980, 1987a) has had a considerable influence on students of community organization and is of some relevance here, especially his concern with the linkages between donors and indigenous organizations. According to Korten, "linkage design" to facilitate the learning process should proceed through three phases: effectiveness, efficiency, and expansion. Most suggestive is his finding that the administrative styles of most governments and also large official financial donor agencies conflict with such a sequence. In a recent paper, Brown and Korten (1989) offer a good typology and suggest ways for donors to improve the developmental performance of NGOs. They single out a category they call voluntary organizations, or VOs, whose main task is grassroots organizing. Brown and Korten also point out that many of the weaknesses of VOs are a function of the same characteristics that give them their distinct advantages. The developmental role of VOs in empowering the poor is further elaborated by Korten (1990).

Relevant work on international development has also been done by a group of Dutch sociologists working out of Leiden. Galjart (1982) looked at the nature of reciprocity relationships between base-level groups and second- or third-level associations. He characterizes these relationships as direct exchange, or pooling of resources, which may encompass non-tangible or political exchanges as well. The Leiden group has also made relevant contributions to the understanding of participation and to the conceptualization of the role of the external change agent in capacity building (van Dusseldorp 1981). In one of these papers, Grijpstra (1982) points out the necessity of external initiative and support for the creation of groups with a participatory structure—one of the main issues in this book: "Paradoxically, top-down planning and organization may be needed for the poor to participate from the bottom-up" (p. 201).

In a brief document written for USAID, Hellinger et al. (1983) reviewed information from seventy primarily nongovernmental institutions with a focus on multiple collective units of beneficiaries. The review suggests that such organizations have characteristics in common, including a two-tiered internal structure with site-specific project development and facilitating functions backed up by central administrative and technical support. Unfortunately, the document presents no specific data or cases.

One of the most useful publications is another contract study for USAID prepared by a team of authors from Development Alternatives, Inc. (DAI) and Cornell University (1985). The foci of this study are two large U.S.-based private voluntary organizations: International Voluntary Services, Inc. (IVS) and the Institute for International Development, Inc. (IIDI). Much of the analysis is based on case studies of indigenous organizations assisted by expatriate private voluntary organizations, including samples from Ecuador and Costa Rica. This report is especially relevant here because it is one of the few published works that explicitly addresses the role played by indigenous intermediary and intermediate-level organizations and is particularly concerned with the issue of capacity building. Methodologically, the DAI/Cornell group has made an important contribution by developing thirty-four institutional development indicators. Organizations were rated on a scale of zero to five. One of the main conclusions of this report is that although the comparative advantage of international private voluntary organizations over other service delivery mechanisms is their ability to work at the grassroots level, their effectiveness to promote local institutional development may be enhanced by working with and through national intermediaries.

The PISCES (Program of Investment in the Small Capital Enterprise Sector) study (Farbman 1981) makes a significant contribution to the understanding of organizations that promote urban microenterprise. This is one of a very few reports based on excellent case material. Seven Latin American organizations, all of which can be considered intermediaries, are covered. The PISCES study identifies a number of organizational features that account for good performance, such as decentralized implementing structure, autonomy of field staff, modest size, and flexibility.

Judith Tendler's work on NGOs has been particularly insightful and stimulating for this study, especially the comparative perspective that infuses her work. In 1982 she reviewed seventy-five evaluations and other documents for USAID in order to assess the strengths and weaknesses of NGOs. Most of this material referred to the work of U.S.-based private voluntary organizations, but her critique, which suggested that they were not particularly participative, innovative, or apt to reach the poor, has challenged subsequent NGO analysts (1982b). Tendler's study of the early years of União Nordestina de Assistência a Pequeñas Organizações (UNO) in Brazil (1983a) and her reports on Bolivian cooperative federations (1983b) and on Fundación Nicaragüence de Desarrollo (FUNDE) in Nicaragua (Tendler, Hatch, and Grindle 1984), the latter two for the IAF, identify the many internal contradictions inherent in Latin American NGOs and offer unconventional views on performance criteria, evaluations, and donor attitudes. Among other provocative ideas, Tendler has argued for elite co-optation rather than confrontation, cooperation with governments, a minimalist approach to services, and urban rather than rural strategies for poverty alleviation.

A useful comparative study of a segment of the intermediary NGO spectrum is Sally Yudelman's review of five women's organizations—all IAF grantees—in *Hopeful Openings* (1987). In addition to offering some conclusions specific to women's role in development, this study identifies other general dilemmas applicable to GSOs, such as the conflict between service and policy change, the problem of strong leadership, and the issue of too many activities and sound management.

As the number of NGOs has grown dramatically in Latin America over the last ten years, many of the larger and older organizations engaged in development research-action-advocacy (*centros de promoción social*) have agreed to meet together periodically. An outgrowth of these meetings has been an incipient intellectual effort to document and describe what these NGOs are and what they do. From this community has come a series of inward-looking papers and thought pieces examining the origins, roles, motivations, and relationships of NGOs in their national context. As expected, there is no agreement about what to call these organizations; however, researchers do recognize that important differences exist. Sergio Gomez's study (1989) of rural support organizations in Chile and Mario Padrón's work on Peru (1982) and on Latin America in general (1986, 1987) are initial efforts to sort out the confusion —by setting out the existing institutional map and examining key elements (the goals, strategies, sectors, clients, and functions) of each organization. Padrón's designation of nongovernmental development organization (NGDO) comes close to the definition of GSOs used in this study. Although these papers and thought pieces exhibit a number of methodological difficulties, they also serve as a useful base for understanding the range and density of these organizations in specific countries. The most recent report (Arbab 1988) is based on a year-long collaborative learning experience by nine Latin American organizations that call themselves by Padrón's term, NGDOs. This unusually frank self-critique, carried out under the sponsorship of Private Agencies Collaborating Together (PACT), analyzes the role of NGDOs in relation to their grassroots clientele, their donors, and their governments. A shared purpose is identified as capacity building at the base.

In 1986, a conference on intermediary voluntary organizations was held at Cambridge, Massachusetts, under the auspices of the Lincoln Institute for Land Policy and the Kennedy School of Government, Harvard University. The report of this conference, which consists of several conceptual papers and country case studies, presents some interesting generalizations: (1) the traditional distinction between "welfare" and "development" is diminishing as intermediary support organizations (ISOs) find it attractive to act in both dimensions; (2) in the production field, the extension of existing technologies is more likely to succeed than the introduction of new ones, but in social service, new techniques are more likely to meet with success; (3) when ISOs have something that the governments want, instead of being petitioners or dependents, they can develop independent strength, leading to a good bargaining position (Carroll and Montgomery 1987).

Also notable is a collection of papers issued as a special supplement to *World Development*, which were presented at an NGO symposium in London in March 1987 (Drabek 1987). Although the main focus of the symposium was on North-South relations, a number of the papers dealt with the emerging role of national intermediary-type NGOs. In searching for effectiveness criteria, sustained capacity building was suggested by a number of Southern NGOs, and donors were urged to provide more core funding for this purpose.

Of methodological relevance is an evaluation of the African Development Foundation by the U.S. Office of Technology Assessment (OTA 1988). The evaluation team assessed a sample of twelve projects, eight of which were carried out by intermediary organizations. Performance was judged and scored under four sets of criteria: participation, results, sustainability, and replicability. Complementarities and trade-offs were also noted in the analysis.

In an important new study, *Learning from Gal Oya*, Uphoff (1992) recounts in great detail how tens of thousands of irrigators in Sri Lanka were helped to change from a disorganized self-destructive state to one of effective cooperation in a remarkably short time. Although the change agents in this case were a combination of academic and intellectual activists and government field agents, this work is relevant to the capacity building theme of NGOs in this book, both empirically and theoretically.

In a retrospective analysis of the evolution of Latin American intellectual history during the past generation, David Lehmann (1990) provides a sociological macroframework for the phenomenon of GSOs. In tracing the broad ideological developments since the post-World War II period he explains the origins of the new type of social movements and of *basismo*, in which self-help development projects as well as lobbying and protest became more legitimate and part of a search for a more open, more equitable civic society. In Lehmann's opinion, Latin American post-Marxist intellectuals now place less reliance on the state sponsorship of local organizations, because "the sources of solidarity lie neither in the state nor in a mythical pre-capitalist commune" (1990, p. 197). This signifies an evolution toward a modern liberal and less corporatist view in which grassroots organizations can coexist and have reciprocal relationships with the state. He observes that the professionalization of grassroots movements and of their leadership helps to render the bureaucracy more responsible and avoids "the colonization of that apparatus in the time-honored style of Latino politics" (Lehmann 1990, p. 197).

Lehmann thinks that to become effective, grassroots organizations have to acquire higher-level and large-scale operating affiliates and that GSOs are needed to bridge the gap between base organizations and government. He is somewhat pessimistic about the managerial potential and sustainability of grassroots organizations, concluding that the strengthening of GSOs may be seen as elitism by some, but it is potentially the most effective way of improving the management of popular organizations and achieving greater stability of participatory self-help initiatives, which are successful in great part precisely because they are not formalized.

Consensus and Controversy

What are the main lessons that may be drawn from the relevant literature, and what are some of the major currents of thought that reinforce the frame of reference of this book?

First, although a great deal has been written about NGOs, there is little scholarly analysis of intermediary NGOs and of those that offer developmental services to grassroots groups. Studies based on primary observations and field research are especially scarce. Little is known about how these organizations interact with their beneficiaries or partners and with the power centers in their countries. This lack of documentation is disproportionate to the growing importance of GSOs and MSOs in the developing world.

Publications on NGOs tend to lump many kinds of organizations together so that lack of discrimination diminishes their usefulness. The heterogeneity of the universe of NGOs defies most analysts. There is either too little useful discrimination or there is too narrow a focus on specialized entities. The nomenclature is confusing: there is no agreement on typologies or on the use of the acronyms invented by various authors. With respect to performance, most evaluations deal with projects rather than with organizations, and there is a tendency to see the effectiveness of NGOs in terms of black and white. There are too many ardent admirers and also a good number of skeptics who minimize or dismiss the importance of NGOs.

On the positive side, the literature offers some convincing arguments for the existence of grassroots support institutions that are neither governmental nor business. It also justifies the evolution of their development functions. However, the NGO literature suffers from a strong case of antigovernment bias, to the point where NGOs are seen not only as opposed to the state but as alternatives to the state. This attitude is fueled by neo-conservative "rational choice" theorists, by celebrants of the informal economy, and by the strong U.S.-led push for privatization by means of the microenterprise sector. However, more balanced views are now emerging, in which some of the utopian and confrontational attitudes are moderated, so that GSOs are encouraged to interact with both the state and the market. Such a linking role for GSOs—support linkages rather than the usual control linkages (Leonard 1982b)—is highlighted and developed in this book.

A less rigid ideological attitude is also evident among the intellectual leaders of the Latin American GSOs (or *centros*) as they have matured and become more professionalized and as state repression has diminished. More is now heard about the need to improve the government's performance in social services and public goods, akin to the earlier theme of scholars in development management about bureaucratic reorientation (Montgomery 1988). Hope is even expressed about the possibility of a depoliticized grassroots support system that could function without paternalism and without outside interventions necessarily leading to dependency. At least in Latin America, NGOs and their self-help projects are beginning to be seen less as a sideshow and more as central elements in the move toward a more just and participatory society (Lehmann 1990).

On the other hand, there is less consensus and more controversy on some of the issues that are at the heart of the relationship between intermediary support organizations and their base constituencies. One such recurring question is the "organizability" of the grassroots population of the poor. This, in turn, is part of the broader ongoing debate about the viability of popular institutions based on cooperative behavior. During the late 1980s, profound pessimism prevailed about the future of cooperation. The dominant paradigm extolled the virtues of individualism and competitive behavior, favoring institutions based on such behavior, especially as socialism disintegrated in Eastern Europe. Yet the 1990s opened with a somewhat greater optimism about the potential of collective action, especially in resource management but also in other dimensions, as long as the internal and external environment was favorable ("enabling") to the release of the requisite "social energies" (Hirschman 1984; Uphoff 1992; Putnam 1992).

The potential of grassroots groups and their aggregations to develop sustainable management skills is once again affirmed, but only if these can develop effective support linkages. However, there is still too little knowledge about and solid theorizing on the optimum levels and scale for self-management tasks. Nor is there any consensus on the ultimate role of self-help participatory structures within the modern technologically sophisticated economy.

These gleanings from the literature will be used throughout this volume, partly to illuminate and interpret the findings of the study and partly to endow this work with greater comparability and general applicability.

Note

1. Brown and Korten (1989) divide NGOs into four types: voluntary organizations (VOs), people's organizations (POs), public service contractors (PSCs), and hybrid governmental/nongovernmental organizations (GONGOs). In this scheme, VOs are value driven, with their members contributing time and money to a cause; PSCs are market driven and offer services to clients. Developmental intermediary GSOs, as used in this book, do not fit into Brown and Korten's categories. They are neither as purely visionary as VOs nor as commercial as PSOs. However, MSOs can be accommodated in the Brown and Korten typology as higher-tier POs.

2

Selecting and Rating the Organizations

Thirty Good Performers

A study of thirty intermediary organizations regarded by Inter-American Foundation (IAF) staff as effective and competent forms the basis of this book. Most of the organizations have had a long-term relationship with the IAF and have received multiple grants or substantial amendments to their original grants. Collectively, they have received a little over $24 million of IAF grant funds and have represented, over the years, a major financial and professional commitment by the foundation.

The universe analyzed here, therefore, has been identified by the IAF as "well-performing" in some respects. This positive a priori judgment has in most cases been confirmed by the study, even though a number of organizations in the sample rated somewhat lower according to one or another of the criteria employed by the author and his research associates. (One set of commentators identified the gamut of private voluntary organizations as ranging from saints to scoundrels [Brown and Korten 1989]. Presumably, the scoundrels have already been eliminated from this sample by the IAF.) Thus, although the sample is deliberately drawn from high-quality institutions, their mixture of strong and weak features and their fluctuating life histories make them somewhat typical of the whole class of organizations. It is hoped that this study not only identifies the characteristics of good performers but also contributes to an understanding of grassroots support organizations (GSOs) and membership support organizations (MSOs) in general.

The fifteen organizations profiled in Part Two were studied firsthand by the research team in the field. Information on the other fifteen came from project files, evaluation reports, and discussions with IAF staff and some of the organizations' past and present leaders.

Of the thirty organizations, six are located in Peru; six in Costa Rica; four in Chile; two each in Bolivia, Colombia, and Brazil; and one each in Argentina, Ecuador, Guatemala, Mexico, Paraguay, Nicaragua, St. Vincent, and Uruguay. Although the IAF is the only donor for a few of these organizations, the majority have several outside sources of funding—further testimony of the approval and confidence they enjoy in the donor community. In the case of some of the older, well-established organizations with diversified funding, the IAF was an early supporter when the organizations were fragile, risky ventures.

Seven of the thirty organizations are MSOs: four agricultural cooperative federations; one association of farmer societies; and two hybrids, in which control is vested in a mixed board of members and nonmembers. The remaining twenty-three are GSOs. Of these, sixteen are focused on productive income/employment-oriented activities, while seven work primarily in the field of social promotion, education, or ethnic advocacy. Since the majority of the organizations covered in the study are GSOs, it follows that much of the analysis concerns them. Table 2.1 presents key information about the thirty organizations.

Common Features

Although diverse, these GSOs and MSOs have some common overall elements in addition to being good performers. All are predominantly rural oriented. Urban organizations were deliberately excluded from the study to keep it within reasonable bounds and to attempt to generalize about rural-oriented intermediaries. This was not difficult because, until the early 1980s, most of the IAF's grantees were rural organizations or at least organizations with a rural clientele.

Whatever their ultimate objectives, most of the organizations try to achieve tangible benefits by supplying services that are needed or requested by the beneficiaries, and most support beneficiary groups (rather than individuals or families) or are actively helping to organize them. Most consider working with locally constituted groups not only a matter of efficiency in the scale of services but also a commitment to collective empowerment as an independent value.

It follows that most of these intermediaries are committed to some notion of a self-sustained development process, in productive and organizational terms. They do not conceive of themselves as distributors of food, clothing, or medicines, as many international private voluntary organizations do. Finally, it is important to note that although some of their staff members may be politically active, the organizations themselves are independent of any political parties or movements.

The majority of the organizations reviewed here carry on classical intermediary-type functions in which they "mediate" or build bridges between their beneficiaries and the institutions holding financial, economic, and political resources. They exemplify the kind of brokering, negotiating, and risk-shouldering activities that make this institutional sector so useful to poor and isolated beneficiaries and so appealing to donor agencies.

All provide advice and assistance—sometimes accompanied by tangible resources and sometimes not. In addition, they carry on a number of less visible functions. They not only transfer resources downward and transmit beneficiary demands upward, but also support beneficiary groups in their efforts to gain legitimacy, make claims upon the system, and defend their interests. As advocates, these organizations assume an activist, representational posture on behalf of collective beneficiary interests. An important variant of the advocacy role is protection, that is, forestalling or blunting aggression or hostility directed against a specific group of the poor. Among the organizations reviewed here, these protective functions have been extremely important, but the groups see themselves most often as advisers and teachers of the poor rather than as protectors or mediators. However, much of what they do involves mediation.

The organizations in the study mediate between the base groups they assist and the upper reaches of the government bureaucracy, centers of technology, the business sector, and, of course, the international donor community. Being represented and supported by an effective GSO or MSO lends legitimacy to a grassroots organization. In repressive regimes, in which all grassroots organizing is suspect, this mediating function is especially important. This also holds true where neo-conservative economic policies have supplanted populist governments and where large segments of the only recently organized rural and urban labor force subsequently have been abandoned.

Evaluation Criteria

Commonly, evaluators of GSOs, MSOs, and other similar organizations have applied either "hard" or "soft" criteria. They have looked either at the effectiveness and efficiency with which the organizations channel services and resources to the grassroots or at the more intangible goals of participation, raised awareness, and enhanced self-reliance. By focusing solely on one or the other, evaluators miss many relevant aspects of intermediary NGO activity and performance, especially the interaction between some of the performance elements, the time dimension, and indirect effects. Thus, in this study, a number of evaluation concepts were used for which both hard and soft indicators were developed.

The criteria used to measure performance of the organizations were gradually developed in the course of the research. These encapsulated the experience of the IAF staff and also reflected recent critical work by scholars and evaluators.[1] Three sets of criteria were used, both for

Table 2.1 Basic Data on Selected Organizations

Organization/Country	Type/Scope	Clientele	Main Focus
ANAI/Costa Rica	GSO Prof/Tech Regional-Atlantic Coast	Unorganized small cultivators	Tropical agroforestry system
ANTISUYO/Peru	GSO Prof/Social Multiregional	Traditional/ethnic handicraft producers	Quality craft promotion, ethnic creativity
APCOB/Bolivia	GSO Prof/Social Regional	Ethnic minority communities in the Oriente	Social organization, technical assistance, training
CACH/Costa Rica	MSO* Public/Private Prof/Tech Regional	Small commercial producers	Multifunctional
CAMPOCOOP/Chile	MSO Coop Federation National	Members of land reform cooperatives	Technical assistance, credit, legal assistance
CAPS/Guatemala	GSO Prof/Social Church-related Multiregional	Highland Indian communities with very small land base	Credit, education, extension training
CEDECUM/Peru	GSO Prof/Tech Regional—Puno	Indigenous communities and semisubstance producers	Integrated rural development, agricultural diversification
CENTRAL/Peru	MSO Coop Association Regional—Piura	Land reform production cooperatives	Agricultural input supply

(continued)

Organization/Country	Type/Scope	Clientele	Main Focus
CET/Chile	GSO Prof/Tech Multiregional	Marginal urban households, small farmers	Low input agrobiological technology, housing models
CIDE/Chile	GSO Social/Action Church-related National	Other NGOs' educational programs	Popular educational materials and methods, community development
CIPCA/Peru	GSO Research/Action Church-related Regional—Piura	Diversified agricultural reform co-ops, campesinos	Multifunctional training, communication, agricultural technology, research
CPC/Paraguay	GSO Prof/Tech National	Small farmers	Local organization, production credit
EL CEIBO/Bolivia	MSO Second-tier co-op Regional	Local co-ops, cacao farmers	Processing/marketing, credit
FDN/Peru	GSO Prof/Tech Consulting Multiregional	Diversified small semicommercial farmers	Production credit, technical assistance, marketing
FIDENE/Brazil	GSO Research/Action Multiregional	Small farmers, landless co-ops, rural unions	Multifunctional technical assistance, training, social promotion, planning, research

(continued)

Organization/Country	Type/Scope	Clientele	Main Focus
FMDR/Mexico	GSO Prof/Tech Nat Dev Foundation Multiregional	Small semicommercial farmers	Production credit, technical assistance
FOV/Costa Rica	GSO Educational Coordinating National	Rural and urban women's productive groups	Production credit, training, networking
FUCODES/Costa Rica	GSO Prof/Tech Nat Dev Foundation National	Small commercial urban and rural entrepreneurs	Production credit, technical assistance
FUNCOL/Colombia	GSO Prof/Tech National—14 Depts.	Ethnic communities	Legal services, (especially rights in land), some health, lobbying
FUNDE/Nicaragua	GSO Prof/Tech Nat Dev Foundation National	Small semicommercial farmers	Production credit
INDES/Argentina	GSO Prof/Tech Multiregional	Small semicommercial farmers	Multifunctional rural development
IPRU/Uruguay	GSO Prof/Tech National	Small semicommercial farmers	Credit, technical assistance, marketing

(continued)

Organization/Country	Type/Scope	Clientele	Main Focus
ORD/St. Vincent	GSO Prof/Tech Local	Small cash farmers	Input supply, marketing, technical assistance
PROTERRA/Peru	GSO Prof/Tech Regional	Small commercial farmers (ex-land reform co-op members)	Legal assistance, credit extension, technical assistance
PURISCAL/Costa Rica	MSO* Public/Private Prof/Tech/Social Regional	Small semicommercial farmers	Supply store, credit, social services
SADECSA/Chile	MSO* Prof/Tech Local	Small farmer associations in dryland area	Farm planning, technical advice, training, credit
UNIDAD/Ecuador	GSO Social/Prof Regional—Chimborazo	Indigenous Andean communities	Literacy education, small-enterprise training
UNO/Brazil	GSO Prof/Tech Multiregional within NE	Urban and rural small enterprise	Credit, technical assistance
URCOOPAPA/Costa Rica	MSO Co-op Federation Regional	Small commercial horticultural producers	Processing, marketing
USEMI/Colombia	GSO Social/Prof Regional	Ethnic communities	Education, technical assistance

* These MSOs are hybrids, i.e., control is vested in a mixed board of members and non-members. However, they will be considered MSOs for the purposes of this study.

comparative purposes and to discover patterns: (1) development services, (2) participation, and (3) wider impact. Each set was then further subdivided, as explained below.

There is a certain evolutionary sequence in the three sets of criteria. The first set—delivering development services to the poor, the isolated, and the disadvantaged—measures GSO and MSO performance as it is traditionally viewed and represents the more proximate or short-term dimension of performance. The second set, which focuses on participation and empowerment, represents a more indirect and complex dimension of performance; it reflects the democratic ethos of the IAF and other process-oriented donors. The third set of indicators, which looks at the wider impacts of the organization, grew out of the recent interest of the donor community and scholarly critics in trying to ascertain how the recognized microeffect of NGOs could be expanded or "scaled up," and even linked to the macrolevel.

The criteria reflect the main goals of the NGOs themselves. As in the case of donors and scholars, the dominant philosophy of the NGO community has also undergone evolutionary changes. The early work of intermediaries was predominantly in the relief and welfare tradition, concerned with the supply of basic necessities—first social services and later economic help. The Spanish term *asistencialismo* is often used to characterize this role of NGOs. Concern with participation and empowerment followed, as influenced by currents of thought from community development, liberation theology, and social mobilization. This goal structure is commonly expressed in Spanish as *acompañamiento*, which roughly translates into "supportive partnership." Having an impact on larger constituencies or systems and policy reform are relatively recent NGO aim, not universally followed or even accepted by individual NGOs, although increasingly espoused by networks and consortia.

The following sections explain the criteria in more detail.

Development Services

Service Delivery. Providing useful services and resources to the poor is the key to strong performance. The services should be appropriate and of high quality so that they meet the beneficiaries' current needs. They should be provided in such a way that they build a foundation for other accomplishments. One also looks for evidence that the services have enabled the recipients to improve their living conditions. Further, the services should complement those provided routinely by the public sector, not replace them. If the nature of "service" can be standardized (such as in organizations that specialize in delivering credit or in literacy classes) and if it is possible to apply costs to a unit of output, the main attribute in this category may be termed organizational cost-effectiveness.

Poverty Reach. A complete evaluation of effectiveness in service delivery must include a consideration of the socioeconomic status of the population that is being assisted. This is seldom done in evaluations, partly because it is difficult to ascertain the status of a given group. To win the highest marks for effectiveness, GSOs and MSOs must be able to reach down to assist the relatively more vulnerable, asset poor, or disadvantaged segments of the population.

Participation and Empowerment

Responsiveness/Accountability. Participation is both a means and an end. It is easier to observe it as a process than an outcome: One can evaluate the relationship between those who are providing the assistance and those who are receiving it. To assess participation, questions such as the following must be asked. To what extent have GSOs and MSOs helped beneficiaries become more adept at articulating their needs in an operational way? How actively and how widely do local groups participate in decisionmaking in matters affecting their welfare? Have they enhanced the sustained involvement of beneficiaries in the development process, especially after the initial assistance by the outside organization has ceased? The values implicit in this line of questioning stress the greater independence and autonomy of those assisted by GSOs or MSOs, but reciprocity is also implied, by which the relationship between clients and service providers gradually becomes a give-and-take rather than a one-way process.

Participation can also be thought of as accountability. The donor's goal here is to enhance the capacity of members to hold their leaders accountable and to facilitate the emergence of leaders who are responsible and sensitive to members' interests. In practice, these processes are extremely complex and difficult to evaluate. However, in a comparative study such as this, the differences among GSOs and MSOs in these dimensions are quite striking.

Reinforcing Base Capacity. The heart of participation is growth in the capacity of a group to create new systems and mechanisms to accomplish its goals. It is the ultimate manifestation of the social learning process. Growth in group capacity is not simply learning how to accomplish certain technical tasks, but also adapting to new circumstances and dealing more effectively with a dynamic external world. It is the function of GSOs and MSOs to strengthen the organizational and management capacity of beneficiary (grassroots) organizations or to help them create new local representative groups for collective action.

Group capacity manifests itself as self-help, or the internal ability of groups to manage their own resources and operate enterprises destined for collective benefits, and as mobilization for influencing the outside environment, or claim-making. This latter capacity is the ability to make demands on the system and to negotiate with the outside world. The institutionalization of group capacity is the key element in sustainability, which sometimes appears as a separate criterion in evaluation reports, but is treated here as part of other criteria.

Wider Impact

Innovation. The notion that intermediary NGOs should have a broader impact is relatively recent within the donor and scholarly community. Many intermediaries themselves contend that their strength is quality through smallness and that scaling up or widening their impact is not their responsibility. Nevertheless, the ability to innovate and to transfer ideas, methods, and techniques (the demonstration effect) and the ability to influence the policy process are used as indicators in this book.

To what extent have GSOs and MSOs designed and tested new technical and institutional approaches or systems for solving specific micro-developmental problems? Have such systems or processes become widely shared and diffused? If they have not, do they at least have the potential to be widely diffused? These questions must be answered to assess the wider impact of a GSO or MSO.

Policy. The ability of intermediaries to exert an influence beyond a limited number of directly assisted beneficiaries or communities implies moving from the strictly microeffects of distinct projects to the macropolicy arena, where it is possible to influence the economic, political, and social context within which intermediaries and base groups work. Such a broader impact may be manifest at the regional, sectoral, or national level.

How the Organizations Measure Up

Chapters 3 through 7 apply these criteria to the organizations in the study sample and discuss the strengths and weaknesses uncovered. The remainder of this chapter reviews the overall ratings of the thirty organizations, keeping in mind that they were selected a priori as good performers. After the field visits, the author and his research associates rated the organizations for each performance indicator on a scale of one (low) to three (high). The ratings were arrived at by consensus among the three researchers. A rating system of twenty subindicators developed by the researchers served as the basis for arriving at a cumulative score for each of the six criteria. The twenty elements are listed in the appendix.

In the case of older organizations, the ratings refer to their current status. In the case of multifunctional and multisite organizations, the ratings either refer to the dominant activity or reflect an average of the two or three main program components. For the policy criterion under the

Table 2.2   Performance Ratings of Selected Organizations

Criteria	Distribution of Scores			Combined Score	Average Score
	High (3)	*Medium* (2)	*Low* (1)	*(max. = 90)*	*(max. = 3.0)*
Service Delivery					
Service effectiveness	24	6	0	84	2.8
Poverty reach	12	18	0	72	2.4
Participation					
Responsiveness/ accountability	12	13	5	67	2.2
Reinforcing base capacity	12	8	10	62	2.1
Wider Impact					
Innovation	13	12	5	68	2.2
Policy (actual)	6	11	13	53	1.8
Policy (potential)	15	13	2	75	2.5
Overall					
Actual	—	—	—	—	2.3
Potential	—	—	—	—	2.4

wider impact rating, the organizations were rated two ways: on their actual performance and on their potential. The results of the ratings are displayed in Table 2.2.

The interpretive nature of the numerical scoring process should be emphasized. Individual scores can vary according to some absolute standards or the choice of comparables used. In each rating, the evaluator's judgment is also influenced by the variation within the group. Although there may be some ideal standard, in effect each organization is rated against others in the same group. Judgments on performance can also vary over time and may be valid for only one stage in the life cycle of each organization. However, these ratings, applied consistently within the group, are highly suggestive of certain overall patterns.

The organizations in the study rated highest in service delivery (not surprisingly) and in potential policy impact (surprisingly) and received respectably high to medium scores for poverty reach, innovation, and participation. They were given relatively low scores for actual policy impact and group capacity building. However, the rating for group capacity building averaged 2.8 for the eleven organizations that had the highest overall scores (a little over one-third of the sample).

The first two items in the table make it clear why these thirty were selected: none rated low in service delivery and poverty reach. The last three items also show an unexpected result: On the whole, these organizations appear to be much more innovative than anticipated and have respectable scores for policy impact; their potential for wider impact is extraordinary, with only two judged low due to their small size and distance from mainstream activity.

Table 2.3 shows how the scores of MSOs in the sample compare with those of GSOs. The results are interesting but should be used with caution, since the proportion of MSOs is small. There is virtually no difference between the two in service delivery and participation. In group capacity building GSOs have an edge (0.6 points), and in poverty reach they display a considerable advantage (0.5 points). The biggest differences lie in actual policy influence, with GSOs having a 0.8 point lead, and in innovation, where the lead is 1.4 points. The gap for potential policy influence narrows to 0.5 points, even though all but one of the MSOs are regional rather than national in scope.

These scores suggest that, in the sample, MSOs are not necessarily more participatory or more competent in providing services than GSOs led by professionals without formal accountability mechanisms. However, GSOs show a greater ability to reach the poor and appear to offer donors greater opportunities for innovative behavior and policy reach.

How the Criteria Are Related

The three sets of criteria are interdependent. At times they are related dynamically or synergistically and at other times conflictingly. One important finding of this study is that although there are clear conflicts or trade-offs in the short run, the ostensibly conflicting "harder" economic, productive goals and "softer" humanistic, organizational objectives are compatible in practice if properly implemented. They can also be mutually reinforcing. To put it another way, increased professionalization of GSOs and MSOs need not conflict with their humanistic objectives: Institutional/organizational efforts can indeed enhance technical, productive goals. This is convergent with the view of Smith 1987. Another finding is that strong performance moves sequentially: Accomplishing one objective serves as a building block for reaching another, although this is not to say that climbing up block by block is easy.

Though the three sets of criteria are interdependent, they are not equally important. Obviously, the measures chosen and the relative weights attached to the multiple criteria are not value-free. A useful way to make some of these value judgments explicit is by applying a stakeholder's analysis. For example, the client groups stress short-term tangible resources, and the leadership stresses longer-term viability-building achievements. Donors profess to favor reduction of dependency and resource mobilization but, in fact, often favor quick disbursement and reportable results during the project period. Differing concepts of devel-

Table 2.3 Performance Ratings of Selected Organizations by Type

Criteria	Average Scores		
	All Organizations (n = 30)	MSOs (n = 7)	GSOs (n = 23)
Service Delivery			
Service effectiveness	2.8	2.7	2.8
Poverty reach	2.4	2.0	2.5
Participation			
Responsiveness/ accountability	2.2	2.2	2.3
Reinforcing base capacity	2.1	1.6	2.2
Wider Impact			
Innovation	2.2	1.2	2.6
Policy (actual)	1.8	1.2	2.0
Policy (potential)	2.5	2.1	2.6

opment also influence the mix and weights of performance criteria (Carroll and Montgomery 1987).

In addition, both the organizations themselves and outside evaluators assign different weights to each indicator of performance depending on the country and the local context, the ethos of the organization, and the stage of its institutional evolution. Furthermore, in certain situations, GSOs and MSOs have broad roles of overriding importance. They may protect and confer legitimacy on rural groups in hostile regimes or provide environmental protection to fragile ecosystems and populations dependent on them. To achieve such broad aims, GSOs and MSOs may express themselves in strongly partisan terms (as advocates for certain social groups in conflict with dominant or rival groups) or they may, in some cases, support public policies that put them in conflict with some of the same groups whose long-term interests they are attempting to safeguard. Examples of the former are GSOs specializing in advocacy for ethnic minority rights (USEMI or FUNCOL) or those of landless workers (FUNCOL). Examples of the latter are environmentalists such as ANAI or regional planners such as CIPCA. ANAI leaders were profoundly embarrassed when their espousal of national legislation for a seaside park along the Atlantic Coast of Costa Rica ran into strong opposition from settlers whom ANAI was trying to help with agroforestry technology. The point is that although all GSOs and MSOs try to protect and help the weak and the poor, it is not always clear to what extent a narrow partisan approach is consistent with a wider social or public interest.

A recent report based on the serious self-reflection of a number of prominent NGOs from six Latin American countries deplores the tendency of many intermediary centers of social promotion—the name assumed by many intellectually inclined Latin American NGOs—to foster special-interest groups, which, however worthy of promotion, tend to create further inequalities and conflict among the poor:

> The villages are in need of decisionmaking structures that care for the interests of every inhabitant including the powerless child born to their least useful members. They suffer from the lack of structures for maintaining unity, structures that would protect them from divisions caused by every sect, political faction and development project. (Arbab 1988).

Some of these topics are discussed in more detail in the next five chapters. However, three contextual and dynamic dimensions of GSO and MSO performance should be mentioned here because, although they do not fit easily with the six performance criteria, they contribute considerably to the understanding of overall organizational performance.

Contextual and Dynamic Dimensions

In a universe as varied as that of NGOs, where the work of such organizations is intimately embedded in their environment (both spatially and temporally), the rating system outlined in the first part of this chapter is incomplete and too reductionist to capture the whole essence of organizational performance. The case studies prepared in the course of the research for this book reveal this richness and complexity.

Additional criteria are needed to explain certain dimensions of performance. First, to evaluate specialized service providers (for example, credit, literacy, agroforestry, water management, and shelter), sector-specific indicators are needed. The organizational effectiveness of credit providers is not simply a matter of increasing the income-producing capacity of their clients. It also involves achieving high repayment ratios, maintaining the value of revolving capital, and capturing resources for new lending. In irrigation management, the performance of NGOs supporting or representing water-user associations hinges on achieving not only participatory management and canal maintenance but also equitable distribution between irrigators in favored and unfavored locations, distinguished as head-enders versus tail-enders by Uphoff (1992) in his new book on cooperative behavior in Sri Lanka. Whenever they are relevant to this assessment, sectoral indicators are employed. But for purposes of this book, it is neither possible nor necessary to delve too deeply into matters of functional specialization.[2]

The second set of additional criteria focus on context. All NGOs operate within a contextual matrix derived from specific locational and historic circumstances that change over time. Furthermore, there are macrosectoral considerations that have a great influence on NGO strategies. As will be pointed out in subsequent chapters, NGOs operate within a given political-economic "space."

Third, internal organizational dynamics, which are strongly influenced by but not identical to the outside context, are very important. What is the role of an organization as it evolves and faces a new constellation of challenges and opportunities? Different criteria are needed to look at older and younger organizations as well as at those in the process of expansion versus those that have reached consolidation. MSOs that represent and service a fixed membership evolve differently from GSOs that must relate to a shifting and mutating set of beneficiaries.

A consideration of the case of Centro de Investigación y Promoción del Campesino (CIPCA) illustrates how these types of criteria were incorporated in the evaluative research for this book.

CIPCA is one of the very highly rated GSOs in Peru. For its founders (social-activist Jesuits), CIPCA's existence was justified by the many problems left in the wake of Peruvian agrarian reforms. As successors to the giant irrigated private estates, the associative enterprises (supposedly worker managed) were left rich in resources but weak in organization and heavily dependent on the state for inputs and management. Smallholders, landless workers, and traditional communities, largely left out of the reform process, were groping toward their own organization and livelihood.

During the 1980s, the vagaries of economic policies—ranging from neo-liberalism to populism to austerity—created confusion, conflict, and crisis in the countryside. The situation was made worse by growing terrorism and drug trafficking. The production co-ops, beset by a host of internal and external problems, gradually disintegrated without any clear alternative agrarian organization in sight. In the midst of these chaotic events, CIPCA tried to create some stability and order by fortifying promising forms of peasant groups with a combination of educational and technical services. Through its multiple functions (communication, training, extension, community development, technology services, and research), CIPCA has become a significant regional presence—a solid resource institution in the midst of instability.

By fortuitous circumstance, the field investigation of this case coincided with a comprehensive evaluation of CIPCA by its three principal European donors: CEBEMO (Central Agency for Joint Financing of Development Programs) of Holland, COTESU (Swiss Technical Cooperation) of Switzerland, and MISEREOR (Action Against Hunger and Disease) of Germany. Hence, it was possible for the author and his research associates to share the insights of this evaluation and benefit from its conclusions (CIPCA 1987).

CIPCA received excellent marks for its overall performance and especially for its regional impact. However, not all of its specialized functions escaped criticism. CIPCA's educational radio program and its farm machinery workshop were found to be especially successful—the former for its high quality, cultural appropriateness, technical utility, and listeners' approval, and the latter for its learning-by-doing style, cost-effectivenss, and high utilization rates.

But the concept of popular education, which was one of CIPCA's original guiding strategies, was found to be too vague in application, of doubtful effectiveness, and poorly integrated with the organization's other activities. Although the high quality of CIPCA's research program was mentioned, the evaluation suggested a reorientation of research so that the viability of different forms of agrarian organization supported by CIPCA could be tested.

With respect to contextual factors, it was observed that new legislation favoring provincial government and other decentralization initiatives opened up new opportunities for CIPCA to become even more influential. For example, CIPCA's previous experience with peasant associations made it uniquely qualified to increase the capacity of rural constituencies to have an impact on and participate in provincial and municipal governments just when these governments were being given new responsibilities and autonomy.

A related finding of the evaluation was that CIPCA should work with second- and third-level peasant federations and rural unions (MSOs), not only with base groups. CIPCA's reluctance to collaborate with important MSOs in its region may be explained by the often radical politicization of such federations, their heavy dependence on state agencies, and CIPCA's disinclination to get involved in partisan politics. As will be seen later in this book, such an aversion to work with prominent MSOs is common among *basista* GSOs, whose ideology favors self-reliant base communities.

Finally, as to organizational dynamics, it was concluded that CIPCA was at a crucial stage in its own evolution: Its growth, influence, and prestige were impressive, but it needed to rethink its comparative advantage, consolidate its scope, and streamline its strategy. This stage in organizational development often coincides with the stepping down of an inspired and strong leader or founder. This was the case of CIPCA.

In conclusion, at the time of the comprehensive evaluation, the great strengths of CIPCA were its regional presence and in-depth accumulated knowledge of its microenvironment as well as its success in combining key technical services with grassroots capacity strengthening. But its mix of activities had become too diffuse. There were no self-regulating mechanisms. Significantly, well-intentioned donors had contributed to CIPCA's lack of cohesion by funding distinct projects (which were congruent with donor agendas).

The next chapters discuss the organizations' performance according to each of the criteria, starting with what is perhaps the key to success for GSOs and MSOs—service delivery.

Notes

1. The following evaluative papers reviewed for this study were particularly helpful in establishing performance criteria: Development Alternatives, Inc. 1985; Honadle 1981; Tendler 1982b; World Bank 1985, 1987; Paul 1987; Arbab 1988; Devres, Inc. 1988; Office of Technology Assessment 1988; Pastore 1988; Brown and Korten 1989.

2. The most extensive recent literature on specialized intermediary NGOs is in the field of microenterprise credit, sponsored mainly by the U.S. Agency for International Development. Elements of this program bear signs of the Zodiac. It started with PISCES (Program of Investment in the Small Capital Enterprise Sector). The findings of this phase are presented in Farbman (1981) and Ashe (1985). The second phase was called ARIES (Assistance to Resource Institutions for Enterprise Support). The main output of ARIES was Mann, Grindle, and Shipton (1990). The third ongoing phase is called GEMINI (Growth and Equity through Microenterprise Investments and Institutions). One of GEMINI's early reports is Edgecomb and Cawley (1991).

3

Service Delivery

The most direct, observable function of grassroots support organizations (GSOs) and membership support organizations (MSOs) is the provision to their beneficiaries of goods and services that are wanted, needed, or otherwise unavailable. The literature on nongovernmental organizations (NGOs) generally stresses their superior ability to serve populations that are not reached by public agencies.

Delivery of Service: A Means or an End?

Most GSOs and MSOs in this study have set for themselves ambitious and bold goals that inspire and guide them in their work. Some of these goals cover the services they provide; others refer to intangibles such as promoting participation or democratic values or the self-image of members. What these groups actually spend most of their time doing, however, is providing services to base groups. The nature of service varies by type of intermediary, as mentioned earlier. GSOs provide production support, social services, linkages to resources, and networking; MSOs provide technical assistance and representation and central operating facilities.

The delivery of these services is supposed to produce a palpable increase in the well-being of the groups attended. Twelve organizations in the sample (40 percent) can be considered principally service providers. The majority (eighteen organizations, or 60 percent) provide services in conjunction with their roles as development catalysts and capacity builders. Both the recipients and the donors involved with the latter group of organizations believe that it is valuable to make a direct impact on beneficiaries' standards of living. However, that is not usually their main purpose, although it is considered a prerequisite for reaching broader and more distant goals. The problem is that GSOs and MSOs often face so many difficulties and complications in providing services that they tend to neglect their broader goals. Thus, services that were intended as a means frequently become the end. It is interesting to note that this tendency to stress service per se to satisfy short-term needs is often encouraged by both donors and recipients. This apparent paradox is discussed further in Chapters 6 and 8.

This said, the first thing that distinguishes the selected GSOs and MSOs is their outstanding ability to implement projects, an ability rarely found among the national service providers (public or private) in most Latin American countries. This capacity has been built up through hard experience over the years. By the mid-1980s virtually all of the thirty organizations had displayed an impressive ability to get things done on time and with reasonable efficiency. Seed, tools, or fertilizer were distributed before the planting season; credit requests were processed expeditiously; courses or demonstrations were effectively organized; machinery was maintained; and so on. Given that these organizations often control only a part of the system necessary to supply the service and make it usable, their record is all the more remarkable. It demonstrates that for GSOs and MSOs, success involves not only proper internal management but also the ability to influence and leverage others (banks, suppliers, and the beneficiaries themselves).

As long as these organizations are operating almost exclusively on foreign money, the notion that they should replace government in some areas and with some social groups appears untenable. It follows that they should emphasize capacity building or viability-upgrading services, not routine services—a major point in this study. This view is strongly endorsed by Brown and Korten in a recent study prepared for the World Bank. They write, "voluntary service organizations (VOs) . . . perform important social functions, but unless they are developing the capacity of indigenous organizations to replace them in their functions on a self-sustaining basis . . . they cannot claim to be doing development work" (Brown and Korten 1989, p. 11).

Conceptually, it is the idea of self-provisioning that separates GSOs from MSOs. The latter, being organizations of the service users themselves, provide the basis of a self-sustaining delivery system. The institutionalization of the latter implies either eventual coproduction of services with government or the creation of more permanent specialized service agencies with their own sources of income. This trend is clearly visible in Uruguay, where Instituto de Promoción Económico-Social del Uruguay (IPRU), a GSO, has given rise to a whole network of small-farm service entities, and in Costa Rica, where small-farm productive services are performed by a set of mixed private-public regional corporations.

Basic Service Delivery Strategies

A central feature of effective rural social service delivery strategies is compatibility or a "good fit" with the existing rural household and community system. Services fit well if they are sensitive to the interests articulated by peasant groups and based on a thorough understanding of local farming systems and the peculiarities of the local peasant economy. GSOs and MSOs acquire knowledge about seasonal labor demands, migration patterns, cultivation, and marketing practices from field research and through direct involvement in various projects. Regionally established GSOs and MSOs (or decentralized branches of national organizations, such as FDN in Peru) have a special advantage in acquiring this sort of local knowledge, which is discussed in a later section.

Devising effective development strategies is crucial to good service delivery. This includes setting objectives, choosing means, and devising tactics. The services themselves, such as credit, training, and legal help, can be understood and properly evaluated only in the context of the particular development strategy. Four basic strategies for deploying rural development services were employed by the GSOs and MSOs under study: semisubsistence agriculture, small farm-based business, rural nonfarm employment, and social community services. The first three aim at increasing the productivity of the poor by upgrading labor skills, capitalization, job creation, or market penetration, the fourth strategy covers "entitlements," or basic social needs.

Semisubsistence Agriculture

The first strategy is to improve the ability of farm households to achieve a secure family subsistence (especially in terms of food and nutrition) with minimal cash outlays. This strategy often promotes traditional farming practices and makes maximum use of locally available and locally controlled natural resources. Most new output is consumed by the producing families themselves, the remainder being sold or bartered locally. This strategy may be characterized as "inward oriented," the microequivalent of an autarchic macropolicy.

In agricultural development circles, subsistence farming has a bad name because agrodevelopment normally strives to eliminate subsistence and achieve production for market with a reduced labor force. Hence semisubsistence agriculture is an area where neither government nor commercial services are readily available. But subsistence is still a key objective for millions of rural households.

The semisubsistence agriculture strategy stresses basic consumption, nutrition or health, less dependence on the cash economy, and greater security of subsistence. The strong contribution of GSOs working on semisubsistence agriculture is explained largely by the scarcity of public services, the relative poverty and ethnic and physical isolation of the populations served, and, in some cases, by the hostility of repressive governments toward small farmers. MSOs tend not to follow this strategy, as they commonly represent commercial farmers. The major exceptions are ethnic federations, but these were not included in the study sample.

Most subsistence functions are adjuncts to other activities or represent a small component rather than the core program of the organization. They often serve as part of a sequence to reinforce other activities. On the Caribbean island of St. Vincent, for example, the Organization for Rural Development (ORD) uses improved subsistence and basic food crops as the first phase of its technical assistance sequence. Then, after some experience and confidence building, it moves on to the production of local cash crops and finally to specialty and export items, activities that require increasingly greater sophistication on the part of the farmers.

A number of socially inspired GSOs, among them Unidad Educación para el Desarrollo de Chimborazo (UNIDAD) in Ecuador and Ayuda para el Campesino del Oriente Bouviano (APCOB) in Bolivia, place a high priority on improving the nutritional status and providing the basic food needs of the poorest rural families, who have too little land and other resources to earn much cash income from farming. In some cases, this strategy involves restoring the cultivation of historically important native crops, such as the nutritious quinoa of Inca times. Although the original motivation for the reintroduction of these neglected plants was nutrition and ecology, it so happens that some of them (quinoa included) are now in demand as health foods and have thus increased in cash value. Sometimes a nutritionally significant crop is introduced, such as high-protein lysine corn in the case of ORD in St. Vincent.

Some GSOs among the study organizations espouse self-sufficiency as a goal rather than as a transitional state. They tend to have an idealistic, almost romantic vision, promoting self-sufficient attitudes to combat helplessness and dependency and attempting to isolate their clients from the rigors of the market and the "evils" of capitalism and commercialism. This goal is not only unrealistic but, more often than not, contrary to the worldview of the social groups these inspired outsiders assist. Several GSOs in the sample abandoned this utopian position for socioanthropological (ANTISUYO, APCOB) or ecological reasons (ANAI). What remains is a healthy skepticism about the virtues of the "open economy" and a more balanced pragmatic stance that permits strengthening capacities to meet the subsistence needs of vulnerable groups without demanding closure. (In regional economics, "closure" is the internal articulation of a region's economy and a reduction of trade with other regions.) There is not a single GSO or MSO among the thirty whose clients do not have at least one foot in the cash economy.

Perhaps it is more accurate to characterize the semisubsistence strategy as low-input agriculture, in which dependence on purchased inputs is reduced and ecological sustainability is promoted. Asociación de los Nuevos Alquimistas (ANAI) in Costa Rica stresses locally available resources in its tree nursery and other projects. No sophisticated concentrates or fertilizers are used. If a species of tree does not survive with what can be readily obtained locally, it is considered inappropriate for the region. ANAI believes that low-income groups cannot afford such inputs and should not go into debt for them, especially in the initial phase of growth. Subsistence and commercial cropping systems are designed to achieve food security first and to make the system resilient to both disease outbreaks and a steep fall in prices.

The Chilean development organization Centro de Educación y Tecnología (CET) exhibits this pragmatism while seeking subsistence security for its clients. It is a thoroughly technical and professional organization intent on providing the rural and urban families sidelined by the Chilean economic model, based on large firms and unemployment, with a low-cost alternative livelihood. CET designed five basic production systems based on bio-organic recycling, starting with a simple one that can be carried out with a minimum of land and virtually no purchased inputs. These limitations are in keeping with the circumstances of small farmers and rural laborers. The technical package is disseminated by way of local *monitores* trained by CET, and demonstrations and training are conducted at three regional centers. Initial hands-on training is followed up by site visits from CET staff or monitors. Because of the high initial risk involved in switching to an entirely new production system and the labor-intensive nature of the process, many small farmers have been reluctant to adopt the organic methods despite the promises of less dependence on costly inputs and ecological conservation. Rural town dwellers and urban unemployed women and youth, however, have been more receptive, and urban gardens have become ubiquitous features of the *barrios* where CET monitors have been working (see the profile of CET in Chapter 13).

Small Farm-Based Agribusiness

The second development strategy of the organizations in the sample is to provide support services for the more market-oriented production systems of small farm-based agribusinesses, which range from semicommercial farming with one or two cash products (often for regional consumption) to full market production of high-value output for metropolitan and export demand. The services provided are intended to lead to successful diversification and generally involve improvements in basic infrastructure, such as irrigation or land leveling and terracing. These, in turn, require new and adapted technologies suitable for specific microenvironments and demand and marketing channels. In contrast to the inward oriented semisubsistence strategy, this approach is outward oriented.

Most of the intermediary organizations in the sample concentrate on testing and diffusing productive technologies and supplying or facilitating farm inputs. Some of the techniques that explain their strong performance are described below.

Respecting Local Practices. Innovations are carefully introduced into the farming system without replacing key food crops or damaging the local agroecology and with due respect for family and community patterns of labor allocation. Good results have been achieved by extending already familiar practices. Instituto de Desarrollo Social y Promoción Humana (INDES), for example, rather than introducing new crops or other untried techniques, provided its client farmers in Argentina with credit to rent animal power, thus freeing farm laborers for other important tasks. By encouraging farmers to employ familiar techniques rather than new ones, INDES reduced the risk the farmers took to increase productivity.

Some breakthroughs have been achieved by introducing completely new, high-payoff crops (marigolds or peaches in the Mexican state of Michoacán, broccoli and snow peas in Guatemala, spices in Costa Rica). In these cases, functioning marketing channels and agribusiness connections were an absolute necessity to assure a payoff from the new farm technology. The technical complexities of such diversification systems often place too many management demands on both the GSOs and MSOs and the peasant groups concerned as well as increasing the risks and dependence on unstable demand. In some cases, the production of high-value specialty crops (for example, flowers and strawberries for export) has also tended to increase the social differentiation within communities and has embroiled local producer associations in conflicts with private traders and processors. In its attempt to market products from its newly introduced beekeeping enterprises, Fundación para el Desarrollo Nacional (FDN) and the beekeepers' association were faced with intense opposition from private traders (one of whom had previously worked with the FDN and had close relations with some of its board members), who saw the FDN's active role in marketing as a threat to their interests (see the profile of FDN in Chapter 11).

One lesson is that diversification works best when the new activity can build on existing experience and when the support organization has access to critical aspects of the agribusiness system, not simply competence in delivering a single service such as credit or extension. Another general finding is that the more sophisticated the new technology, the greater the risks as well as the likelihood of inequality in the distribution of benefits. The exception seems to be when the new technology is based on a collective rather than an individual enterprise (wool in Uruguay, cacao in Bolivia), in which case a central agroprocessing operation can have significant benefits for individual small-scale producers.

An unplanned bonus from many decentralized diversification programs is the multiplier effect from regional linkages. The impact of using locally produced, low-cost inputs is often maximized with the additional

benefit of enhancing backward supply linkages (carpentry for FDN beehives, hand tools and homemade looms for handicraft projects, local
bricks for UNIDAD bakeries). It is interesting to note that although these
indirect effects are frequently noted in evaluation reports, neither the
Inter-American Foundation (IAF) nor its grantees seem to plan for or try
to enhance them.

The case of Consultores del Campo is perhaps the best way to illustrate the low-cost, risk-reducing strategy employed by some of the top
GSOs. Consultores, a small rural advisory group formed by young professionals, works in the Lake Pátzcuaro region of central Michoacán State
in Mexico, practicing community-based rural development. In a recent
research report, Robin Marsh, using quantitative economic methods,
compared the Consultores model with a more traditional research/exten-
sion system employed by a government program for rain-fed maize
improvement in the same area (Marsh 1991). The PIPMA program, as the
government's program was known, recommended higher levels of
inputs and higher-cost practices. It was a failure, even though it offered
rather attractive guarantees against losses. For farmers following PIPMA's
advice, net benefits barely covered production costs; campesinos affiliated with Consultores had almost 50 percent higher yields and more
than double the per hectare net benefits. Marsh concluded that the community-based nonofficial program run by Consultores was effective in
both improving small-farm productivity and in reducing risks because it
(1) offered technological options tailored to site-specific agroeconomic
conditions, (2) incorporated reasonable estimates of production risk (and
of farmers' attitudes toward such risk) in the formulation of recommendations, and (3) provided for a highly participatory testing and diffusion
of innovations. If the regional benefits obtained with the Consultores
strategy could be obtained statewide or nationwide, a 20 percent increase
in maize production and small-farm income could be achieved.

The significance of this case is even greater than that indicated by the
data. Since the famous Puebla project sponsored by the Rockefeller
Foundation in the 1960s, Mexico has evolved a sophisticated system of
technology generation and diffusion in the dryland farming areas that
were bypassed by the green revolution, where most of the country's
rural poor are concentrated. Puebla was followed by various maize programs assisted by the National Agricultural Graduate School at Chapingo
and later by CIMMYT, the International Research Center for Maize and
Wheat, located nearby. Yet the astonishing evidence from Michoacán is
that a small GSO made up of young university graduates can outperform
a seasoned extension service that was the beneficiary of more than two
decades of experimentation and experience.

Table 3.1 indicates to what extent the community-based rural development system of technology diffusion differs from two other systems:
one characterized as "traditional" and the other as the "farming system"

Table 3.1 Comparison of Technology Diffusion Approaches

Key Aspects	Alternative Systems		
	Traditional System	Farming System	Community-Based Rural Development
Objectives	Maximum yield. More income per hectare.	Improved productivity of total resources of the farm enterprise.	Improved total household welfare. Community empowerment.
Research strategy	Experiment station based. Pursuit of technical optimums.	Field based. Technological packages targeted on agroecological domains.	Optimization of existing resources. Selective adaptation of modern practices to meet community needs.
Extension strategy	Focus on commercial farms.	Focus on small farmers. Reliance on demonstration by progressive farmers. Recommendations for average conditions.	Focus on resource-poor farmer-managed tests and peer diffusion; learning by doing; training in technical, social, and organizational skills.
Credit strategy	Access to commercial credit assumed.	Access to subsidized credit assumed.	Promotion of community-based financial options, revolving funds, cooperative input/output distribution.
Income strategy	Emphasis on mono-crop agriculture	Optimization of all farm resources. Stresses diversification. Off-farm labor is treated as a constraint.	Includes concern for off-farm income, women's status and earnings. Stresses sustainability of resource use.

Source: Adapted by the author, based on Marsh (1991).

approach, which has been in vogue since the late 1970s. The third column reveals the success of the process: Technical services to resource-poor and risk-prone campesinos are effective if they are adjusted to microconditions through participatory means and if they are part of a community empowerment effort.

Developing Alternative Marketing Channels. In areas of high commercial activity, GSOs and MSOs generally seek to promote alternative marketing channels designed either to fill gaps in the existing system or to challenge commercial traders and middlemen to become more competitive.

Several of the organizations studied have sought to stabilize the prices of agricultural inputs and basic consumer goods in rural areas by establishing local consumer stores (PURISCAL), engaging in merchandise wholesaling (EL CEIBO, URCOOPAPA, CENTRAL), or arranging for direct distribution through field agents (IPRU-supported Comisión Nacional de Fomento Rural), with varying levels of success. There are tensions between distributive and commercial goals and, for MSOs in particular, between an exclusive model serving only members and an operation in which both members and nonmembers are served in order to achieve economies of scale. Central de Cooperativas Agrarias de Producción "3 de Octubre" (CENTRAL) and Unión Regional de Cooperativas de las Provincia de Cartago (URCOOPAPA) offer discounts and credit only to members but also sell to nonmembers at regular prices. Other cooperative federations achieve a large volume of sales by being nonexclusive. Cooperative agribusiness is especially vulnerable to macroeconomic crises, as evidenced by Centro Regional de Cooperativas Agropecuarias e Industriales's (EL CEIBO's) severe losses during Bolivia's hyperinflationary period in the mid-1980s.

In their efforts to bypass middlemen and directly market small-farm production, some programs also tend to reduce the availability of production credit, generally supplied informally by these same middlemen buyers. To avert this problem, Centro Agrícola Cantonal de Hojancha (CACH) managed to negotiate with the Costa Rican government to achieve a *zona cafetalera* status in its production area, which thereby opened up a line of credit for its client coffee growers. Freed from dependence on informal credit arrangements, these farmers subsequently organized a cooperative to process and market their production directly. In a similar vein, the IPRU-sponsored Central Lanera Uruguaya (CLU) (Woolgrowers' Cooperative Federation) sought to fill the credit gap by providing advance payments at preferential interest rates to wool growers that committed their harvest to member cooperatives in advance (see Box 3.1). Overall, marketing projects have been more successful when peasants were not traditionally tied to middlemen or when credit could be provided along with marketing services.

Other programs have sought to develop alternative marketing channels through vertical integration, with the GSO or MSO itself serving as intermediary between producers and markets. In one of its early activities, CACH bought vegetables from an agricultural diversification project and sold them to Costa Rican government-supported schools and nutrition centers. However, when a fiscal crisis forced the government to cut back these programs, the enterprise and, consequently, the program failed because CACH had sought no other outlet.

As these examples imply, commercial marketing programs demand sophisticated organization and finance and a thorough knowledge of the commodity system, which calls for specialization within the management of the GSO or MSO. The previously mentioned CLU program is a case in point. This producer-managed second-level organization, with a

membership of thirty-five wool-grower cooperatives, opened a processing center to receive and classify its members' wool production. When
the crop was sold after months of negotiations, CLU returned to the
farmers an average price for each grade of wool, thereby recognizing
quality and evening out short-term fluctuations in world market prices.
CLU's operations have not only secured better prices for cooperative
producers but have also set standards in pricing policies, classification
schemes, and payment schedules to which other wool-market intermediaries have been forced to conform in order to remain competitive.

Because marketing activities call for personnel with special skills, the
marketing components of projects with a different original focus have
generally not worked well. A marketing component may be hastily
thrown in because of donor or beneficiary interest and, as a consequence,
may not be given the necessary attention.[1]

The mixed results of the marketing component of FDN's beekeeping
project illustrate the difficulty of adding such a component to a project
primarily involved in production and credit. Although adept at demand
promotion, quality control, and contract negotiation, FDN had little
experience in developing the capacity of the beekeepers' association to
administer the collection of produce for sale. Lack of attention to this crucial element, as well as strong resistance from middlemen, severely ham-
pered the development of the beekeepers' marketing potential. (A profile
of FDN can be found in Chapter 11.)

In general, micromarketing projects show a high failure rate due
largely to heavy dependence on exogenous macrofeatures such as price
and trade policies, urban subsidies, or exchange-rate restrictions. But
farmer-run marketing associations or co-ops have frequent internal problems as well. Corruption and double-dealing are tempting. In the case of
CENTRAL, a forceful leader exposed the endemic practice of personal
under-the-counter deals with large private suppliers. The FDN case mentioned above shows that elite support was readily mobilized for production (bees were useful to the owners of large orchards for pollinating
their trees) but not for marketing, where the interests of small beekeepers
and local merchants diverged. Yet, with the above caveats, GSOs and, in
particular, MSOs have a special role to play in supporting base groups in
marketing. Given the evidence, this role should involve assistance in
dealing with the market more effectively and developing new sources of
demand rather than taking over marketing and processing activities.

Relying on Agricultural Extension. The GSOs and MSOs in the sample
make full and effective use of field extensionists familiar with local conditions and languages, along with farmer experiments and demonstrations. The experiences of these organizations contradict the notion of
some rural development researchers who maintain that investment in
agricultural extension has little value when compared to research or
credit (Perraton et al. 1983; Hayami and Ruttan 1985).

Box 3.1   IPRU: Cooperative Marketing Promotion in Uruguay

Instituto de Promocíon Económico-Social del Uruguay (IPRU), a classic GSO that provides leadership and skill training to the Uruguayan cooperative sector and supplies expertise to the small-farm sector in general, has been a key element in designing and implementing a system of alternative marketing for small-farm production. Working with first- and second-level organizations in rural Uruguay, such as Central Lanera Uruguaya (CLU), IPRU has strengthened cooperative marketing capacity by providing education, training, and evaluation services as well as brokering arrangements between these organizations and external funding agencies. The organization has also encouraged active farmer participation in collective marketing operations and decisionmaking.

Originally founded in 1966 by a group of business leaders and professionals to assist both rural and urban grassroots organizations, IPRU was forced to refocus its operations toward rural areas to escape the new military regime's increasing repression and intimidation of urban participatory groups. In one of its first efforts, IPRU provided support and technical assistance to the Comisiõn Nacional de Fomento Rural (CNFR), a national representative organization of small farmer societies, in implementing its contracted crops program. The program involved the formation within each society of producer committees, one for each commodity, which supervised the channeling of CNFR-provided production credit and agricultural inputs, coordinated the provision of technical assistance, and, at the national level, participated in decisions made on prices and marketing. Though the program itself met with mixed results, the positive impact of the revival of formerly inactive farmer societies and the experience gained through farmer participation in democratic decisionmaking was significant in the long run.

The Sociedad de Fomento Rural de Durazno, a dairy farmer cooperative, drew upon its experience with CNFR's program to expand its collective processing and marketing capabilities. With continued assistance from IPRU in human resources development and negotiations with external funding agencies, the Durazno cooperative is now operating one of three successful producer-managed milk-processing plants in Uruguay.

In another successful effort, IPRU was instrumental in the development of the Federación de Sociedades de Fomento del Nordeste de Canelones, a second-level organization with a membership of six *minifundista* cooperatives that promoted the production and marketing of alfalfa as an alternative crop. By providing technical assistance in administration and brokering IAF funding in support of the federation's service delivery, IPRU enabled Canelones not only to introduce, develop, and market a successful new cash crop, but also to become a defender of the interests of small farmers in the region.

In implementing its small-farm development strategy with limited resources, IPRU has sought to forge links, both horizontal and vertical, among base groups and cooperatives, second-level organizations, and other development organizations, including external funding agencies. Its coordination of these linkages has served to broaden the impact of this and other similar development initiatives in Uruguay.

Essentially, the GSOs and MSOs in the sample have changed the traditional nature of extension services. Instead of relying on outside specialists to disseminate a package of information and techniques, many have employed field promoters with an excellent knowledge of the language, circumstances, and people in the areas in which they work. These promoters tend to function as problem solvers rather than as only technology disseminators (the traditional role of extensionists), working with beneficiary groups to identify their needs and link them with the appropriate resources. Through this responsive approach and sensitivity to beneficiary circumstances, these new-style extensionists gain the trust and respect of their clients.

In Peru, for example, Centro de Desarrollo para el Campesinado y del Poblador Urbano-Marginal (CEDECUM) extension teams, working in a region of predominantly Aymara-speaking subsistence farmers, were made up of staff fluent in Aymara. Thus, they were able to conduct all courses and organizational meetings in terms most familiar to the beneficiaries. Also, by living within the community receiving support, CEDECUM staff became more or less intimately acquainted with the beneficiaries and their needs and gained their trust by responding to those needs. In fact, due to CEDECUM's staff shortage, more time was actually spent on organizational issues and strategic problem solving than on technical dissemination (see the profile of CEDECUM in Chapter 11).

Because many of the sample GSOs and MSOs employ rather small staffs, they utilize various strategies to stretch their capacities. Some seek to train monitors, or paraprofessionals, within participating communities to further spread technical information and distribute agricultural inputs. Others, such as Centro Paraguayo de Cooperativistas (CPC) in Paraguay, have established demonstration plots and experimental farms that serve not only as training and research centers but also as a means to lessen the risks perceived by small farmers in adopting new techniques.

Most of the organizations engaging in extension prefer to deal with groups or group leaders rather than individual farmers in order to achieve the most impact with their scarce resources and elicit greater levels of participation from their clients. This is a feature of all the cases, especially those in which credit is combined with extension (FMDR, FUNDE, UNO, and CAPS, for example).

A number of organizations in the sample have successfully implemented basic literacy and numeracy training for adults in conjunction with normal extension services. For instance, in its efforts to strengthen the capacity of Peruvian peasants to manage and increase the productivity of their newly acquired lands, Centro de Investigación Promoción del Campesino (CIPCA) started with a small program of adult literacy before moving on to provide technical and credit support. In a Latin America–wide study, nonformal rural education has been found to be positively related to the diffusion of technology (Figueroa 1986).

Providing Legal Services. Legal and administrative services provided by GSOs or MSOs to achieve security of land tenure are increasing in importance. Governments are notoriously slow and inefficient in this field, employing cumbersome practices marked by political favoritism and petty corruption. Protection of occupancy for settlers, squatters, or ethnic groups and clarification of land titles in postreform situations provide a foundation for all sustained efforts to upgrade farmer income. Legal services, especially those concerning land tenure and water rights, address a fundamental issue of many small farmers: security. If security is not established, beneficiaries hesitate to make investments. In a number of instances, a tenure security program has served as a base for an organization to launch other activities.

An outstanding example is provided by Instituto Tecnológico Agrario Proterra (PROTERRA), an organization that works with groups of Peruvian land-reform beneficiaries in the Lurin Valley near Lima. Caught up in the general dissatisfaction with collective enterprises in the post-Velasco period, the *parceleros* (smallholders) of Lurin faced a double threat. If they dissolved their production cooperatives without setting up some legally sanctioned substitute, they would not be able to obtain credit and other needed assistance to make it on their own. Also, as individuals, they were exposed to the claims of former landlords hoping to repossess their holdings. Working first with collective groups, and later with individuals, PROTERRA's legal team developed a strategy for processing the necessary titles quickly. In this effort, PROTERRA did not simply serve as a *pro bono publico* lawyer, but it took up the whole cause of the *parceleros*. Armed with a thorough understanding of the legal and bureaucratic processes and options available, PROTERRA applied subtle but consistent pressure on key individuals in the appropriate agencies, leveraging concessions, commitments, and procedural changes that ultimately speeded up the titling process and educated both farmers and agencies responsible for land tenure on how to work together more effectively. Once titles were secure, PROTERRA continued to serve its clients with agricultural extension and credit assistance so that the *parceleros* could make the successful transformation from collective workers to independent small producers.

This whole process was embroiled in ideological and political controversies, through which PROTERRA has managed to maintain a balanced pragmatic role. In fact, this is a case that redefines the concept of an "intermediary." Rather than acting as a retailer of donor resources, or even as a substitute *patrón* to perform a brokerage role for its clients, PROTERRA has developed into an invaluable resource for both peasants and the government. This GSO not only made the connection, but, through legal research and superior expertise, it has greatly improved the service itself (see the profile in Chapter 11).

Although the above discussion of legal services is in the context of enhancing tenure security for small farms, there are a number of important organizations that extend legal protection and advocacy in other realms such as human rights or the environment. Fundación para las Comunidades Colombianas (FUNCOL) is a good example. FUNCOL's work with indigenous populations in rural Colombia began with legal aid to individual Indians involved in civil and criminal cases, many related to questions of land tenure. As FUNCOL's lawyers gained the respect and trust of the Indians, the judges, and the communities at large, the legal team began taking on cases to assist entire Indian communities in recovering, defending, and legalizing land and in obtaining *personería jurídica* (incorporation as legally recognized entities) in order to receive credit and other forms of government assistance. FUNCOL's activities later expanded to promote the drafting and enforcement of legislation affecting indigenous groups and to educate the public about Indian rights and struggles. Through its continued efforts, FUNCOL has achieved some notable legislative successes (for example, the passage of a bill to reform the national Indian education system), and its services are in high demand.

General legal services GSOs, although representing a small share of the IAF's portfolio, appear to be solid, highly effective organizations. A review of ten years' funding by the IAF for legal services confirms the position taken in this study: Specific legal aid to the poor by private voluntary groups is a stepping-stone to collective advocacy, legislative reform, and improvements in the accessibility and performance of the legal system (Liebenson 1984).

Nonfarm Employment

The third strategy for rural service delivery is to generate nonfarm employment either in the countryside or in small rural population centers. GSOs have excelled in assisting craftspeople, not only by helping them market or improve their handicrafts but also by encouraging them to maintain the intrinsic artistic and symbolic quality of their traditional crafts, which might otherwise disappear. Asociación Civil Antisuyo (ANTISUYO), an anthropologist-led civic association in Peru, is an interesting example. Having found markets for fine Amazonian crafts, the association has seen an amazing burst of creativity among the native potters and weavers (Ricca 1987). In turn, this burst of activity has created numerous employment opportunities within the rural communities ANTISUYO serves.

Outside of handicraft production, GSO activity in rural industries is still limited but very promising. Activities that use local materials and fulfill a local and regional demand, such as baking, brick making, or

---

Box 3.2   FUNCOL: In Defense of Indian Rights

Fundación para las Communidades Colombianas (FUNCOL) is a GSO that has made its mark since the early 1970s in promoting the social and economic development of Colombia's Indian populations through legal assistance and, more recently, health programs. Beginning as a branch of the Asociación Colombiana Indigenista, FUNCOL has been working to foster Indian pride and self-awareness and to call national attention to problems faced by Indians, with a view toward revision of Colombian legal codes to advance Indian interests.

In its first years, FUNCOL's team of lawyers handled 829 individual cases, mostly related to land conflicts. Many of these dealt with recovery of lost tribal lands and legalization of lands currently under Indian control but threatened by encroachment. As FUNCOL's operations expanded to include populations in other geographic areas, it took on more cases involving communities, helping them in their appeals to establish *personería jurídica*, or incorporation as legally recognized entities, and in collective legal cases involving land. Although FUNCOL does not promote grassroots organizing as such, it does provide already established organizations with legal aid, thus strengthening the basis of their associations and enabling them to gain access to the government and financial system.

In 1980, FUNCOL sponsored the first national conference of Indians, in which 100 Indian leaders met under the same ceremonial pavilion for the first time in modern history. This conference laid the foundation for the Organización Nacional Indígena Colombiana, an independent national indigenous organization. Furthermore, several regional associations of Indian groups were established as a result of this forum. FUNCOL provided each of these with the legal advice and representation needed to gain governmental recognition and begin operations.

Its activities also extend to research on and dissemination of legal issues pertaining to Indian rights as well as lobbying on the national level. In 1980, Adolfo Triana, FUNCOL's director, published *Legislación Indígena Nacional*, the first compilation of laws affecting Colombia's indigenous population. FUNCOL representatives have also been major advisers to the national government on indigenous affairs, at one point sitting on the Ministry of Government's permanent committee, which advises on all aspects of the government's relations with indigenous peoples. In addition, FUNCOL has lobbied against several large-scale development projects that would have displaced thousands of Indians and damaged the ecology in their areas.

Since 1978, FUNCOL has also supported the development of Indian populations with its health programs, providing both direct health care and training of indigenous health promoters. It has also produced a simple health manual for use by the promoters in native communities. The manual emphasizes the need to combine modern health techniques with traditional ones in order to provide the best treatment possible.

One of FUNCOL's greatest weaknesses lies in the organization's dependence on the strong leadership role played by two of its founders. Their firm guidance and political connections have led to the expansion of FUNCOL's programs and have enabled it to make a mark at the national level. Yet their domination has also created internal tensions and raised the issue of organizational sustainability.

hand-tool manufacturing, have been especially valuable. In its work with Quechua Indian communities in Ecuador, for example, UNIDAD has achieved great success in establishing communally owned and operated bakeries through its Bread for Education program. In addition to providing employment for an average of seven people per community, these small bakeries also benefit the entire community by producing high-quality, low-cost bread and by channeling a portion of the profits to other community projects and to a scholarship fund that enables local students to continue their education.

Another alternative is piecework on specific labor-intensive industrial processes, such as shoemaking or sewing clothes. The work is performed in the villages—usually by women—and then transported to a market town where the business is based. Many of the most promising rural enterprises are located in small towns and market centers, where infrastructure, transport, and some market outlets already exist and where other employment is available for rural workers. União Nordestina de Assistência a Pequeñas Organizações (UNO) in Brazil is one of the very few in the sample that links rural and urban enterprise development (for example, lace makers). UNO has an outstanding record for generating nonfarm employment in rural areas not only directly, but also indirectly through supply linkages to locally made inputs.

In general, assisting nonfarm activities appears to be a very important but neglected activity of rural-oriented GSOs. Evidence is accumulating that a significant share of peasant family income is now coming from sources other than farming (de Janvry et al. 1988) and that in *minifundia* areas, agricultural production-based programs, even if successful, may not contribute sufficiently to the household income of the poorest. As a recent evaluation of rural development programs in the northeast region of Brazil pointed out, the neglect of rural nonfarm enterprise may be due to the tendency of this initiative to cut across traditional disciplines: "Those specialized in agriculture are not trained or particularly interested in non-agricultural growth matters, and those specialized in industrial development are not interested in the more rustic, dispersed, and smaller-scale forms of manufacturing associated with agricultural growth" (Tendler 1988, p. 119). On the other hand, the same study reports that the state of Ceará has changed its procurement practices, for example, by commissioning the manufacture of desks for rural schools from carpenters in rural towns (rather than sponsoring a national bidding competition, which usually resulted in purchase from the richer south). The employment effect is similar to that induced by the beekeeping program reported by FDN in Peru to manufacture beehives and other components locally. (See Chapter 11 for a profile of FDN.)

In contrast to rural enterprise that is only indirectly linked with farm production, agroprocessing is a better understood and often favored category of rural industry. The most successful agroprocessing endeavors involve simple techniques to add value and increase output. Some of the GSOs and MSOs, especially cooperative federations, have become involved in more sophisticated agroindustrial processes, but these have succeeded only to the extent that they have been capable of adopting strict financial and business-management practices. Successful peasant-managed agroprocessing enterprises emerge after years of struggle and many failures. EL CEIBO in Bolivia is a remarkable example of just such a success story. After ten years of trial and error, this federation of small farmer cooperatives now collectively manages and operates a complex of cacao processing-related activities that annually makes $1.5 million and employs over 100 peasants (see Box 3.3).

These agroprocessing enterprises also tend to do better within a sympathetic (or at least neutral) national macroenvironment, especially with regard to price policies and long-term financing. In most countries, among them Costa Rica, Mexico, and Peru, the potential for small farm-based, vertically integrated agribusiness is considerable. Still, the comparative advantage of most Latin American GSOs and MSOs that concentrate exclusively on the poorer peasant strata does not at present extend to trade-based, vertically coordinated associations of small producers. Commodity-based federations have been notably successful under private or quasi-governmental auspices. Examples are the Windward Islands Banana Growers' Association (WINBAM), Federación de Cafeteros de Colombia (FCC) in Colombian coffee, the Henequeneros Association in Yucatan, and the CLU for wool in Uruguay. (For a description of the latter, an IAF-supported organization, see Ferrin 1989.) Commodity associations are viable mainly because they are able to retain a share of revenue from marketing, processing, or shipping the products they handle.

However, most are not really GSOs and most cater to both poor and not-so-poor producers. Perhaps the cases in the study that come closest to this model are the CLU in Uruguay and one of the family of Costa Rican cooperatives that specializes in and has a quasi-monopoly over some specialty crop, such as Cooperativa Agrícola Industrial de los Productores de Chayote (COOPECHAYOTE) (Avina et al. 1990).

Social Community Services

The fourth rural development strategy of the GSOs and MSOs in the sample consists of providing social community services—some related to basic household consumption, others to nonformal education, cultural identity, and community health.

A popular community service is to operate a village store that sells household staples. Several GSOs and MSOs from among the thirty are running such stores, although it is not their main activity. For example, the agricultural input store in Puriscal, Costa Rica, also sells consumer

**Box 3.3   EL CEIBO: A Peasant-Led
Agroprocessing Enterprise**

The most remarkable example of an MSO engaged in agroprocessing activities is Centro Regional de Cooperativas Agropecuarias e Industriales (EL CEIBO), a second-level cooperative federation operating in the Alto Beni region of Bolivia. By 1986, with thirty-five affiliated cooperatives with a combined membership of 850 peasants, EL CEIBO controlled a transport division with ten twelve-ton trucks and four pickups, an agricultural extension/popular education division providing services to some 500 small farmers, business offices and rudimentary processing plants in two separate locations, and two medium-sized factories that manufacture cocoa, chocolate, and cocoa butter. This impressive complex of activities employed over 100 peasants and provided services and economic benefits to thousands of small-farm families (Healy 1988).

Yet EL CEIBO's integrated marketing operation did not coalesce overnight or without financial, administrative, and other problems related to Bolivia's macroeconomic crisis. It was the federation's flexible, participatory management style and access to external funding sources that enabled it to recognize and effectively respond to member needs and organizational opportunities as they arose. An IAF grant to cover operating expenses and the purchase of a large truck, for example, allowed EL CEIBO to use its new capacity to garner control of 60 to 70 percent of the cocoa beans transported between the Alto Beni and La Paz, and thus to become chief price regulator in the region. A later IAF grant to finance the purchase of a secondhand factory enabled EL CEIBO to further diversify its production potential and explore new markets. The success of this plant inspired the rental of a second. When cacao production declined because of the spread of a disease of the cacao tree, the federation formed COPROAGRO, its agricultural extension/education division, to disseminate techniques to combat the disease as well as to assist in other agricultural and organizational improvements. EL CEIBO's ability to undertake and integrate new ventures has been a significant factor in the formation of its agroprocessing enterprise.

One of the keys to EL CEIBO's success has been its highly participatory style. The membership of its administrative council changes at frequent, regular intervals and, within the council, responsibility for the various divisions of the enterprise is widely shared. This gives cooperative farmers lots of opportunities to participate in administration and decisionmaking. To avoid discontinuity in operations, new council members undergo a period of apprenticeship during which they learn by sharing in administrative duties. Three times a year, the general assembly of cooperative delegates meets for three days to discuss problems, solutions, and strategies. Broad participation is further bolstered by yearly turnover in the personnel of the Sapecho offices and processing plant as well as COPROAGRO paraprofessionals. All employees, except those in the transport division, are recommended by their respective cooperatives and receive equal wages. Through these and other innovative mechanisms, members are able to participate in and collectively control the development of their enterprise, and thus their livelihoods.

items. Experience has shown that village retail stores have a high failure rate, even when a central umbrella organization buys stocks in bulk.[2] Furthermore, consumer stores, unlike farm input supply stores, have few beneficial linkages to other rural income and employment enterprises and therefore produce little in the way of spillover benefits. Typically, to achieve a sufficient volume of business, consumer stores attempt to diversify both their merchandise and their clientele.

Virtually all of the organizations discussed in this study have educational/training components in their programs, but only a few—mostly church-inspired organizations—consider themselves educational specialists (UNIDAD, CIDE, CAPS, CIPCA, FIDENE). Both "popular" and "nonformal" approaches are used, most often in tandem. In popular education, which grew out of the Paolo Freire tradition, learning is linked to consciousness-raising about one's social situation and the forces that limit or facilitate the development of human potential. Freire's *Pedagogy of the Oppressed* (1970) has been used extensively as a starting point for many social-activist GSOs, most of which have gradually moved beyond it. Nonformal education refers to training outside the formal school systems in literacy, numeracy, bilingual communication, and other practical skills, commonly conducted in conjunction with productive activities. Like popular education, the nonformal approach often seeks to stimulate critical thinking, cultivate alternative visions, and, ultimately, transform society (Shifter 1984).

Tracing the effects of popular education remains elusive. For Lehmann, the key concept is "communicative competence." Reviewing the experience of popular education in Chile, he writes:

> Such activities open up a space in which individuals can become persons, in which a "climate of affect and respect" reigns, in which participants acquire a vocabulary of competent and skilled social interaction enabling them to regard themselves and each other as citizens, as equals, rather than, by implication, as dependent and interstitial operators. (Lehmann 1990)

The popular education approach is practiced by UNIDAD, previously noted for its Bread for Education program. UNIDAD uses *Ferias Educativas* as its entry point into Indian communities. In these *ferias*, teams of musicians, incorporating traditional songs and dances, present sociodramas, which raise social issues in the context of Indian values and culture and encourage the local villagers to be proud of their culture, to assert their rights, and to develop practical solutions to their problems. From this point, UNIDAD expands its involvement into other areas, including nonformal education programs such as literacy training and skills training for income-generating projects (see Box 3.4).

In some cases, tensions between the two approaches arise as popular education programs become more technical and skills oriented. An illus-

Box 3.4   UNIDAD: Education, Cultural Revival, and Livelihood

How education can be enlisted in the service of cultural reaffirmation and community-based income enhancement is demonstrated by the story of Unidad de Educación para el Desarrollo de Chimborazo (UNIDAD). This Ecuadorian GSO has a unique approach to building the capacity of the Quechua Indian populations to take pride in their identity and to promote their own socioeconomic development. Using its *Ferias Educativas*, musical and dramatic presentations dealing with social and cultural themes, as a point of entry into the indigenous communities, UNIDAD encourages existing organizations to get involved in literacy programs, community development projects, and income-generating activities.

UNIDAD is interesting not only because of its sequence of services, but also for its unique straddling of the public and private realms. Founded in 1978 by the Ecuadorian Ministry of Education and Culture as a regional unit to promote the literacy of the Quechua people, UNIDAD has developed methodologies in education, training, and community development that have come to be adopted nationwide by various ministries and by the Instituto de Cooperativas Ecuatorianas. When the government changed in 1984, however, UNIDAD fell out of favor with the conservative administration. It was resurrected by UNIDAD's staff, comprised primarily of Indians who have roots in the areas served, as an NGO under the name of the Servicio Ecuatoriano de Voluntarios—Chimborazo. Now under a more sympathetic administration, the ministry's program once again features the old UNIDAD approach, and the public and NGO functions may merge again. In the meantime, the capacity of the Indian communities themselves has been built up so that a network of representative organizations is emerging in the region that can carry out part of the work of the original "outsider" institution.

UNIDAD's efforts initially focused on educational activities. Its programs included adult literacy, training of bilingual teachers in primary schools, technical training for promoters in Indian communities, publication of a newsletter and a biweekly supplement, preparation of bilingual texts for use in primary schools, and the previously mentioned *Ferias Educativas*. These programs sought not only to build the Indians' capacity to function more effectively within a bilingual society, but also to encourage the villagers to be proud of their culture and to assert their rights.

In response to the need expressed by these communities for economic empowerment, UNIDAD developed a set of programs including communal bakeries and handicraft production workshops to improve their income-generating capacity. The artisan workshops employ craftspeople, an administrator, and sales agent, and also offer technical training for those wishing to engage in craft design. Although these economic programs have been popular and clearly fill local needs, so far there has been little success in having them taken over by the communities on a sustainable basis.

Perhaps the most potentially significant spin-off of UNIDAD's activities is the generation of horizontal links among the Indian villages. From these informal links have emerged five regional federations of Indian communities, which, with UNIDAD's brokerage and support, have become eligible for direct grants from the IAF and other assistance from national agencies.

trative example is the case of Centro de Investigación y Desarrollo de la Educación (CIDE) in Chile (see the profile in Chapter 13). In the early 1970s, CIDE was highly influenced by Freire's popular education ideal and adopted the "horizontal model," a participatory learning methodology that drew heavily on the resources and daily experiences of low-income groups. In 1974, CIDE launched the pilot Programa Padres e Hijos, which sought to apply this new methodology by encouraging families to deal with problems such as alcoholism and nutrition. Also, through simulation games, booklets, and participatory exercises, families were taught to tend to the social and educational needs of preschool children. The following year, CIDE began incorporating more technical, or "harder," materials in its action programs to boost the skills of base-group participants. But as the subject matter became more technical, the effectiveness of the participatory learning process came under scrutiny. For example, in CIDE's Educación Campesina program, an integrated community development effort that included the study of gardens, trees, and animals, many questions came up that could not be adequately answered within the group itself. Base-group participants not only demanded greater technical expertise, but also called for more formal instruction in these matters, the latter representing a departure from CIDE's approach. Although the popular and more technical approaches are not entirely incompatible, some compromise may be necessary.

Evaluating the impact of rural education services is not as clear-cut as evaluating agricultural diversification projects. Shifter, in his 1984 evaluation of CIDE's programs, notes that there is some controversy over whether these services should be judged for their palpable benefits, such as literacy or increases in income and productivity, or for less tangible effects, such as heightened awareness and self-confidence. Although some education services show clear, direct results, such as literacy, numeracy, increased frequency of listening to radio programs, or learning a new skill such as farm machinery repair, evidence of more far-reaching impact is generally lacking.

A large number of social-activist organizations among the thirty employ some variation of the community development approach to rural development (reviewed by Alliband 1983; Midgley 1986), in which the educational process is designed around "mobilization," or the identification and implementation of relatively simple tasks of common interest, usually with considerable voluntary labor contributions by members. The rural community development movement, which had its heyday during the 1960s, was inspired by external aid agencies and spearheaded by village-level community development social mobilizers. The movement was subsequently criticized, mainly because it had no economic/productive core and no linkages to social/structural change and because it was accused of creating new forms of dependency (Holdcrof 1978). The more militant and reform-minded consciousness-raising efforts were put forward precisely to promote social/structural change. Economic linkage is now a standard feature of GSO/MSO strategies.

Several of the thirty GSOs and MSOs studied have provided health-related rural community services, primarily as adjuncts to other programs (CIPCA, USEMI, APCOB). Their experience suggests that regional federations of local health committees can be very effective in holding the public health establishment more accountable for community needs. In Panama, for example, a minister of health sympathetic to community involvement in public health services spearheaded the establishment of regional health federations whose leaders were accountable to the local committees in their districts. These federations created two kinds of linkages: vertical between health committees and health officials and horizontal among the committees themselves. First and foremost the federations functioned as a bridge between the health committees and regional or local public health authorities to solve community health problems. They were also instrumental in shifting the system's attention from curative to preventive health services. According to a study carried out by La Forgia, three-fourths of the petitions dealt with by the federations involved preventive health (aqueduct/well construction, latrines/septic tanks, sanitary inspectors, and so on). Significantly, the federations also provided financial and technical assistance to communities for such things as well-drilling equipment or burned-out water pumps (La Forgia 1987; see also a broader report on the Panama health committees, La Forgia 1985). The Panama case is one of the very few instances in which a second-tier health-care user group was formed into a federation, a sort of MSO. Normally a GSO works with a number of local community health committees. (For a summary of the extensive experience in the field of primary health care through community action, see Martin 1983).

Problems in Evaluating Service Delivery

One might think that evaluating service delivery is a relatively straightforward process when compared with the complications of assessing performance in less tangible dimensions. But this is not really true, because providing a service is just the starting point in a chain of events that should ultimately end in an increase in the well-being of users. Most of the indicators of successful service provision refer to some intermediate point in the chain of events, generally when the service is placed within reach of the beneficiaries, or "delivered." Judgments on performance are based on the suitability and utility of the service to the users' situations and on the speed or frequency of actual use, rather than on the resultant changes in their well-being.

In the economic realm, the effective delivery of services should ultimately result in an increase in income. Still, it is hard to attribute changes in income to specific interventions. Moreover, GSOs and MSOs do not collect the information needed to track changes in income, and most donors, including the IAF, do not request it or help to collect it. In addition, if the GSO or MSO were to put an adequate evaluation system in place, it would have to expend much of its resources on research and experimentation in the early project stages when benefits have not yet materialized.

Another problem in evaluating service delivery is the sequencing issue, in which experience building and trying out new approaches (which by themselves may appear unfruitful) lay the foundation for future positive achievements. The payoff on intimate knowledge of the local reality is the ability of intermediary organizations to launch or support successful diversification projects in which different income and employment sources complement one another. The need for GSOs and MSOs to spend time and money in an area to acquire local knowledge and credibility means a heavy investment in staff and beneficiary relations. Most donors, as will be illustrated later, are reluctant to support longer-term "up-front" investments with longer expected payoff periods.

In the search for effective income-producing projects, there may be a number of failures or wrong moves. Such projects are usually selected on the basis of trials by the organization's staff without adequate study and consultation. (Before ANAI's excellent agroforestry program, it failed in fish farming; before URCOOPAPA's profitable vegetable marketing scheme, it failed with a potato-washing operation.) In fact, a number of failures seems to be a prerequisite to finding something that clicks. These historic failures and learning experiments are seldom documented.

It is often extremely difficult to evaluate the benefits of vaguely defined activities. This poses a particularly severe problem in credit services, a common feature of market-oriented strategies, in which use of the loan funds is not designated. One explanation for the success of GSO/MSO-administered credit is precisely the relative lack of specificity and control over loan funds compared to that exercised by official agencies and banks. Typically, such credit is granted on the basis of the borrower's character, usually vouchsafed by a local solidarity group (*convenio moral*). In such cases it often does not matter what the funds are used for in the short run, as long as the productive goals of the project are ultimately fulfilled and repayment is made. But although a high repayment rate is a good indication of uptake, it is only a proxy for an enhanced income stream.

In this respect GSO/MSO credit systems resemble very much the operation of private moneylenders. In general, the success of the credit function of GSOs and MSOs, as in marketing, is not in the service itself, but in the linking of beneficiaries to other sources. Because donor funds for credit are strictly limited, these projects cannot possibly replace regular credit sources, as is sometimes implied in evaluations of microenterprises. GSOs and MSOs should be evaluated for their ability to bring new methods into the system (especially in reducing transaction costs), raise their beneficiaries' capacity to work with credit, and act as a catalyst between poor clients and regular sources of loans. The creation of solidarity credit groups is now seen in the development literature as an important means of overcoming the costly and risky information problem faced by lenders (Hoff and Stiglitz 1990). A small credit group that is liable for the debts of each member has incentives to undertake the burden of selection, monitoring, and enforcement that would otherwise fall on the lending institution.

In the productive realm, as alluded to before, effectiveness is associated with a microsystems approach in which key elements of an interlocking production or marketing system are tackled. It is, of course, not feasible for a small private organization to get directly involved in all important elements of the system, although there are good examples of two-or three-pronged operations. PROTERRA works on land titles and agricultural extension, CIPCA on irrigation and farm machinery, and INDES on both marketing and credit. Note that these "prongs" are not in separate projects but within the same project. Several GSOs and MSOs combine technology, credit, and marketing. The tendency to bring everything under the control of one agency or project has been the bane of official integrated rural development programs. Successful organizations do not have to manage the whole system, but they understand it and are able to influence those components they do not directly control. "Smart" GSOs know how to link their beneficiaries to needed services that they cannot provide themselves. ANAI's decision not to expand into marketing the specialty crops it had introduced was a wise one, but the organization made sure that the nursery groups it sponsored got the proper advice.

The discussion of the service function of GSOs and MSOs brings out very clearly the ambiguous but intriguing position of these organizations, which operate somewhere between the state and the market. Their work appears to be a response to both bureaucratic and market failure to serve the poor.

Although the market is driven by demand, state service organizations are generally driven by supply; they try to induce clients to consume what is judged to be good for them. The cases in this study demonstrate that poverty-reduction efforts would be greatly enhanced if they were energized more by demand rather than by supply (Salmen 1990).

The services provided by the highly rated intermediaries are effective because they fit well into the particular situation of the beneficiaries and are demand driven, even if the process is not initiated from below. GSOs and MSOs are able to develop cost-effective solutions to specific problems as yet unperceived by the poor, to articulate demands, and to expand the scope of choice.

The most bothersome issue for these organizations is finding a way to turn a successful delivery system into a sustainable development process, given the impermanence and limitations of NGO funding. The "projectized" form of donor financing virtually mandates that by the end of the project period the service provided should (1) no longer be required, (2) be turned over for routine continuation to other institutions, or (3) be performed, at least in part, by the beneficiaries themselves. During the time that the GSO and MSO carries out the project, something "developmental" is supposed to happen, with the intermediary organization that provided the services serving as a catalyst.

Some of the more sustainable or permanent outcomes associated with service delivery have been highlighted in this chapter, such as the establishment of useful linkages between beneficiary groups and technical and financial resources or the institutionalization of agribusiness activities. However, most of the other developmental aspects for which the service function is a catalyst are dealt with in later chapters.

This leads to the more general conclusion that while service delivery has a strong *intrinsic* value, it should really be evaluated on the basis of its *instrumental* value as a catalyst for other developmental changes.

Notes

1. This was also one of the conclusions of Lynn Gilleland's study of 179 marketing projects carried out by IAF grantees. She writes:

> Agricultural marketing components are often tacked onto a project in order to ensure its grant approval. . . . There is also a belief that agricultural marketing will take care of itself and is a passive partner in production. (Gilleland 1988, p. III–1)

2. The strengths and weaknesses of community stores are reported in detail by Flora and Flora (1985).

4

Poverty Reach

The direct beneficiaries of the thirty grassroots support organization (GSO) and membership support organization (MSO) programs under examination in this study tend to be the "middle poor," those at the third and fourth quintile of the income-distribution spectrum. However, many poorer households are indirect beneficiaries, and some types of community services have a wider reach and encompass the most disadvantaged groups. This is because the beneficiaries of GSOs and MSOs are generally from poorer regions and live in poorer villages, making it more likely that the indirect effects of the services will have a positive effect on income distribution.

In general, the clients of GSO-supported productive services for semi-subsistence households represent an income stratum lower than that occupied by the clients of rural development programs sponsored by governments and financed by international agencies such as the Inter-American Development Bank (IDB) and the World Bank. The income standards used by international lending institutions are quite generous in that the poverty line is determined by reference to national income data. For example, the IDB eligibility standard for softer loans is a project family income seven times the minimum wage (see Faller 1984; Ayres 1985; World Bank 1987; Jourdan 1988). For those GSO/MSO programs for which income figures are available (for example, in the extensive evaluations of FMDR and FUNDE or baseline socioeconomic surveys done for FDN, CAPS, and CPC), the ex-ante income level of beneficiaries tends to be below the equivalent of two full-time minimum wage earners, and in many cases is under one full-time minimum wage. In other words, although the income and socioeconomic level of GSO/MSO beneficiaries vary widely within and among countries, on the average, the target families served had lower incomes than those in which between one and two members worked full time for unskilled rural wages.

Not the Poorest of the Poor

Even the highest rated among the thirty GSOs and MSOs have relatively few direct beneficiaries among the poorest rural households. There are several explanations for this finding. The programs of most of the GSOs and MSOs involve small semicommercial agriculture based on initial access to some productive land, but those at the lowest rural income level have no land and are generally assetless occasional workers and squatters. *Minifundistas* and holders of collective rights to the land are the preferred beneficiaries. The position of the landless can be permanently upgraded only by massive land reforms or by effective national employment-generation policies, neither of which is in vogue today. There are, of course, temporary work programs, such as the Programa de Apoyo al Ingreso Temporal (PAIT) in Peru and the Programa de Empleo de Emergencia (PEM) in Chile. Scurrah (1987) thinks that these programs have a negative effect on small-enterprise development.

A second explanation concerns the self-selection process, which is a feature of most GSO and MSO programs (and of the Inter-American Foundation itself in making grants to base groups). This process tends to bring forward those who are more experienced, active, and willing to take risks—those who, in the best spirit of the participatory, bottom-up ethos, are likely to make the greatest immediate contribution to successful development projects. To organize and to be organized demands certain prerequisites, which once again restricts participation of the poorest.

In two countries (Peru and Chile), a number of high-performing GSOs and MSOs have worked with the beneficiaries of recent land reforms, after their respective governments abandoned the reform cooperatives or even promoted counterreforms. The withdrawal of former state support has created a crisis for the members of the reform co-ops. Bankruptcy and dissolution of their collective enterprises threatened members with loss of livelihood, thus justifying nongovernmental organization (NGO) assistance. But the original beneficiaries of these reforms carried out in the 1960s and 1970s tended to be not the poorest but the middle peasantry or plantation workers.

To a great extent, the observation that land-reform beneficiaries are not the poorest also holds for countries that experienced earlier reforms, such as Mexico and Bolivia. Although these more revolutionary reforms did originally benefit whole communities, over time, the de facto landholding system has become more uneven, and the clientele of GSOs and MSOs includes only those subgroups from among the reform *ejidos* or *sindicatos* that are able and willing to engage in special productivity-enhancing efforts. The poorest among the original reform beneficiaries have long since fallen by the wayside or have reverted to laboring status. Today's poorest include many of the descendants of former land-reform beneficiaries as well as those who provide occasional labor for productive reform units without having access to land of their own.

All GSO/MSO-assisted base groups and households in a given area encompass a spectrum of income levels, with some of the very poor mixed with the less poor. This is especially true of collective group projects (for example, dairy farming). Interviews conducted for this study have repeatedly shown that many organizations do not really know who the real beneficiaries of their projects are, as compared to the target beneficiaries. Even if good records are kept, as in credit projects, the socioeconomic status of the families and their relative income levels are not known. As a general rule, GSOs and MSOs choose areas and population groups that are poorer than the average, and many tend to work in remote rural regions that are seldom or poorly covered by government programs. However, within these areas or communities, the socioeconomic status of the families assisted tends to be mixed. As in other dimensions, regionally well-established GSOs or MSOs with ongoing local research (such as CIPCA) can target poorer beneficiaries better. Some (CEDECUM, CAPS) are definitely more poverty sensitive than others, and although initially they may not differentiate among the socioeconomic levels of people within the communities they assist, with experience, they tailor their projects more toward the poorest. Centro de Autoformación para Promotores Sociales (CAPS) for example, has broken through the barrier of most Guatemalan projects that work heavily with *ladino* (mestizo) villages where Spanish is spoken and where the rationale is that more "progressive" communities are also more receptive to development inputs. CAPS has managed to concentrate on predominantly indigenous, native-speaking villages, most of which are much more isolated and impoverished than the average. Not only are the villages poorer, but within each village the specific participants are also drawn from the less affluent (although still not the poorest). The insistence on group processes and frequent meetings tends to turn off the village elites, and the credit limits are too small to interest those in a better economic position (Murray 1985). (See Box 8.1 for more on CAPS).

Poverty-Reach Variation by Type of Project

In small-farm diversification projects, where credit is included in the service package, beneficiaries are spread over the middle three quintiles of the income range. The larger GSOs or MSOs with more diversified programs have distinct lines of activities and projects destined for clients at different income levels and social status. Credit data from evaluations of typical small-farm upgrading projects show that the average preproject family income of participants is less than the equivalent of $1,000 a year ($150 to $200 per person). Similar magnitudes are reported by Kilby and D'Zmura (1985). This level is lower than the equivalent of one full time minimum farm wage. Some Fundación Nicaragüense de Desarrollo (FUNDE) data also indicate that after three or four years in the program (with reasonable macropolicies), family income from farm production tends to rise by one-quarter to one-third, which, at that level, is very significant and tends to reduce the need for labor migration (Tendler, Hatch, and Grindle 1984). Some successful diversification programs have raised postproject family income by 50 to 100 percent, pushing the recipients into the first or second quintiles in the rural income-distribution range (Diskin, Sanderson, and Thiesenhusen 1987, for FMDR). (See profiles of PROTERRA and FDN in Chapter 11).

Agricultural production projects often have significant spillover effects from direct beneficiaries or more exclusive groups to nonclients or nonmembers who tend to have fewer assets and less income. Input supply stands out as a service with particularly high external benefits. Spillover from new technological farming systems depends on whether it is possible for a cultivator to apply parts of a system, without taking the whole package. For the poorer peasant this is often difficult. For example, in the Organization for Rural Development (ORD) program in St. Vincent (see Box 6.2) or in the Asociación de los Nuevos Alquimistas (ANAI) program in Costa Rica (see the profile in Chapter 12), the productivity of farmers greatly increased when they planted better varieties of specialty crops, even though they did not necessarily adopt all the other practices recommended. Where GSOs or MSOs have made available simple but crucial innovations that do not require changing to a whole new system (such as improved or disease-resistant varieties of crops already widely grown), the spillover is likely to be very high. In Centro de Educación Tecnología's (CET's) program in Chile, urban gardens have had better success than systems designed for small-farmers, probably because the urban models could be applied more partially and flexibly by those of scarce means (see Chapter 13).

There is some evidence in evaluation reports that farm diversification programs such as dairy farming or pig raising, which are featured by many of the organizations studied here, have reduced the need of very poor *minifundistas* to supplement farm income by hiring out as occasional wage laborers. Some farm diversification programs can provide remunerative labor opportunities for family members throughout the year. The Fundación para el Desarrollo Nacional (FDN) honey program has benefited landless workers who get supplementary income from hives located on their employers' land. (In this case, the landlords gladly accepted because the bees pollinated their orchards and the laborers moved around less). On the other hand, some commercial production systems with very high peak demands for labor, such as exports of fruits and vegetables, create a temporary and unstable demand for labor and tend to have a negative effect on the poorest stratum of the rural population.

In general, marketing activities are of the greatest interest to the poor peasants who are most vulnerable to the vagaries of the seasons, prices, and middlemen's sharp practices. However, marketing activities benefit the not-so-poor disproportionately. The exceptions occur in two systems: one in which a valuable specialty crop can be produced in very small quantities and then purchased, bulked, or processed by the marketing enterprise or cooperative along with the output of larger producers (for example, EL CEIBO for cacao, URCOOPAPA for potatoes) or one in which access to garden and household production is opened up through urban periodic markets (the ubiquitous *ferias* in Latin America). In the latter case, the role of the GSO or MSO is not so much in the bypass model, but in negotiating with municipal and national authorities for better physical facilities, price information, control of weights and measures, and transport to and from the *ferias*. In the sample, PROTERRA in the Lurin Valley of Peru and CAPS in highland Guatemala facilitate such market town access. However, this rural-urban connection has not enjoyed the emphasis it deserves from private voluntary organizations and from donors.

Because off-farm rural employment benefits the landless, it can reach down more deeply into the income pyramid. Developing rural nonfarm enterprises is an attractive possibility, especially in small market towns and district seats. Jobs created there have the additional advantage of being near the rural residence of workers who are thus saved from the difficulties of long-distance migration.

A very interesting case of nonfarm enterprise in the sample is ANTISUYO, mentioned in the previous chapter. The Amazonian tribes of the Peruvian jungle may not be landless in the conventional sense, but their hunting and gathering lifestyle provides only bare subsistence. An important source of income is from distinctive handicrafts, especially from the celebrated polychrome pottery of eggshell delicacy. ANTISUYO has found a special market niche for this pottery, as well as for weavings. By paying cash for these items immediately, this GSO has significantly boosted the income of jungle communities.

Cultural, literacy, and ethnic defense programs tend to have the widest poverty reach, as do rural health services, probably because such programs target specific needy groups or make their services available as a public good on a communitywide basis. (These services are also offered free of charge). A number of cooperative federations have managed to combine productive and social activities in such a way that the economic benefits from the commercial business can subsidize social services that do not earn revenue (see the description of EL CEIBO in Box 3.3 and the profile of PURISCAL in Chapter 12). In the PURISCAL case, attempts to combine social and productive activities failed until the input store was put on a sound financial footing based on the contributions of the more viable members. Thus, the organization was able to become a sort of income distributor, in which the economically strong contributed to the support of the weak.

A significant number of GSOs or MSOs with a strong regional presence have gradually moved toward assisting the poorer segments of the rural population: from irrigated to dryland areas, from land-reform beneficiaries on former haciendas to indigenous communities, from valleys to highlands. This move toward serving the poorer groups within a region is due in part to accumulated experience with the less poor (it is wise to start with the less difficult cases and after initial success move on to the more difficult ones), in part to more intimate knowledge of the socioeconomic characteristics of the region, and in part to new demands from more isolated groups that are requesting assistance as the organization becomes more widely known. In some cases it is also a function of pressure from donors. In Peru, this greater poverty reach also reflects GSO/MSO disillusion with government-created reform enterprises and a search among the indigenous communities for the simpler and more spontaneous forms of peasant organization that were bypassed by the original reforms.

A Larger Presence among the Poor

Can we conclude that the thirty organizations covered in this study are on the whole more poverty oriented than similar organizations in the same countries? Probably not. However, the GSOs and MSOs in the study sample have a larger presence among the poorest and most isolated rural groups, and it appears that, in their choice of strategies, these organizations have managed to benefit a sizable number of the poorer groups indirectly.

It also appears that a significant number of the older organizations (such as INDES, CIPCA, and UNO) have gradually become more poverty oriented. In the case of Centro de Investigación y Promoción del Campesino (CIPCA) (see the profile in Chapter 11), two factors seem to have been responsible for this shift. The first is a gradual disillusionment with the Peruvian land-reform cooperatives that were CIPCA's original target group. As mentioned earlier, members of these reform enterprises were better off than the average peasant, but, despite this, most of these supposedly self-managed enterprises foundered because of their top-down organization and lack of sustained support from the government. The second factor was CIPCA's gradual maturing into a regional action/research role and its self-confidence in helping other less visible and politicized rural groups in the interior of the province. In this case, CIPCA's donors also contributed to steering the GSO toward the "mainstream poor," thus avoiding the temptation faced by many organizations to work with either the most visible cases of reform or settlement beneficiaries or with small pockets of communities in the most isolated and neglected corners of the region.

In the productive/economic realm, there is an evident trade-off between financial viability and benefit distribution, seen most clearly in the Costa Rican MSOs. The transformation of Unión Regional de Cooperativas de la Provincia de Cartago (URCOOPAPA) from a socially motivated group-based scheme into a business enterprise based on individuals illustrates this general dilemma, analyzed previously by Tendler for the Inter-American Foundation (IAF) (Tendler 1981, for credit projects; 1983b, for cooperatives). When member cooperatives were unable or unwilling to contribute enough to secure the federation's financial stability, URCOOPAPA became a hybrid organization renamed HORTICOOP, admitting individual farmers and workers as well as cooperatives and accepting funding from the National Production Council, a government/business policy group, in exchange for a seat on the cooperative's administrative council. Thus, in an effort to place itself on a sound financial footing, URCOOPAPA/HORTICOOP withdrew from its original intent to provide low-cost service and support to the region's small-scale farmer cooperatives (see the profile of URCOOPAPA in Chapter 12).

One of the largest rural development GSOs in the sample, the Fundación Mexicana de Desarrollo Rural (FMDR), has also struggled with this issue. FMDR has invented a term, the *estrato promovible* (or "promotable" stratum), as a benchmark to establish the lower limits for its clientele, below which agricultural production credit cannot possibly be absorbed, usefully employed, or repaid. FMDR's rationale was that if clients did not meet its viability tests, credit would make them even worse off—more chronically indebted—than before. FMDR's concept of the *estrato promovible* dictates the proper identification of those groups that are currently not eligible for official programs, but that have the potential to graduate to become regular credit users. This potential can be realized by means of a large dose of technical and organizational assistance in combination with carefully monitored small loans.

Nevertheless, FMDR was harshly criticized by an IAF evaluation team for having chosen the upper poor as clients and for having pushed the income levels of their beneficiaries into relatively high brackets in the distribution spectrum (Diskin et al. 1987). The same evaluation admits, however, that the vast majority of those who are poorer than FMDR clients cannot possibly absorb and eventually repay production credit, even with the GSO's assistance, and that the concept of *estrato promovible* is entirely correct. What we have here is a development model that is valid for most economically focused GSOs or MSOs, especially those that work with production credit: Select the potentially viable (or encourage them to self-select) and boost them above the line of viability, in the microenterprise sense, so that they have a good chance of "making it" on a sustained basis once the special assistance or subsidy ceases. The special GSO/MSO ingredient in these cases is not the resource transfer but the carefully nurtured educational process and experience or, in FMDR's language, the technical and organizational *promoción*.

The evident trade-off appears when the initial resource endowment or predevelopment income level of the *estrato promovible* is lowered:

Costs go up and the rates of failure and default rise. Thus, farm credit may not be suitable as a means to relieve deep poverty. In her 1981 paper, Tendler even questions whether microenterprise credit is a proper function for foundations such as the IAF, given the specialization and control that successful credit operations require. Credit can, however, have an indirect or spillover effect on nonborrowing community members, and it can have a wider income spread if lending is extended to projects of community interest and to nonfarm employment.

In recent years attempts have been made to adopt the celebrated Grameen Bank model, pioneered in Bangladesh, in Latin America. This is a system in which very small amounts of money are lent to very poor people. So far, most of the promotion of poverty lending, also called village or community banking, has come from U.S.-based private voluntary organizations, but efforts are under way to establish country-based "apex" institutions that aggregate the community-level banks into a sort of a service cooperative or, using this book's terminology, an intermediate-level MSO.

The Latin American version of the Grameen Bank was first developed by the Foundation for International Community Assistance (FINCA). After six years of experimentation, a prototype has evolved, variants of which are being applied by other private voluntary organizations such as Catholic Relief Services, Save the Children Federation, and Katalysis. Their model has the following features:

- It targets the poorest of the "productive poor."
- It provides a series of very small, very short-term loans, with weekly or monthly repayment schedules.
- It includes compulsory savings. The repayments are capitalized into a revolving fund.
- Individuals get loans from their community groups, and the groups collectively guarantee repayment.
- Women are preferred as borrowers.

The heart of the financial system in village banking is the so-called internal account, represented by the group's savings plus weekly amortization of capital and interest, which forms the bank's capital and from which future loans to members can be made.

By early 1991, FINCA had 270 village banks with over 7,000 members in seven countries (about 60 percent of the membership is in Costa Rica). In four countries, repayment rates were 100 percent, with the lowest rate being 84 percent in Mexico. National intermediary GSOs have been engaged to help identify interested community groups, to help groups to become operational, and to monitor progress in service delivery and repayment (Catholic Relief Services 1991).

It is not yet clear whether village banking can become institutional-ized. Sharon Holt (1991), in a cross-country study covering five pro-grams, found the following positive results:

1. Poor people, especially women, who are traditionally excluded from formal financial services, have been reached.
2. Projects have been successful in mobilizing local resources.
3. Many of the older village banks have moved from individual business ventures to investments in public goods of commu-nity preference.
4. High repayment rates have been maintained.

On the other hand, none of the village groups has come close to financial self-sufficiency, and few have "graduated" to commercial bank lending (Holt 1991).

There are two alternatives to intermediary apex organizations for scaling up and sustaining the village banking system: One involves a confederation of community programs based to some extent on the expe-rience of credit unions; the second involves transforming a GSO operat-ing with external funds into a permanent domestic intermediary. In the latter role, the GSO would link village banks to other public or private agencies for economic, technical, and marketing services and perform the functions of supervision and auditing.

Some proponents of poverty lending go to great pains to distinguish it from microenterprise lending (stressing the social empowerment func-tion more than the economic function). Others would like to see successful village bank experiences as a stepping-stone to larger loans and gradua-tion to small-enterprise status in which there is less stress on solidarity groups and more on individual entrepreneurship.

As was the case with the original Grameen Bank, the early results of the Latin American projects indicate little increase in employment out-side the family as an outcome of poverty lending. Income gains, although real, are constrained by a ceiling over which household-based productive activities cannot rise. Greater employment and more sus-tained income would require more capital and greater risk and would mean moving into banking for full-fledged business-based productive enterprise, which, of course, would lift it beyond the reach of the very poor.

The mixed record on poverty is partly explained by the nature of the sample: the thirty cases are biased toward productive services, in which the absolute poor, especially the landless, are not well represented. Had the sample of organizations featured more GSOs in health, education, nutrition, or women's rights—that is, social and cultural services not eas-ily appropriated by the better-off—the score would have improved.

Preventive health is a well-suited activity for GSOs and MSOs and has an immense potential to reduce the incidence of illness and the cost of medical care.[1] Nonetheless, these findings do raise a question: How can developmental NGOs reach more of the truly poor?

Techniques for tilting benefit distribution toward the poorest do exist, especially in practices that are unappealing to the elites. But, because the rural poorest have few assets and derive most of their income from occasional or seasonal wages, the main improvement in their economic situation must come from fuller and more remunerative employment. Self-employment in small nonfarm businesses, which is the goal of a number of microenterprise programs, is important, but it can benefit only a limited number of rural families. Village banking is a promising approach. Voluntary labor contributions by the poor toward the building of social infrastructure (wells, latrines, schools) are a standard feature of community development efforts, but they do not put cash into the pockets of the volunteers. The bulk of the needed income gains will have to come from remunerative wage employment, much of it originating in market towns and secondary cities.

The construction of labor-intensive infrastructure can generate much wage income among the poorest. The segmented and malfunctioning labor markets are perhaps even biggger obstacles to poverty alleviation than are the more commonly cited failures of the product markets. It is curious how little NGO activity and grassroots organization occurs in the field of wage employment. (Labor unions are bargaining agents of the already fully employed—they are usually unconcerned about expanding employment). Donors and NGOs alike need to focus much more on this sector and explore institutional innovations, such as self-contracting by community groups to promote labor-intensive practices and policies. Asian countries are far ahead of Latin America in this respect.[2]

Notes

1. Sandra Huffman, in reviewing 100 health-related projects, found that community health care can be expected to handle up to 90 percent of the needs of the people locally and that it can be financially self-sufficient, because the poor currently spend substantial sums on traditional health care by indigenous practitioners and midwives as well as on the purchase of over-the-counter medicines or traditional herbs and cures (Huffman 1981). These conclusions are also echoed by Martin (1983).

2. During a mission to Sri Lanka, the author was able to observe an interesting program to enable community-based construction groups to bid for and to execute infrastructure contracts. This involved not only forming viable local groups with sufficient skills to undertake such ventures but also removing legal and financial obstacles that effectively excluded such groups from entering the bid-

ding process and obtaining contracts. Although the Sri Lankan experience was in an urban setting, there is no reason why similar projects could not be initiated with a small-town or rural orientation. Most of the relevant literature is contained in a series of studies by the International Labour Organization (ILO) and generated by its Special Public Works Programme. See Gaude et al. (1987).

5

Participation

Participation has become a ubiquitous concern in international development work, affecting even the largest donor agencies. (Relevant experiences of the World Bank are discussed by Paul 1987). The effectiveness of
participation in projects of the U.S. Agency for International Development
(USAID) has been reviewed by Finsterbusch and Van Wicklin (1987). Nongovernmental organizations (NGOs) are celebrated in great measure
because of their ability to elicit participation by the populations they
serve. Participation can be direct or indirect; it can range from simple
day-to-day tasks to broad political processes. However, as generally
understood, it means the direct face-to-face involvement of citizens, usually the disadvantaged, in decisions that affect their own welfare (Midgley
1986). As it refers to development projects, participation has been
defined as a "process of change in which the members of the project
group by common effort gain an increasing influence in the decision
making of their organization" (Buijs 1982). This narrower and more specific definition is used in this book. This research stresses organized participation by looking at beneficiary organizations created and managed
by the members themselves. Uphoff et al. (1979) gives a good basic
framework for analyzing rural development participation; the most comprehensive treatment of induced participation in rural development is
offered by van Dussseldorp (1981) and Uphoff (1989a).[1]

As suggested earlier, participation can be viewed as both an input
and an output of GSO/MSO activity. In evaluating the performance of
the intermediary organizations, participation was viewed as a *process*, in
which beneficiary involvement was rated along four dimensions: (1) initial decisions, (2) implementation, (3) accountability, and (4) resource
mobilization. Participation as a *result* is an increase in the beneficiary
group's ability to influence decisionmaking and the extent to which the
process has become more regular and institutionalized in terms of norms,
procedures, and organizational structures. Progress along these dimensions is reported in the next chapter under capacity building.

It was the original intention of the research team to find out whether beneficiary participation was genuine. There is much controversy in the literature over how much "real" participation is possible in strong inegalitarian settings. Some even suggest that, where elites are entrenched, efforts to elicit local views can actually make things worse for the poor (Midgeley 1986; Lurie 1986). Since it was not possible to interview a representative sample of beneficiaries, the assessment of this dimension was left to informed judgment. Inter-American Foundation (IAF) representatives and local in-country support staff closely familiar with the intermediary organizations gave valuable insights.

As an indication of performance, participation may be viewed as the enhancer of other goals, as an associated goal, or as a goal in itself. Among donors, the IAF is unusual in favoring intermediaries that have a clear participatory style. The IAF tends to value participation as an independent goal, desirable for its own sake, but it also recognizes that beneficiary involvement can lead to better services, enhance project outcomes, and contribute to sustainable microdevelopment.

The thirty organizations in the study scored significantly lower in participation than in service delivery. In fact, the majority (eighteen) scored only medium or low on the scale; only twelve scored higher in participation than in service delivery. It appears that some GSOs and MSOs perform valuable services without much active involvement by their beneficiaries. This may occur when the organization operates at such a high level that it does not deal directly with the base groups (for example, CAMPOCOOP, a national third-level MSO), or the nature of the service is such that direct decisionmaking by the beneficiaries is not feasible (for example, the legislative defense work of FUNCOL), or direct participation is not necessary, as in the case of credit dispensed to individual small enterprises. This is where MSOs have an edge, at least potentially: Although they need not be participatory in the usual sense, they can still be accountable to elected representatives. At least this is what the IAF expects when it favors MSOs over GSOs. The reasons why MSOs are often less participatory are discussed later in this chapter.

There is no clear pattern of organizational features associated with either high or low participation of the thirty organizations studied. As expected, small groups with social/community development origins tend to be more participatory, and the larger, more technical and business-inspired ones seem less so.

In spite of considerable variations, most of the GSOs and MSOs in the sample have acquired an operational style that relies on knowledge of local practices and customs and involves a continual dialogue with beneficiary groups. As a result, the rural services performed and facilities established tend to be compatible with the existing socioeconomic system and more readily accepted and internalized, both when projects are successful and when they fail. In the latter case, the beneficiaries, having become partners in the enterprise, cannot blame the GSO or MSO but must accept coresponsibility for the failure. For example, when ANAI's initial efforts to market condiments by the cacao farmers failed, the development effort did not collapse, but new initiatives were spurred with a better knowledge of the intricacies of selling specialty crops.

Investment of Local Resources

One way to evaluate participation is to observe to what extent local resources are mobilized. Although many evaluations have documented resource mobilization, few have been able to prove that the GSO or MSO can take credit for stimulating local contributions or for assuring that the flow of benefits will be maintained after the original assistance terminates.

If GSO/MSO-supported grassroots activities are to be sustained, there must be a cumulative investment of local resources by the beneficiaries themselves. This aspect of participation is uncommon, but it does show up among the organizations in the study. For example:

- In Sociedad de Asistencia Técnica, Comercialización y Desarrollo, Sociedades Agrícolas del Secano Ltda. (SADECSA), member societies have agreed to set aside two hectares of land for production to serve as income for the second-level association. Part of this income is channeled back into individual societies in the form of credit or training courses, and part is designated for services and expenses provided and paid for by the organization.
- Asociación de los Nuevos Alquimista (ANAI) runs a nursery program that uses a counterpart policy that requires beneficiaries (as a group) to contribute land, materials, and labor as a precondition to receiving seeds and technical assistance. The expenses of representatives from each group that participates in regional meetings are paid by their nursery groups. In turn, these "monitors" are responsible for serving the community upon completion of the course.

GSOs and MSOs have supported the construction of physical facilities such as wells or canals with vigorous local participation, but this initial momentum has often not been sustained to include the maintenance of these facilities. The more general point is that projects that depend on contributed labor require regular maintenance as well as more complex and skilled labor inputs beyond the initial phase of construction. Therefore, they are not easily sustainable. Successful cases are found among already well-organized, cohesive traditional groups and business-minded co-ops where labor obligations have been replaced by financial contributions. It seems easier to mobilize unskilled labor for community tasks than to elicit cash contributions, especially on the recurrent basis needed to maintain a base organization or a physical facility. This is so probably because social pressure is more effectively applied in the case of work contributed. However, it is not realistic to expect regular maintenance to be performed by voluntary labor. An exception may be irrigation, in which the incentive for eliciting labor from members of a water-user group is assurance that water as a public good will continue to make private production possible. There are many instances of voluntary labor contributions by irrigation associations toward "preventive maintenance" (Uphoff 1992).

It is also interesting to note that in the cases reported here, social infrastructure (community centers, village clinics, schools) tended to be better maintained than productive resources, probably because of social controls. Trucks, machinery, or canals require a stronger sense of collective responsibility and an ability to deal with the "free rider" syndrome, members who do not contribute their share expect to benefit anyway from the effort of others.

Cost recovery is seldom on the agenda of NGOs, but it is of utmost concern to development economists and to aid agencies. With the exception of microenterprise credit, the GSOs in this study are making only sporadic efforts to charge for services. When tangible assets and materials are provided there may be a nominal charge, but the transaction costs of the services are virtually never recovered. However, experience from elsewhere indicates that if the service is reliable, recipients are quite prepared to pay for it. For example, Agua para el Pueblo (APP), a Honduran GSO working in community water supply, has created an ingenious local tax base, with each household paying the equivalent of one to two dollars a month for the water it receives. APP makes community loans for the inputs it provides, with repayment on a sliding scale depending on the income-earning potential of each group. After repayment (within eighteen to twenty-four months) 25 percent of the utility fee is set aside for the maintenance of the new system, and the rest is capitalized to expand service or to start a new development activity (Weber 1991).

Management Style

How and under what conditions does a participatory project promoted by a GSO or MSO lead to a more generalized increase in base-group capacity? The donor community (including the IAF) assumes that projects initiated by local groups and a style of assistance that encourages them to experience "ownership" of their projects lead directly to capacity building. It follows, according to this view, that the facilitator or sponsoring organization should play a passive or "reactive" role. However, the case histories examined for this study indicate that an active—not a passive—stance is consistent with a participatory style of management and, in fact, is essential for positive outcomes. Sponsoring organizations can take an active role in guidance, training, and promotion of helpful linkages.

An outstanding example of a GSO that has adopted an active participatory style throughout its various programs is Fundação de Integrãçao, Desenvolvimento e Educação do Noroeste do Estado (FIDENE) in Brazil's Rio Grande do Sul state. FIDENE is an interesting blend of academic social activism and a civic support structure for popular movements. What originally started out as a rural community school program, in which community decisions on the operation and maintenance of schools were encouraged, later evolved into the Institute for Peasant Education, which worked primarily with rural grassroots groups and urban labor and community associations in the barrios. Eventually, FIDENE's work gave rise to a full-scale regional university (Universidade de Ijui), in which the various academic departments have their own active outreach programs in health, agrarian reform, employment, and agricultural technology and diversification. What distinguishes FIDENE is primarily its ability to involve more or less organized popular groups in all phases of development projects and to provide organizational as well as technical support on a sustained basis. (See Box 5.1.)

If the main motivation for participation is improved project implementation rather than eventual empowerment, one cannot expect too much carryover from initial learning experiences. For example, it appears that solidarity groups in credit projects are useful in promoting better identification of creditworthy individuals and in facilitating repayment. But such groups may not develop the basis for cooperation in other fields.[2] One exception is the well-publicized case of the *tricicleros* (delivery people on tricycles) in the Dominican Republic, described by Hirschman (1984). Initially organized into small *grupos solidarios* to vouch for one another's repayment, they soon created an intergroup association, a full-fledged MSO, and took on a number of other social and economic functions. In this case it was the association that sparked the new collective activities: Leaders took a stand against municipal and traffic departments that harassed the *tricicleros* and organized a health insurance scheme. Some writers offer a more optimistic assessment of the social importance of solidarity groups in small-enterprise programs (Otero 1986; Blayney and Bendahmane 1988). At any rate, projects that call for early involvement of the beneficiaries in the planning process (ANAI, CEDECUM) or in which a productive system is widely understood throughout the membership (EL CEIBO, CIPCA) enhance learning and the ability to tackle tasks unrelated to the original activity.

Nevertheless, credit groups, which are a feature of virtually all business-oriented GSOs and MSOs, are still a valuable resource. Wenner

---

Box 5.1 FIDENE: Grassroots Capacity Building
in a Brazilian Region

Fundação de Integrãçao, Desenvolvimento e Educação do
Noroeste do Estado (FIDENE) is a university-linked nonprofit foundation with over twenty years of experience in participatory development
efforts in the Brazilian state of Rio Grande do Sul. FIDENE is unique in
the sample GSOs because it combines educational, research, technical,
organizational, and public advocacy functions, and also because it has
evolved into a civic organization that is governed by and accountable to a
broad-based coalition of business, government, and popular representative groups.

Originally focused on educational programs, FIDENE rapidly
became involved in development projects with grassroots organizations
such as cooperatives and rural unions. FIDENE kept one foot in each
realm, improving its own educational institution while supporting the
growth of local institutions in the region. By 1985, FIDENE had become
an academically accredited, full-fledged university with a modern cam-
pus and a new name—Universidade de Ijui. In a rather unique arrangement, FIDENE's projects are now part of the outreach programs of
individual departments. For example, the department of administration,
finance, and economics is giving training and technical assistance to local
governments, cooperatives, and unions. Its department of natural science
is working with other GSOs and MSOs, local unions, and farmer associations in experimental farms, soil conservation, and crop diversification.
Its education department runs a model training school for rural teachers
and sponsors workshops on nonformal education and teaching methodologies. The health department promotes the creation of rural health clinics and organizes programs in health education. The social science
department is responsible for FIDENE's work in participatory planning.

FIDENE, as one IAF representative put it, "operates more like a
cooperative than a foundation or university." FIDENE tries to ensure that
its actions will be dictated by the concerns of its client population. Its
general assembly is made up of representatives of many social sectors,
including the unions of urban and rural workers, associations of elemen-
tary and secondary teachers, the church, the local literary society, the
state and several municipal governments, the Chamber of Commerce,
and student representatives from the major university departments. The
assembly elects the administrative councils of FIDENE from among its
members. The board of directors is composed of thirty-two members
drawn from the same constituencies mentioned above.

FIDENE's participatory and capacity-building philosophy has permeated all its activities. For example, the organization considers accountability in government critical. It attempts to keep regional and local
government bodies efficient and honest by encouraging citizens to
acquire skills to run for office or to at least understand and participate in
the process of governance and to put pressure on the system to remove
corrupt or inefficient government officials. FIDENE helps to build local
self-reliant groups that reduce dependency on outside capital and technology and encourage local ownership and investment. To strengthen
existing groups, it puts emphasis on sound management and has trained
many persons to lead and manage local organizations.

An example of a FIDENE activity that illustrates the synthesis between participatory planning, research, and capacity building is its agricultural diversification project designed to counteract the negative effects of the mechanized soybean industry on the regional economy. FIDENE, in consultation with farm unions, cooperatives, and state ministries, began a program of research and extension to determine the alternatives to soybean monoculture. Using the results of the research, FIDENE and local cooperatives and unions developed strategies for crop diversification and the establishment of locally owned agribusiness for specialty products. Experimental sites for crop diversification were created in fifteen locations in five municipalities.

FIDENE's efforts to involve all sectors of society in the development of its region have led to the birth of a new organization, Movimiento para o Desenvolvimento Regional (MDR), which deals with the priorities and direction of local and regional development. At a 1983 FIDENE conference organized to focus on administration and participatory planning, the discussion evolved into a far-reaching debate among representatives of regional institutions over local and regional development. The result was a resolution to forge a united effort of municipal government, cooperatives, unions, merchants, and so on to draw up an integrated plan for the economic recovery and future development of the region.

That FIDENE was able to develop and expand its grassroots activities even during a twelve-year period of repression by the military government attests to the strength and viability of its participatory methods. By engaging various sectors of society in the collective development process, FIDENE built a consensus that was able to withstand attempts to undermine its objectives.

(1989) calculated the cost of participation in one group credit scheme in Costa Rica, sponsored by Fundación Integral Campesina (the Costa Rican national affiliate of FINCA) and found that when compared with the cost of applying for an uncertain state bank loan, the cost of gearing up for a FINCA loan (meetings, travel, and the like) was much lower. Jointly liable groups are identified in economics as innovative institutional devices to bridge the information gap, and hence reduce costs. The gap is especially wide with formal lending because banks, unlike moneylenders, are unable to observe the creditworthy characteristics of certain socioeconomic groups. However, to maintain participation, the perceived benefits from mandatory meetings with FINCA promoters (opportunity to share information, organize for community action, learn new skills) would have to be quite high. What this indicates is that the success of extending the scope of solidarity groups beyond credit hinges on the discovery of what type of activity has the greatest perceived benefits.

The horizon for future benefit opportunities expands if the initial experience of participation proves to be positive and is accompanied by the group's greater confidence in tackling new tasks. This sequence was often confirmed in the case studies and will be examined further in Chapter 6, which deals more fully with the issue of capacity building.

Day-to-Day Interactions

The cases indicate that GSOs and MSOs can effectively provide services to the poor even though they have no systematic mechanisms for holding leadership accountable to clients or members. In general, formal mechanisms of client or membership participation in decisionmaking, such as board representation, are not as important as informal day-to-day interactions. Sensitive, respectful attitudes are crucial, as is a code of behavior that stresses mutual responsibility. A number of GSOs that rated high in participation have a code of ethics applicable to all members of the organization. Every staff member is expected to keep appointments with beneficiaries, making it a point to be on time. The quality of communication and coordination both within the management structure of the GSO or MSO and between the staff and the beneficiaries is crucial. Open communication (*transparencia*) is pursued, and it may include access to financial information. One of the key factors in this process is access to information in usable and understandable form. This is consistent with the findings of other studies (Honadle and van Sant 1985; Gow et al. 1979).

When both the participatory ethic and technique have permeated an organization, it is observable in almost all day-to-day activities, as it was in FIDENE and CAPS, both of which rated high in terms of participation. Yet, even in those organizations that did not receive top ratings in participation, some evidence of the participatory ethic can be seen. Here is an example of the participatory process of a large GSO (FMDR in Mexico), which was not rated as especially participative:

> The process can be painfully slow, as it was in July 1984 for one group of the eight in the JADEFO area that were moving in the direction of cattle enterprises. The groups were expecting their loans when the planning process was complete, but the *promotor* did not rush to conclusions and was careful not to push the discussion farther than the members of the group Lázaro Cárdenas were willing to take it:
> "What about getting a loan for a trench silo?"
> "Many of us have seen this buried silage spoil." Since no decision could be taken on whether the silo was really worth the investment this matter became a subject for technical assistance some time in the future. If it can demonstrate usefulness the idea might be carried further at some later time.
> Then, "Should the cows we get be for dairy or for fattening?"
> The consensus: "Dairy makes slaves of us, but at least there is some money each day."
> "Should the operation be collective?"
> "No, definitely individual."

"Should each get loans for the same number of cattle?"

"Absolutely, we are all equal."

The *promotor* skillfully set the agenda for next week's meeting:

"Talk among yourselves to decide how many cows each would like to have and I will take your ideas and requests back to the office in Guadalajara. Also, be sure you are in agreement about the fattening versus the dairy cattle issue. Next time we will figure out how many resources each person in the group has and see whether they are sufficient for the number of cows you want.

"It is a little like getting married," he said cheerfully. "Each must think of the contributions to the union of the other partner."

Clearly this was an example of democracy in action. The *promotor* was aware of his duty to listen to the peasants. But the *modelo* clearly did come from the center level and only the strategy was likely to vary from group to group. (Diskin et al. 1987, pp. 141–142)

Momentum

Some GSOs and MSOs introduce services initially without much active participation from beneficiaries even if they are committed to a bottom-up approach. This often occurs before any base organization is established, when consensus building is incompatible with implementation schedules or when members or leaders are in conflict. However, eventually such organizations are able to spark greater beneficiary involvement and dialogue.

In other cases, being able to select activities for which a clearly perceived demand exists depends almost completely on the ability of the leadership to identify problems and to match them with potential solutions. Among the thirty cases, "sharp" leaders were able to elicit the interests of beneficiaries right away by launching an activity that satisfied one or two of their specific needs even though strategic and planning considerations would have dictated another course. In this way a form of accountability was established and a positive dynamic was created for tackling more difficult and complex tasks later. Centro de Investigación y Promoción del Campesino (CIPCA) gained access to a set of communities by responding to a request for assistance in staffing and equipping health clinics, although this was not CIPCA's field of expertise. In some Andean villages, Unidad de Educación para el Desarrollo de Chimborazo (UNIDAD) installed sports facilities and arranged for transport to and from religious *fiestas* as gestures of goodwill toward the Indian communities. Centro de Autoformación para Promotores Sociales (CAPS) in Guatemala was pressured into giving credit before its sequence of group-consolidation activities could be completed. Of course, this sort of yielding does not mean that the base-group members always get what they want, especially if their local wants are not widely shared, but pushed only by some leaders. But it does mean that in tailoring programs and services to well-articulated needs, the best GSOs and MSOs have learned to respond even if it means modifying their original agen-. das. They have had the flexibility to experiment and change paths if necessary and have mastered the art of responding and leading, listening, and teaching. This important attribute, referred to here as "sensitive guidance" or "assisted self-reliance," may seem contradictory but works well in practice. The process is well documented in the profile of ANAI in Chapter 12 and in a corresponding article in *Grassroots Development* (Carroll and Baitenmann 1987).

The Fear of Paternalism

The IAF and other donors working with NGOs often worry that GSOs or MSOs will be paternalistic or control oriented. The IAF has always placed great emphasis on accountability, participation, and reinforcing the autonomy of grassroots groups. In fact, the "responsibility tenet" (Reilly 1985) has dominated IAF grant-making strategy for many years. This tenet poses a dilemma: If the GSO or MSO is expected to act strictly in "response" to a beneficiary request, then it truly becomes merely a financial intermediary with a restricted role. If, on the other hand, it is expected to offer initiatives and guidance and help in capacity development, then there is always the possibility that it will become paternalistic and domineering.

Another dilemma is in the already-mentioned poverty stratum. If the donor and its intermediary act mainly on request, the recipients are likely to be those who have more resources, access to greater information and experience, and are already "organized." If, however, the challenge is to seek out the poorest, the most isolated, the least informed and organized, then the sponsor has to intervene and take a more active role. What actually happens at the level of intermediary GSOs and MSOs is that a workable compromise is struck between activism and reaction.

It is particularly interesting that the linkages are between the support/facilitator organization and grassroots groups rather than individuals. This bias is partly explained by the fact that most of the IAF's grantee GSOs and MSOs work with base groups, and partly by the theory that vertical linkages between the giver and the receiver should not preempt the horizontal bonds between poor people but rather reinforce and hence strengthen their cohesion and autonomy.

This theory, along with a number of provocative observations on paternalism, has been articulated by Grace Goodell (1985). One of the interesting features of the literature on paternalism is that it focuses on government bureaucracies and large financial and international aid organizations. Private developmental organizations, it can be argued, can be more effective because they are less paternalistic. But is this really so?

"Can one-way help be given without jeopardizing the beneficiaries' integrity?" asks Goodell. An answer is provided by Donald Emmerson; he observes that the effect of a "gift" depends on its nature, how it is tendered, and how it is justified, and that the giving helps to strengthen the recipient's future autonomy (in Goodell 1985). (The question of capacity building is specifically addressed in the next chapter.)

From the case studies and discussions with GSO and MSO leaders, it appears that the secret of nonpaternalistic giving is mutuality—in obligations, contributions, and benefits—and the right to question or to protest (*reclamar*). Under conditions of "sensitive guidance," the provision of resources helps strengthen the recipients' future autonomy when mutual legitimacy is recognized as part of the exchange.

The question of paternalism is especially relevant when the beneficiaries are isolated ethnic groups that may have good internal self-government but may engage in notoriously dependent relationships with outside assistance organizations. Sensitive GSOs (such as FUNCOL, USEMI, CEDECUM, and ANTISUYO) have managed to extend assistance to such groups without fostering dependency. With outside support, indigenous or ethnic social groups have gained self-confidence and have started to make claims on the official system. The case studies show that in organizations that rated high on participation, there is a lot of give-and-take between the staff and local groups; initiatives from either side are constantly discussed, and there is much consultation, even if formal accountability mechanisms are absent. One of the top-rated Peruvian GSOs—CEDECUM—has a quasi-formalized consultative mechanism; it has sponsored assemblies in each of the *multi-comunales* where community members can raise issues important to them, such as the choice of activities and the performance of staff. *Multi-comunal* leaders and CEDECUM staff agree that the assemblies were well received by participants, and they are now a regular part of the evaluative process. (See the profile of CEDECUM in Chapter 11.)

GSO-MSO Relationships

The relationship between intermediaries and their grassroots clientele is quite complex and is often mediated through second-level MSOs (such as federations of cooperatives). The interface between MSOs and GSOs and the desirable division of labor between the two are dynamic and delicate processes. Some donors tend to view GSOs as dispensable, once there are genuine representative support organizations. This is also the position of some members of the IAF staff—the *basistas,* or those who maintain faith in the primary representative group and who are suspicious of "outsiders." Yet the fieldwork for this study suggests that MSOs are more prone to mismanagement, corruption, political cronyism, or co-optation than GSOs, whose leaders and staff do not depend on the type of reward system that prevails in membership organizations where formal accountability mechanisms can be circumvented more easily.

David Bray, writing about small-farm organizations in Paraguay, highlights the emergence of an alliance between GSOs and multitiered peasant organizations and cites a number of cases in which such alliances have been attempted. In one case, a GSO was instrumental in removing the upper of three tiers from a peasant organization that had become alienated from the membership, concentrating assistance on the lower levels with fewer members and more common interest. In another case, an MSO was established with a mixed board of equal representation from small farmers and professions, ensuring that peasant members had a voice from the very beginning of the process. This structure resulted in the eventual absorption of the GSO into the MSO (Bray 1991).

Another important role of GSOs is to unobtrusively mediate disputes, dissensions, and personal and political rivalries among MSOs. It was even suggested, in the course of the interviews, that in situations of internal conflict the leaders of MSOs can use their quasi-dependency on GSOs to enhance *their* accountability to the membership. The process is similar to the one discussed by Tendler in which leaders who are constrained by internal kinship and political ties use sympathetic outside support agencies, or "hatchet men," to do unpleasant things, while they remain in the membership's good graces by blaming outsiders (Tendler 1982a).

This mediating role is especially important in indigenous communities where rivalries with neighboring groups are often intense. In the case studies, a substantial complementarity generally existed between GSOs and the fledgling MSOs they helped to create and continued to nurture. Among the thirty cases, this is best illustrated by the delicate relationship between Ayuda para el Campesino del Oriente Boliviano (APCOB), a GSO, and Central de Pueblos y Comunidades Indigenas del Oriente Boliviano (CIDOB), a second-level federation established by the Guarani-speaking Indians of eastern Bolivia. It was due to APCOB's influence in the first place that CIDOB managed to unite native groups that have different ethnic, linguistic, and socioeconomic characteristics. APCOB suggests and provides backstopping for projects, but they are always managed by the *Capitanías* (the Indian village government) or by CIDOB itself. Even though APCOB is run by skilled anthropologists, there are always conflicts and misunderstandings, so that APCOB's task of maintaining the confidence of the Indian groups and assisting without appearing in the role of *patrón* is most sensitive. (For an insider's view of APCOB-CIDOB relations, see Hirsch 1988).

A study by a consortium of NGOs in Latin America came to the same conclusions, not just on the crucial role of outsiders in conflict-ridden situations at the base, but also on the contradictions that such a relationship engenders (Arbab 1988). The study found the dilemma to be between devolution of responsibility versus accountability to donors. An example from Honduras is used to illustrate this relationship. In the course of an integrated development program, Asesores para el Desarrollo (ASEPADE), an outside professional GSO, tried to involve Federación Hondureña de Mujeres Campesinas (FEHMUC), a well-known women's MSO, as a ploy to gradually transfer management responsibility to the implementers. ASEPADE hired FEHMUC senior staff as promoters and supervisors. However, this double role of being supervisors and constituents placed such a stress on FEHMUC that the relationship soured. ASEPADE finally (and in its view prematurely) turned over the administration of the whole project to FEHMUC. ASEPADE's leadership admitted that they "allowed themselves to be carried away by their fears that standards of success, mostly imposed by the conditions of donors, would not be met if they (as responsible intermediaries) did not control the administration of the project."

Shared Decisionmaking

Technical projects do not easily lend themselves to shared decisionmaking, at least not initially when beneficiaries are not organized and have little knowledge of and experience with the new technologies. But among the sample GSOs and MSOs, even those with the most technically sophisticated projects were very responsive to their beneficiaries and attempted to solve their problems whenever possible. The willingness of these organizations to offer assistance beyond the formal project framework has proven to be a good way to build trust. These "side activities," which frequently involve education and health needs rather than productive activities, have prompted involvement of the beneficiaries in more demanding tasks, as mentioned earlier.

MSOs with structured member participation in decisionmaking and organizational tasks are paradoxically often less participatory than GSOs, though there are some outstanding exceptions (EL CEIBO in Bolivia and SADECSA and CAMPOCOOP in Chile, for example). Centro Regional de Cooperativas Agropecuarias e Industriales (EL CEIBO) has managed to delegate responsibility and evolve a democratic management style, which is quite remarkable, given this cooperative's scope and complexity. EL CEIBO has instituted a system of yearly rotation of most leadership positions. This process facilitates the upward mobility of the rank and file and also provides the base cooperatives with experienced leaders after they have served in central management tasks (Healy 1988). In SADECSA, a small homogeneous federation, each local member group elects both male and female delegates to serve on the central board, and leadership positions are rotated. Confederación Nacional de Cooperativas Campesinas (CAMPOCOOP), a national federation in

Chile, learned the value of accountability to its member co-ops through bitter experience in the early years, when affiliates defected. Its current structure is highly democratic, and decisions are decentralized to regional federations. (Profiles of SADECSA and CAMPOCOOP are in Chapter 13.)

More typical is the position of the MSO Central de Cooperatives Agrarias de Producción "3 de Octubre" (CENTRAL) of Peru, an association of land-reform cooperatives. CENTRAL's leadership positions tend to rotate among small cliques within the base cooperatives, which are so large and centralized that the members do not attend the assemblies. In some, outside administrators with ties to powerful private businesspeople have successfully manipulated local leaders and split the membership. CENTRAL's main task, the purchase and distribution of agricultural inputs, is both complex and technical, and it absorbs the resources and energies at the federation level. For a number of years, CENTRAL has flourished under the persuasive leadership of a dynamic campesino member. In this instance, rotating federation leadership (as desired by the IAF as a donor) may be seen as more participatory but less efficient (see the profile of CENTRAL in Chapter 11).

The case studies show that in MSOs representation is not identical to participation. For example, the Unión of Ejidos Lázaro Cárdenas (UELC) did have effective representative leaders, but little power was devolved to the rank and file because the leaders did not encourage direct membership participation in ongoing activities. Perhaps typically, the president of UELC saw organizational success exclusively in terms of leadership performance (Fox and Hernandez 1989). Furthermore, mobilization for protest does not necessarily establish institutionalized member involvement in development activities. This was clearly shown in the case of the Paraguayan campesino organizations (Bray 1991) and in the case of the Brazilian rural labor federations (Maybury-Lewis 1987).

One theory is that participation in MSOs can be stronger if the members have homogeneous backgrounds and a strong identification with their community. Another is that early mobilization and successful weathering of external conflicts promote participation. Yet another is that more than sporadic membership involvement becomes possible when peasant federations move from protest to development concerns (Bray 1991).

A good illustration of the fusion of technology and participation in MSOs comes from the Province of Chimborazo in the central Ecuadorian Andes. This is an area of significant supra-communal peasant organization, supported by external donors, including the IAF. As described by Bebbington (1990b), the current organizational bases of these federations were laid during the period of agrarian reforms, when the relationship between the base organizations and their national unions (MSOs) was strong, because of the universal struggle for land. Subsequently, the national unions' continued rhetoric about land (without much action) stimulated less and less grassroots interest and weakened relations with the bases. New regional groupings came into prominence, organized more around access to technology and negotiations with the state to obtain inputs and economic services. These MSOs are now successfully engaged in participatory technology generation and extension activities, in which both the choice of the technical package and the system of testing and dissemination are to a large extent communally determined.

All the regional federations were originally formed around nontechnical concerns; now they all employ trained agronomists; run simple experimental trials; offer training for promoters in crop management, animal science, and accountancy; and interact with sympathetic government agricultural agencies. The promoters are Quichua-speaking paratechnicians, chosen by and working in their own communities. There is some data on the coverage and distributional effectiveness of these MSOs. In one *cantón* (parish or county), two federations actively assist thirty-eight base communities and cooperatives; the Ministry of Agriculture's programs do not extend to any communities in this area. In another *cantón*, the federation reaches eighteen of the twenty-two base organizations; the official programs work with only seven. Seed distribution is another indicator. Three of the farmer federations distributed 625 quintals (hundred weights) of certified potato seed, the region's most important food and cash crop, among twenty-four communities in just one *cantón* during the 1988–89 season. In the same period, the ministry was able to make available only 480 quintals of certified seed to just six farmers in the whole province (Bebbington 1990b). Bebbington also points to a very important by-product of the technology programs carried out by the indigenous federations: The locus within the "Quichua landscape" for information and inputs is being reoriented away from the provincial cities toward the smaller rural towns, which are more spatially and culturally accessible.

It is notable, though not surprising, that all the GSOs and MSOs that received high ratings in both service delivery and participation are headed by strong single leaders or competent managers with extraordinary vision and personal commitment. Although reliance on a charismatic personality has been deplored in and out of the IAF—an early IAF staff paper warned of the "Lawrence of Arabia syndrome" (see Toth and Cotter 1978)—strong central leadership has been essential to the survival and strength of these organizations and has generally not spawned the autocratic, paternalistic relationships often attributed to it.

In summary, active participation represents a cost to individuals, which is not likely to be incurred unless there is a perceived benefit. GSO/MSO strategies that provide tangible benefits in the short run are often used to stimulate the process of participation but do not automatically lead to long-term growth in participation. There is less correlation between participation and service effectiveness than expected: Service can be reasonably effective without much active involvement by the beneficiaries. However, it seems important to match initial interventions with beneficiary interests even if the outside promoters would have preferred to start with other activities.

Formal accountability mechanisms (ownership and representation) are not as important as commonly believed. Many of the most sensitive and accountable of the organizations in the sample rely on open consultative processes and have a code of ethics that guides their attitudes and behavior toward their clients. The GSOs that made up the sample have largely avoided paternalistic and dependency relations, partly because of their internal ethos and partly because the services they offer are not permanent (or, in the case of cooperative facilities, not mandatory). Strong leadership does appear to pose a dilemma: On the one hand, it is closely associated with viability, but on the other hand, it may perpetuate a more autocratic stance. In practice, however, dependence on a charismatic leader is less damaging for participation than for loss of flexibility and dynamism in later stages of organizational development.

The MSOs in the sample were significantly less participatory than the GSOs. This appears paradoxical, as MSOs are supposed to be representative of their membership. But behind the formal structure there is often little democracy, alienated membership, and, at best, domination by an "active minority" (Fox 1989). MSOs in the sample also appeared less participatory because most of them are regional cooperatives performing centralized agroindustrial services that require little direct day-to-day involvement by their constituent base co-ops.[3] Yet another case of a failed regional milk co-op illustrates premature federation without solid community experience at the local level. In this perhaps not unique case, the MSO was unprepared to take on a complex project with a weak base, and the project offered so few benefits that it could not generate broad support (Pezullo 1988).

However, a number of the MSOs that grew out of local initiatives (rather than being imposed by the government) show that participation is possible through accountable MSOs. In this case the "group," that is, the membership, need not be permanently involved in the face-to-face cooperative activities that are so hard to sustain, but can meaningfully affect decisions through elected representatives.

Notes

1. Too much of the literature is concerned with trying to justify participation and too little deals with how participation can be successfully elicited and promoted under different circumstances. Although participation is often equated

with the functioning of a democratic political system, the developmental connection is ambiguous and the meaning of "participation" varies by country and cultural context. "It makes more sense to think of a range of participatory possibilities that operate (and can be improved) in all societies" (Guggenheim and Koch-Weser 1991). In the GSOs reviewed for this book, participation tends to be direct (meetings, referenda, joint decisions, and consensual member contributions), for MSOs, participation tends to be more indirect, channeled through represenative bodies or delegated authorities. What unifies the experience of the thirty cases across countries and sectors is less the particular form that participation takes than the extent to which local majority interests enter into the decision-making process.

2. Summarizing the findings of the PISCES research on microenterprise development, Ashe reports another drawback of solidarity credit groups: Although the main advantages of the solidarity group is that it has proved effective for encouraging high loan payback, the disadvantage is that the owners of fairly well-established businesses tend to be selected. The "pre-entrepreneurial" group, generally, is effectively excluded (Ashe 1985). The relevance of this selectivity to the relative poverty level of the *estrato promovible* is clear. Tendler (1981) also doubted that credit was a good organization builder among the poor, quite apart from the regressive income-distribution implications of credit programs in general. Tendler was particularly critical of the IAF's belief that credit was a good first step in the organizational sequence. She felt that the many unsuccessful credit funds did not lead to "better things."

3. This point is well illustrated by the regional Mexican *ejido* federations, an important set of MSOs. "Regional control over development activities is often economically necessary, [but] it inherently creates a source of leadership power not directly linked to the membership assembly, thereby potentially distancing the leadership from its base. To carry out regional economic projects while minimizing loss of leadership accountability then, community-level organizations must take conscious and deliberate steps to sustain their own autonomy and membership participation" (Fox and Hernandez 1989, 15).

6

Group Capacity Building

The most crucial dimension of performance by grassroots support organizations (GSOs) and membership support organizations (MSOs), but also the most difficult to accomplish or even to measure, is their contribution to capacity building for collective action. Within the list of criteria, group capacity building is paired with participation. The two concepts are related but not identical. A participatory style is essential to the gradual strengthening of base capacity, but many forms of participation, such as open communication or broad consensus, do not of themselves build capacity. Group capacity, as the term implies, is the ability to act together, not once but consistently, to "get ahead collectively" (Hirschman 1984).

It is paradoxical that, although group capacity is highly valued by the Inter-American Foundation (IAF) and most of the GSOs and MSOs themselves, little analytical work or systematic documentation exists on how local institution building occurs over time. The thirty organizations show a mixed record. Some that are competent in service delivery and poverty reach are more comfortable working on individual capacity building than on group empowerment, which they either do not seek as a goal or see as leading to political entanglements.

Some intermediary organizations, of course, deliberately seek the political role of challenging national and local power-holders through base organizing, although, under repressive regimes, such organizing is given a technical raison d'être. Among the thirty organizations covered in this study, the most politicized (not in a party sense, but ideologically) are from Guatemala, Brazil, and Chile, where at times all organizing was regarded with suspicion. This often created delicate problems for these GSOs and for their donors. Based on his work in Colombia, Smith (1990) believes that NGOs allowed to operate under authoritarian regimes are co-opted or innocuous, but Lehmann (1990) thinks that NGO base mobilization in Brazil and elsewhere, especially that inspired by the liberation movement of the Catholic church, is a significant democratizing force.

Some organizations assume that helping base groups obtain services for which there is a strong demand contributes automatically to capacity building. Hence, they do not expend much effort to promote it. But those that share the IAF's ethos work hard on capacity building and design special programs to enhance group cohesion, leadership, and management skills. Of course, some GSO or MSO activities cannot be accomplished without collective action (or joint endeavors); others can be done individually, with only a minimum level of local organization.

Capacity-Building Domain

Figure 6.1 attempts to explain schematically why some organizations rated high on the group capacity building dimension and others did not. In the figure, GSOs and MSOs are divided into five species, three of which fall under the genus "service provider": retailer, aggregator, and cooperator. The *retailer* is an intermediary that provides mostly individualized services to households or enterprises, typically the business-oriented national development foundations, for example, FUNDE, FMDR, FUCODES, and FDN. Most are GSOs. As already stated, retailers tend to be less participatory and, therefore, they lie mainly outside the capacity building domain.

The *aggregator*, on the other hand, is an intermediary that, like a processing plant or cooperative, provides services through a centralized facility—a buying, selling, or trading operation performed at the intermediary level rather than at the base. Aggregators are typically MSOs (for example, CENTRAL, PURISCAL, URCOOPAPA). These have been previously identified as not particularly participatory, in spite of their formal accountability mechanisms. In the figure, aggregators are half inside and half outside the capacity building domain. (The notable exception is EL CEIBO, which has continually stressed not only membership participation in all realms of operation and decisionmaking, but also strengthening the capacity of its member cooperatives to keep the federation accountable). The need for these aggregators to focus more attention on their own capacity to operate effectively at the central level is functionally more important than attending to the capacity of their member groups.

The third type of service provider is the *cooperator*, a GSO or MSO that favors group-based services and, hence, lies entirely within the capacity building domain. Because the activities of cooperators primarily involve collective groups, their potential for high performance in this dimension is greater than that of other GSOs or MSOs. This species makes up the majority of the sample of thirty.

Another species is the *advocate*, an intermediary that espouses the causes of certain underprivileged groups, providing cultural, legal, or environmental services or supporting women's rights. Organizations

Figure 6.1 The Capacity-Building Domain

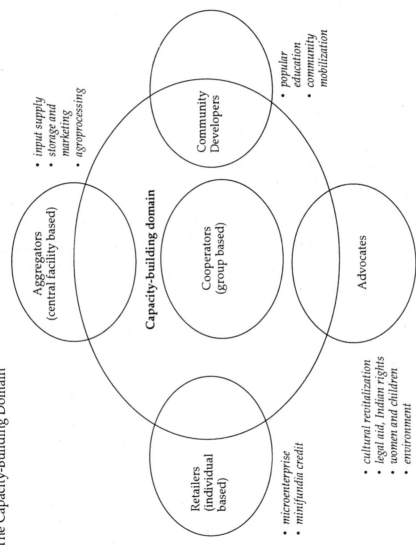

from the sample that fall within this category include FUNCOL, USEMI, CET, and FOV—all GSOs. The advocate group lies half in and half out of the capacity-building domain; some of this group's activities lend themselves to collective activity, but others do not. PROTERRA can be characterized as both a "retailer" and an "advocate." For its role in agricultural extension, PROTERRA is in the retailer group, while for its legal services, it belongs in the advocate group. However, in both dimensions of its split personality, this GSO lies outside the big circle.

The fifth and final species incorporates what this book terms the *community developer*. This kind of intermediary has been previously identified as a member of the social awareness school: educators, self-help promoters, and social mobilizers. Most are GSOs. Although one might expect that community developers would also fall squarely within the capacity building domain, this is not the case. Centro de Investigación y Desarrollo de la Educación (CIDE), for instance, produces educational materials and engages in social communication work that is highly valued but does not directly affect the empowerment of base groups. Hence, this species lies slightly outside the capacity building domain.

GSOs and MSOs falling outside the domain of the large circle—mainly retailers and aggregators, but also some advocates and a few community developers (in the sample, a total of twelve)—are not interested in capacity building or their work does not lend itself to it. This explains why all these organizations have consistently rated lower on participation and group capacity than the eighteen that fall well within the domain of the large circle.

Internal and External Dimensions of Group Capacity

It is important to distinguish conceptually two dimensions of group capacity evident in the cases. The first is learning how to manage resources collectively, or the internal dimension. The second is learning how to negotiate with and make claims on the government, banks, and other power holders, the external dimension. Examples of the former are group management of tree nurseries (ANAI, CACH), irrigation (CIPCA, CEDECUM), marketing and agroprocessing (EL CEIBO, IPRU), nonfarm community enterprises (UNIDAD), and group credit (FMDR, CAPS). Examples of the latter are legal petitions (PROTERRA), Indian rights (USEMI), union benefits, and defense of smallholder interests (FIDENE). Common to both dimensions is the capacity to work effectively as a group, interact democratically, reach a consensus, manage conflict, limit corruption and free ridership, and forge networks.

It is less difficult to mobilize for claim-making than for group management, which requires a more sustained activity, many costly member contributions, and complex trade-offs between selfish behavior and group-centered behavior. Also, group management efforts can be jeopardized if internal divisions exist or collective endeavors do not yield expected benefits. However, even limited successes often generate a surprising amount of "social energy," as in the Bolivian, Guatemalan, and Paraguayan cases in which local organizations have resurfaced even after years of hostile circumstances (see Hirschman 1984, ch. 5).

Social and Business-Inspired GSOs

The predominant ideology of GSO leaders—the extent to which they favor individual or group approaches—obviously has a strong effect on organizational objectives and strategies. MSOs are, by definition, federations of base groups, and this issue does not arise, except when spillover effects from cooperative activity are made available to nonmember individuals. Hence, the subsequent discussion is centered on GSOs. Typically, business-inspired intermediaries are not preoccupied with questions of organization and group capacity building (FMDR, FUNDE). They favor working with individual entrepreneurs. Even when pressed by donors, they often fail to deal with organized beneficiaries.

The Fundación para el Desarrollo Nacional (FDN) beekeeping program in Chiclayo, Peru, illustrates this failing. The FDN, a competent university-related GSO, agreed, as a condition for receiving IAF funding, to promote a beekeepers' association that was gradually to take over the management of the program, especially in marketing. The FDN proved itself competent in the credit and technical backstopping of the program and successfully marketed the high-quality honey produced by the beneficiaries through special outlets. However, the FDN had no skills or experience in group promotion, and the beekeepers' association, which was dutifully created, never got off the ground. In fact, the top-down style of the FDN, combined with the emergence of a beneficiary leadership that also had financial interests in honey marketing, created tensions and confrontation. The FDN never seriously addressed the issue of self-marketing by the group. After the grant period, when the individual loans were all repaid, FDN ceased to market honey, and surpluses accrued to individual traders. The result was that technical assistance, which was to have been paid for out of the profits from marketing honey, had to be discontinued. The sustainability of the program was undermined because the organization was unable to further develop beekeeper technology and find uses for valuable by-products without outside technical help. (See the profile of FDN in Chapter 11.)

Intermediaries that depend on donors for short-term projects, especially those whose mainstays are credit and technical assistance to microentrepreneurs, have insufficient time and lack incentives to nurture local organizations. In contrast, those with strong religiously inspired and socially committed leaders tend to be involved in popular education and local movements based on group solidarity. Such movements are generally oriented toward mobilization and claim-making, rather than self-help. Although this has given them a firmer and more permanent anchor in local communities where they work, their efforts have often been too vague and diffused to create much capacity. (In a private communication with the author, Martin Scurrah called these "otherworldly objectives: heaven or the revolution.") Some critics of traditional community development practices insist that the core of capacity building, especially in its sustainable dimensions, must be based on the management of income-producing activities, such as the acquisition and control of natural resources.[1] The evidence from this study indicates that capacity can also be built on the basis of social services, as long as they provide concrete benefits.

Over time, however, an interesting dynamic shift toward convergence can be perceived. Initially, many of the social GSOs disdained productive activities and focused on popular education and consciousness-raising. Meanwhile, the typical enterprise-oriented organizations ignored social promotion. But now it appears that the business-connected GSOs are becoming more aware of the organizational dimensions of their work and are even becoming radicalized or socialized by their field staff. Meanwhile, many of the social GSOs are acquiring more professional skills and now focus their education and training programs on income- and employment-related activities in response to beneficiary demands for tangible services and concrete results.

Incremental Strategies

Group capacity is strongly influenced by experiences accumulated over many years, exceeding the duration of a normal grant. The path is seldom linear, as there are frequent setbacks caused by both internal and external events. Some GSOs have constantly managed to pursue capacity building strategies in such a way that donor-supported projects sequentially contribute to long-term capacity-related objectives. This strategy can be called "incremental capacity building." In activities aimed at incremental capacity building, concrete tasks of value to the membership are combined with specific educational and organizational training followed by other tasks that demand more collective actions. About a third of the organizations in the sample have implemented such strategies with good results. Learning is enhanced when member contributions lead to greater collective rewards.

The case of Asociación de los Nuevos Alquimistas (ANAI) in Costa Rica (see Chapter 12) is especially instructive. This GSO has managed to initiate a sequence of events in which new technology is the incentive for a group effort that in turn is the carrier of technology. An excerpt from a *Grassroots Development* article illustrates ANAI's unique approach to participatory capacity building through the establishment of communal tree and plant nurseries called *viveros:*

> Both intermediary organizations and donor agencies might benefit from understanding the strong synergy that results from linking technological innovations with efforts to build up the capabilities of local groups.
>
> The key to managing that process is in the finely crafted sequencing or staging evident in ANAI's work. The progression of tasks and activities not only follows a sound management path, in which each step is a prerequisite for the next, but is flexible enough to incorporate participatory decisions and feedback loops. For example, ANAI decided to begin the project with only three nurseries, while at the same time upgrading staff skills through training at CATIE (a Central American tropical agricultural research center located in Costa Rica). By concentrating their efforts on organizing the first three *viveros* and making them work, regional interest was boosted, and ANAI staff felt better prepared to take on larger numbers of groups. This first phase also showed that *viveros* with larger memberships performed jobs more quickly and had higher morale. As a result, new nurseries were required to have at least 15 volunteers.
>
> The strength of the initial infrastructure allowed ANAI to expand very rapidly, after which the organization took time to consolidate the entire project. ANAI managed to speed up or to slow down the diffusion of technology whenever necessary by carefully monitoring feedback from the nurseries. The number of cacao plants, for instance, was reduced whenever a nursery group could not care for all its seedlings with each volunteer providing one day of work per week. And while ANAI had originally planned to distribute over 70 varieties, they now concentrate on the half-dozen or so crops with the greatest commercial potential.
>
> Once the nursery groups reach a certain level, ANAI helps them move on to the next stage by providing additional services. (Carroll and Baitenmann 1987, pp. 19–20)

Many GSOs often employ strengthening activities like training in accounting or group leadership without having a systematic strategy. Sometimes they tend to overload beneficiaries with tasks that are supposed to help them become self-managers but that are too complex or on a scale that is too difficult to manage for groups with relatively little experience. Denise Humphreys (1989) wrote to the author from her recent Guatemalan experience:

> Often what new, young base groups need is a small amount of money to gnaw on in order to organize themselves and sort things out. This approach requires close supervision by the GSO, which is often lacking. I have seen several repentant GSOs here in Guatemala with long sad histories take this issue much more seriously and adopt a tougher stance. As a result, they find the groups they assist on much firmer ground.

Incremental capacity building, therefore, involves knowing when to be loose and permissive and when to be demanding and tough and to insist on a quid pro quo.

A vexing issue in grassroots development is the relative exclusiveness or inclusiveness of the base groups. Unfortunately, this is often glossed over in the IAF documentation. The impression is fostered that the beneficiaries of a given project are synonymous with the community or ethnic group where the project is located, or are representatives of a broad social and economic class with common interests. There are some cases in which the beneficiaries are indeed a village, or a tribe, a whole locality, as in the case of health and water supply programs or in the restoration of native land tenure rights. But more commonly the beneficiaries are only a subgroup of a social class or of a population aggregation that has either joined together in a process of self-selection or has been selected by the GSO according to some eligibility criteria.

Therefore, the "organizability" of grassroots groups depends very much on the degree of shared interest and motivation among members. It is also influenced by the degree of homogeneity among the membership. Most analysts believe that groups that include relatively well-off and more powerful individuals may be more organizable but tend to be less democratic, less participatory, and hence less sustainable. This is why the combination of small, more homogeneous base groups and one or more upper tiers of MSOs is seen as a successful organizational system in which both solidarity and scale can be obtained.[2] The value of mutitiered organizations is confirmed in the present study, although it is clear that capacities needed at the base are different from those required at the upper levels. (See Box 3.3 on EL CEIBO, the Bolivian cacao-processing federation, in which the two tiers perform different functions.) The federation is generally the technically and managerially sophisticated hub of the system, and the constituent local co-ops concentrate on buying and distributing. In other MSOs the roles are reversed: The base performs most of the service functions, and the upper levels concentrate on lobbying, fund-raising, and procurement. This study also indicates that homogeneity of status is less important than commonality of interest. This explains the great value that commodity-based federations place on their poorer members, who may benefit relatively less than those with larger holdings and more production, but who benefit nonetheless in proportion to their market share.

Local capacity can be promoted successfully when beneficiaries see very clear gains in group action and when the local organizational models are based on socially accepted forms of solidarity, incentives, and sanctions. A new model of such community-based cooperation is the *rondero* system (a sort of self-defense committee originally started to prevent theft of livestock, which later assumed other tasks) in the northern Andes of Peru, which is the basis of CIPCA's new programs.

Base groups were created and nurtured by an impressive set of GSOs among the thirty organizations: UNIDAD in Ecuador, INDES in Argentina, CAPS in Guatemala, and CIPCA and CEDECUM in Peru. IPRU's work to strengthen the farm cooperative movement in Uruguay is especially notable. It has provided skill and leadership training for cooperatives and was the originator of FUNDASOL, a development bank for cooperatives, which also offers educational and technical assistance to its borrowers.

The importance of these considerations for capacity building is that the groups that are most likely to become empowered or enabled are also likely to be task specific and, therefore, exclusive, with a more restrictive benefit distribution than one would wish.

Special Role of GSOs

A more general argument can be made for the special advantage of outside organizational facilitators or GSOs in helping to get things done in groups and in building institutional capacity at the grassroots. Anne Hornsby, a sociologist working in the Bogota barrios with community organizations under an IAF doctoral fellowship, has pointed out that at the local level there is a tremendous opportunity to learn better ways to run meetings, make decisions, solve conflicts, manage relations with other groups, grow larger without losing control and disintegrating, and convince members to "buy into" the group process. She writes:

> What I have observed in my small, informal, all-volunteer groups *is a lack of information about how to maneuver within the environment of Bogotá* to get what they want; and a lack of experience in and/or facility with basic processes for getting things done, for coordinating consciously with others so that everyone has a voice or participates in some manner, and for ensuring that decisionmaking actually results in effective actions. It seems to me that the failures to get things done can be, in part, attributed to the way these folks run meetings, the way tasks are distributed (e.g., not clearly assigned), the way good ideas are lost because the two people in the corner cannot make themselves heard (especially the women), the restricted notion of "leader" as the one who dominates rather than the one who also must listen and synthesize at times, the lack of follow-up (i.e., the common trap of just having meetings to feel like the group is getting somewhere, even when not enough work is done outside of meetings), and so on. (Hornsby 1989b)

Another useful concept in grassroots capacity building is the idea of "free space" as an environment in which people are able to learn a new self-respect, a deeper and more assertive group identity, public skills, and values of cooperation (Evans and Boyte 1986). It cannot be assumed that such learning happens automatically or that such free spaces are permanently available. Even groups that start out being highly participatory can lose that feature over time because of a dominating leader or some external feature, such as shifting regional political alliances. Hornsby points out that an outside facilitator who is not part of the regular relationships in an organization can open up this space again. Fox (1989) also stresses the importance of such free spaces for the generation of internal leadership from below in the case of a regional Mexican peasant federation. The Chilean organizations in the sample show that in a repressive situation this space can be very narrow indeed and exploited only through outside help.

Another way to conceptualize the special quality of "outsiders" or GSOs is in their role as brokers and mediators. In this sense, GSOs are change agents who insert themselves from the outside to mediate exchanges, negotiate resource flows, and, most important from the point of view of capacity building, help the organization develop strategies for dealing with other actors in the external environment. For example, INDES and IPRU were notable in linking their member cooperatives to financial and marketing centers in the Southern Cone. PROTERRA in Peru and FUNCOL in Colombia provide legal defense services and, in the process, confer credibility to the causes of the groups they assist.

The suggestion here is not simply that the best GSOs are those that provide links that their clients need but are unable to forge themselves. The ability to deal effectively with the environment must be transmitted to the groups themselves, along with techniques to make the functioning of this process more democratic. Thus, the key is that an outsider, a facilitator, carries these techniques and insights into the organization. In this context it should be recognized that local organizations are generally not fixed or stable, so capacity building at this level often implies sustaining and reinforcing networks of individuals and informal groups of people, such as neighbors, fellow activists, friends, or professional colleagues. These multiple, fluid, often overlapping networks form the organizational base within which specific forms of aggregations appear, disappear, and reappear. What is important is that such networks hold collective experience long after a particular organization has ceased to exist because it is through the cumulative learning and relationships that the potential for future mobilization is kept alive. This notion is very close to what Albert Hirschman has so vividly described as the "principle of conservation and mutation of social energy" (Hirschman 1984; see also Annis and Hakim 1988; and Uphoff's further elaboration of this theme 1992).

This notion of a fluid and mutating local organizational network, although helpful in explaining how the process of capacity building actually occurs, complicates evaluation. It is hard enough to follow the evolution of a group over time, but it is much harder to trace its mutations or reappearances in such a dynamic setting and to attribute some causality to the growth in group capacity. So it is not surprising that process stories are very scarce among the data on the thirty cases, and in the IAF files in general.

Perhaps the Costa Rican cases reveal the most: It is evident that households belong simultaneously and sequentially to a number of different organizations, which may have different purposes, leadership, or appeal (similar to the variety of civic associations to which people in more developed countries belong). This relative density of civic groups may be associated with the great degree of democratic experience and pluralism in Costa Rica. What impressed the research team there, especially in the ANAI story, is that even in isolated areas people seem to have options or choices and that the legal system is not an obstacle to joining new types of associations (as is often the case elsewhere). Even within the Costa Rican sample, a number of organizations had recently split off, merged, changed functions, or reconstituted themselves. Although this instability certainly arises partly from obvious failures (such as the ill-fated potato-washing experiment of URCOOPAPA), one can also interpret the Costa Rican scene as rather resilient and potentially favorable to the accumulation of organizational effectiveness. The downside is that local organizations in Costa Rica seem more adept at building clientele relations with the state than improving the status of the very poorest social groups.

It may be that the phenomenon of resurfacing "social energy" can be more readily observed in an urban, rather than a rural setting (Friedmann and Salguero 1987; see also a review of community participation in urban projects in Moser 1989). Hornsby provides the following observations from a barrio in Bogotá:

> In some of the groups with which I work, the inevitable tensions are reduced because the members have shared many years of working together in a variety of different organizational settings. Twelve years ago one network was involved in political groups doing land invasions; ten years ago, a subset of this network organized to protect a recreational area from being destroyed for use as commercial storage; eight years ago another piece of the network, along with some new faces, formed a street theater group; and today this network of friends/activists is spread across a wide range of community groups and local or city-wide organizations. (Hornsby,1989a)

It is, of course, not possible to trace how much of this cumulative process can be credited to GSO facilitators. What is clear is that although the staffs of a number of GSOs in the sample have strong organizational skills, such skills are not commonly found in GSOs. The ubiquitous training component of GSO programs generally includes courses in accounting or technical subjects but seldom includes instruction on how to work together more productively, creatively, and democratically; in other words, it lacks a micro-organizational institution-building element. However, the IAF has often included leadership training as an element in its assistance package.

Because GSOs often work with base organizations created by land reform programs and thus lack cohesiveness or homogeneity, it is not uncommon to find failures in capacity building. In the organizations studied here, agricultural production cooperatives or collectives generally fail in this area. Most of these joint enterprises were imposed by government reforms. They are especially vulnerable to the "free rider syndrome" and lack incentives for members to promote cooperative effort. Collectives are also prone to internal and external disruption. For example, in Peru, GSOs have underestimated the strong post-reform tendency in the countryside to reject imposed cooperative organizations, especially in the productive sector. GSOs working with organizations originally created by government fiat have been forced to decide whether the organizations should be supported, rehabilitated, or dissolved so that members can regroup on their own initiative. Peruvian GSOs are now experimenting with support for informal groups and more "natural" or spontaneous forms of local organization. They are also attempting to identify activities, such as irrigation committees, that offer more opportunities for beneficiary cooperation and collective action than existed in the land reform sector.

Another heritage of the once-celebrated member-managed collective enterprises in Peru and elsewhere is the tendency for local groups to assume a bargaining stance based on union tactics. Many of the land reform collectives have a heterogeneous membership, often made up of former wage workers. The use of pressure tactics against the government or whatever organization assumes the role of authority or is the source of financing has carried over to the GSOs or MSOs themselves in some instances. This has made their job of promoting self-reliance and self-management exceedingly difficult.

Repressive Environments

GSOs and MSOs have made a positive contribution by keeping the torch alight for alternative values and systems. Under Chile's military regime, any kind of organization among the poor was suspect. GSOs and MSOs strived to keep the surviving rural or local institutions together and functioning to preserve some grassroots organization. But the repressive Chilean environment in some ways helped members see the value of their organizations not only as sources of credit or technical assistance but also as viable problem-solving entities.

Under similarly repressive circumstances, Centro Paraguayo de Cooperativistas (CPC) has worked to organize small farmers into problem-solving committees, consciously avoiding the formation of formal cooperatives. CPC directors found that in Paraguay, as in other countries, cooperatives tended to be dominated by a few better-off members who themselves became intermediaries and tried to control an entire market. To avoid this problem, field staff members work with smaller groups of ten to twenty farmers, illustrating the benefits of collective problem identification and action and encouraging, from the very beginning of CPC involvement, self-sufficiency and self-reliance. An excerpt from an interview with a CPC organizer taken from Wasserstrom's collection of oral histories of social change illustrates the CPC strategy of group capacity building:

> Often they would ask us, "What do we need to form a group?" And we would answer, "You need a president, a secretary, and a treasurer —everything else depends on what you want to do. We can't tell you what kind of structure you should have; that will become clear when you decide what your goals are." At first, people found it strange that we didn't want to take the responsibility for organizing them. But we believe that each group has to stand on its own. We all know plenty of groups that can't function without some outsider standing over them. The only time the group gets together is when the extension agent or the social worker comes to visit and if they don't show up, the group falls apart. We aren't interested in more of those organizations. We want to support people who think about their situation, who follow their own path, who try to solve their own problems, and who can organize themselves. The reason is very simple: any outside group like ours can only provide a limited degree of support, whereas the problems never go away. As soon as one is solved, you have another one to worry about. (Wasserstrom 1985, p. 150)

By stimulating and supporting the formation of problem-solving committees rather than formal, narrowly focused service cooperatives, CPC has generated an environment in which small farmers can act collectively not only within a hostile economic setting but also under a repressive political regime (see Box 6.1.)

It is of interest to consider here the role that rural labor union federations have played in grassroots development. Most unions are urban, but in Brazil, rural unions are important, and they are joined at the state level in federations, a special type of MSO called Federacioes dos Trabalhadores na Agricultura (FETAGs). The military government has allowed these rural unions, or *sindicatos*, to persist and has even given them some developmental functions, such as implementation of health and welfare services, albeit under strict supervision.

Because rural unions are not represented in the sample (or in the IAF's portfolio), one of the IAF's doctoral fellowship holders doing fieldwork in Brazil, Biorn Maybury-Lewis, was asked to explore the grassroots organizing role of FETAGs. He chose the federation in Rio Grande do Sul, representing mainly a smallholder constituency rather than landless

Box 6.1   CPC: The Formation of Problem-Solving Committees

Avoiding the formation of formal cooperatives, which were viewed as another form of exploitative intermediary, Centro Paraguayo de Cooperativistas (CPC) has been working in three departments of Paraguay to organize small farmers, many of whom are among the poorest, into problem-solving committees. Many of these farmers are without title to the lands they till; others have received land from government colonization plans. Facing a situation of repression, threats of land repossession, decreasing prices for cash crops, and inflationary increases in the cost of consumption items, individual farmer families saw new hope in CPC's strategy of collective action.

Founded in 1963 as a GSO, CPC's original goal was to organize formal cooperatives. Through a process of self-reflection by the staff, CPC decided to abandon this idea and implement a new work methodology that assigns priority to other forms of communal organization, a methodology that has been subsequently adopted by many other Paraguayan GSOs.

CPC's methodology functions on several levels, beginning at the base with committees of ten to twenty small-farm families. Initially, a field team of four to five staff members, including organizational promoters, an agronomist, an accountant, and a home economics specialist, visits with potential members to discuss the benefits to be derived from group formation. Once the committee has decided to organize, individual staff members visit at least once a month to conduct specialized courses in their corresponding areas. The organizational specialist, for example, covers issues relating to group dynamics, analysis of problems, and the available means of addressing these problems. Particular emphasis is placed on the elaboration of communal production plans in coordination with the agronomist. Accompanying accounting courses engender concepts of rational management of credit from CPC's revolving loan fund. From the very start of CPC involvement, independence and self-reliance of the committees in all aspects of their development are encouraged and stressed.

As local committees evolve, higher-level zonal committees of ten to twenty base committee representatives are formed to carry out joint commercialization of cash crops and joint purchases of agricultural implements. The organizational training strategy employed at this level is similar to that at the base level, but with courses tailored more toward analysis of links and forms of integration between the committees and the zonal level as well as collective marketing techniques.

Under the auspices of an IAF grant, CPC directed its attention toward the creation of a financially and managerially autonomous regional peasant organization that brought together representatives from five zonal committees. This experiment proved unsatisfactory, however, because of problems with the over-centralization of power and administration derived from running too large an organization in the regional model. CPC's focus then returned to the zonal committees as the ultimate level of peasant organization.

Less than three years after an initial IAF grant (1976), CPC had organized sixty-two local committees with 1,200 small producers and their families into six zonal groups and a regional organization. By 1982, all promotion was handled by these local, zonal, and regional groups. Regional coordinators were making all decisions on the use of revolving loan funds and carrying out all negotiations with banks and marketing outlets. Essentially, CPC had worked itself out of a job by carefully and successfully building the capacities of these organizations to identify and solve their own problems. At the same time, CPC has allowed disenfranchised men and women to create their own forms of democratic participation, even in a repressive, undemocratic setting.

workers, as the most likely FETAG to begin engaging itself in grassroots development. Maybury-Lewis's findings raise doubts that this type of MSO promotes much group capacity at the base or even has a significant development role.

In Rio Grande do Sul, there is little evidence of a federation level effort to coordinate contacts between the base groups and institutions engaged in the work of grassroots development support. Nor does the federation provide services itself that could be considered grassroots support services. The federation spends most of its members' time and its resources on lobbying the government for improvements of welfare services and of agricultural policies. Agricultural policies of chief interest to FETAG-RGS concern price supports, storage systems, credit conditions, marketing ventures, and economic infrastructure improvements. Mediation between *base groups* and superior economic and political power centers is still contained very much in the channels envisioned by the military governors since 1964. The style of syndical activism remains, for the most part, corporatist, patrimonial, vertical, and extremely cautious.

Grassroots work is a type of mobilization activity whose ends are not at all clear to those leadership factions, progressive or otherwise, compromised with the system. They appear to have viewed "excessive base work" as the first step to creating the conditions and leaders that will eventually unseat them. They consider base work, of even a seemingly innocent developmentalist nature, with suspicion. (Maybury-Lewis 1987)

What is remarkable about the Brazil case is not so much that union base organization is politically suspect, but that there is so little interest on the part of the regional union federations to engage their constituent groups in development work. Tendler (1988) also reports that rural labor syndicates in northeastern Brazil have not taken advantage of or made claims on the substantial integrated rural development program of POLONORDESTE, which was certainly much less open to "aggressive" interpretations than the union's stand on land reform.

Complementary Functions of GSOs and MSOs

Some of the group-capacity-promoting GSOs have not only succeeded in building more and stronger base groups but have also been instrumental in the development of second-tier MSOs that represent clusters of base groups. The most visible and concrete cases of capacity building among the sample GSOs occurred when facilitator-type organizations succeeded in gradually creating networks and built up service organizations run by the peasant groups themselves. This process is especially notable in Uruguay, northern Argentina, and Paraguay. But once such indigenous capacity has been built, what happens to the original "outsider" GSOs? Is there a role for facilitator-type GSOs after primary groups have acquired their own higher-order federations?

As suggested in Chapter 5, the two types of intermediary organizations—GSOs and MSOs—are not antagonistic (or alternatives for donor support) but complementary. The evidence indicates that capacity building continues to depend on outside help. In periods of initial group mobilization, GSOs deal directly with base groups or MSOs with membership organizations. Once these base groups become stronger and more numerous, facilitators can and do work increasingly with representative aggregates of base groups or MSOs. More important, because of their independence and superior technical access, GSOs can help MSOs strengthen *their* base groups. There are a number of cases in the sample in which a promising but weak second-tier association was able to reinforce its constituent groups, thanks to the presence of a GSO (CEDECUM, APCOB). Hence, it is the interface between MSOs and GSOs that is of real interest. When a clear differentiation of services or functions is achieved, the "insider" and the "outsider" organizations can fully develop their respective comparative advantages. Such a relationship is not without conflict, however. When MSOs become strong enough to assert their independence, tensions may develop between them and the GSOs that initially helped create them. This sometimes conflictual relationship is illustrated by the interface between APCOB and CIDOB, described in Chapter 5. A similar case is described by Tendler (1983b) in which Acción Cultural Loyola (ACLO), a Bolivian Catholic social-action GSO, founded a cooperative federation and then was keenly disappointed over the way the federation turned out. It was largely a business enterprise serving better-off individual members with no interest in the community. Writes Tendler: "It was as if ACLO had wanted COINCA [the federation] to be successful at a business that benefited peasants without having the business mentality it takes to make that kind of success—a kind of immaculate capitalist conception" (1983b, pp. 250–51).

Even after base groups and their own representative support organizations (MSOs) become stronger, the GSO network of outside support institutions need not wither away as some suggest. In fact, the technical, financial, and organizational needs of the more dynamic membership groups continue to grow and change. A considerable segment of the poorer social groups, even if gradually represented by their own organizations, has come to rely on increasingly sophisticated outside services and support linkages. Some of these services are supplied by the state, as in Costa Rica and Mexico. However, in many countries, state support carries with it dangers of political co-optation or excessive dependency. To the extent that there is pressure from below and some openness at the top, a private or semiprivate grassroots support system can operate and become institutionalized along with a network of responsive membership associations. The emergence of such a dual system is already visible in some countries (for example, Uruguay, Brazil, Ecuador, and Colombia) where membership-controlled networks are supported by specialized nongovernmental institutions in finance, technology, or management.

Modes of Support

It is useful to think of three modes of support: proactive, collaborative, and responsive. Depending on the initial capacity of the base organization, the GSO offers support in varying degrees of intensity (see Box 6.2). When there is very little or no local organization, the dominant mode is proactive, with a large dose of promotion and motivation. (ANAI in Costa Rica and ORD in St. Vincent are good examples.) Early group experiments are carefully monitored and protected. In order to make its technical-assistance component sustainable, ANAI trains one member of each of its tree nursery groups for an entire year. This person is supported by the community during training, but later becomes responsible for providing free technical assistance to his or her fellow farmers. Such a process requires intensive work. When there is some local organization, the dominant mode is collaboration, characterized by extensive interaction and fraught with the possibility of making mistakes. (CEDECUM in Peru and CAPS in Guatemala operate in a collaborative mode.) For mature groups, the support organization typically provides assistance upon request and responds to client initiatives. (INDES and IPRU in the Southern Cone have evolved into this mode.) In practice, support organizations that carry out a number of different activities and work with different groups at various stages of organizational development may act in all three modes simultaneously or sequentially. (For an elaboration of these modes of support, see Uphoff 1986, ch. 7.)

Some fear that a proactive stance by GSOs threatens the autonomy and "genuineness" of local groups. Bebbington observed the effect of two excellent GSOs working in Ecuador's Chimborazo region on collective resource management by *runas* or peasant groups. He writes:

> The implications of these changing relationships (social organization of technology in *runa* agriculture) to institutions are not yet clear. On the one hand they are perhaps creating the sense among *runas* that change can only come from outside, from projects. The peasantry is now well aware of the existence of funding sources for "poor Indians" and is

Box 6.2   ORD: The Evolution of Organizational Strategies

The case of the Organization for Rural Development (ORD) in St. Vincent illustrates the evolution of organizational dynamics and strategies as the needs and capacities of beneficiaries change over time. Beginning with the primary goals of ensuring the subsistence and adequate nutrition levels of small farmers and their families in remote areas of the Caribbean island of St. Vincent, ORD has been able to move beyond these goals to provide support and assistance to promote increasingly market-oriented agribusiness activities.

ORD's origins stem from a 1976 convention of the Rural Youth Council of St. Vincent, where member representatives struggled to devise a solution to the problems faced by rural subsistence farming families. They resolved to promote a coordinated, scientific, and systematic subsistence farming approach, whose primary objectives were self-sufficiency, improved living standards, import replacement, maximum use of local resources, development of rural leadership potential, and establishment of scientific subprojects.

The development strategy of ORD has evolved through three phases. In the first phase, ORD emphasized the increased productivity of subsistence farmers through the introduction of seeds and improved techniques in producing high-protein food crops such as high-lysine corn, peanuts, and soya beans. As productivity increased, the focus shifted to creating a group of semicommercial farmers from the more successful subsistence farmers or, in ORD terminology, "emergent farmers." In this phase, subprojects included the sale of vegetable seeds for kitchen gardens, the use of food preservation and solar drying techniques, and the provision of storage facilities. As the more prosperous emergent farmers exhibited the capacity and willingness to expand their marketable crops, ORD responded with the dissemination of crop intensification techniques and the identification of markets for new crops such as ginger and yams.

As ORD moved through the three phases, some subprojects were abandoned, some modified, and others added. For example, in the second phase, it was determined that the food preservation and solar drying activities should be discontinued because it was more economically feasible to sell the surplus fresh produce in the capital city, Kingstown. The storage facilities, on the other hand, had to be expanded and increased in number as more farmers began producing for the Kingstown market and more farmer housewives became retailers and traders. This agility and responsiveness to the changing needs of clientele have been cornerstones of ORD's success in moving farmers from subsistence to commercial activities.

In order to keep up with changing beneficiary capacity, the technical capacity of ORD's staff and Volunteer Field Corps members had to be strengthened as well. With each phase, staff and volunteer training was modified so that ORD workers could attend to the increasingly demanding needs of emergent farmers. To gear up for phase two, for example, refresher training courses were provided in personnel development and management, market identification, and advanced-level pest- and disease-control methods. Because of their training, staff and field agents were able to continue responding to farmer needs. Consequently, confidence and trust in ORD services and personnel increased and farmers no longer had to depend exclusively on the erratic visits of Ministry of Trade and Agriculture extensionists.

As beneficiary needs and capacities evolved, so did ORD's organizational dynamics. In the initial stages of the ORD program, administration and management responsibilities were highly centralized within the Central Coordinating Committee. In the early 1980s, however, area program coordinators were employed to supervise the local volunteers and fieldwork. These coordinators lived within the communities served and acted as liaison between the farmers and volunteers and the Central Committee. Over time, the balance of power has shifted from the Central Committee and staff to the community committees and extension staff, on whom ORD has placed increased responsibility for decisionmaking, planning, and day-to-day operations.

ORD's work has also stimulated social mobilization and community action in areas outside its purview. For example, in several villages, the old "swap" reciprocal labor teams have been revived. Further, community groups have begun meeting regularly to discuss and devise solutions for common problems. Thus, in addition to increasing the productivity and living standards of an estimated 35,000 rural residents, ORD's efforts have laid the foundation for continued community development in the future.

---

seeking access to such funding by adapting itself to meet the type of requirements financiers require: requirements such as being "well organized." With this there is perhaps the risk that the principle and purpose of organizing are becoming depoliticized in the process, "organization" becoming simply a formal means to gain access to resources and then administer them. On the other hand, the *runa* organizational capacities that are being built up in the process, alongside the institution of norms of responsibilities expected from the state and GSOs may contribute to greater self-awareness and assertiveness among *runas*. Either way what is clear is that all this has made a difference to how *runas* manage local resources, organize this management, and think about it. (Bebbington 1990a)

GSOs are often criticized for hanging on to their beneficiaries for too long and for perpetuating a dependency relationship. The real proof of disengagement is when a self-reliant group contracts and pays for GSO services. This seldom happens, and has not happened in any of the thirty cases, although some of the legal organizations are beginning to recover a portion of their costs from the groups they serve.

Another way of looking at capacity building is to observe what progress GSOs make in weaning base groups from dependence on the services they provide. This process, in which a GSO systemically transfers assets, authority, and training to a grassroots group, is often referred to as the "transference problem" (Bray 1991). This weaning process can be accomplished in a number of ways. Beneficiaries can be brought to the point at which they no longer need the services or they are capable of relying on existing institutions (usually state or parastatal agencies).

New institutions can be established to meet new beneficiary needs. The beneficiaries can provide the services they need for themselves (especially in self-managed groups). Or, as mentioned above, beneficiaries can be encouraged gradually to pay for the services they receive (the financial basis of most cooperatives). Most of these alternatives apply more to GSOs than to MSOs, whose service functions may be considered more permanent. The ability of GSOs to wean base groups also depends on how well organized the base groups are at the time a project is initiated. Often, membership organizations, such as cooperatives, gradually acquire accounting and other management skills so that they are no longer obliged to rely on outsiders for these functions. The most common strategy is "graduation," or the expectation that the recipients of credit, extension, or key inputs will be capable of shifting to the regular public and private business providers of these services by the time the GSO-sponsored programs are terminated. The problem is that although base groups may be ready to use regular services, such services are usually unavailable or unsuitable.

It is also difficult for base groups to make the jump from free or heavily subsidized services to those offered at market rates. Some GSOs have eased this transition by establishing credit guarantee funds at commercial banks, which then lend to the GSO clients. This scheme was successful in the CARE program in Peru. According to information obtained in an interview with Martin Scurrah, the repayment record was good, and after two to three loans, many recipients managed to graduate before the current extreme liquidity crisis. In one of the most impressive manifestations of grassroots capacity, some of the GSOs in the sample (INDES, IPRU, UNO) have managed to reorient state agencies in their areas by putting pressure on government agencies to become more accessible, accountable, and honest. This was also observed in ANAI's agroforestry program in Costa Rica and in the community health federations in Panama described in Chapter 3.

Few Opportunities for Learning

It should be noted that GSOs and MSOs are almost never evaluated on their capacity building performance, and for that reason there is no opportunity to learn what actions under what conditions contribute to the capability of base groups. As alluded to earlier, evaluators lack the means to adequately measure or illustrate progress in organizational capacity. Furthermore, the interaction between "outsiders" and "insiders" is a protracted and subtle process that is exceedingly difficult to grasp and to document. Evaluators would have to observe the interactions between support organizations and their beneficiaries for several years following the termination of a project to find out whether project activities had been maintained and expanded or new activities under-taken. Then they would have to ascertain whether such development had any relationship to the assistance and support received from the GSO or MSO. The IAF staff has periodically proposed just such long-term process evaluations for interesting cases with "learning potential."

Another research issue of great interest is how outside interventions in the organizational sphere are perceived by the "insiders." It is very easy to get trapped in one or the other of two common fallacies: either that the privileged outsiders possess all the scientific knowledge needed for development or that the poor are the repositories of all the wisdom that they need. The dynamics of the real process, of course, is always a combination, and, as mentioned in the discussion on participation, the secret of effective external assistance is not only permanent consultation and two-way information flows but also a process that empowers the members of a local organization to analyze their own situation, figure out what the problems are, what options are available to resolve them, and how to choose workable options. The process is named here "sensi-tive guidance." Uphoff (1986) called it "assisted self reliance." He describes such a process among water-user associations in Sri Lanka:

> The marvel of the program was that it functioned entirely by informal, consensual means, which generated social energy.
> The organizers encouraged constructive behavior with normative and structural reinforcement. They emphasized the *values* of coopera-tion and participation (means) and of equitable sharing as well as efficient use of water (ends). At the same time they facilitated the for-mation of *organizations* which created "public space," where problems could be raised and transformed from individual to collective ones.
> Farmers who had not been other-regarding began changing their behavior because, as one organizer nicely put it, "It is much more diffi-cult to be selfish in public than in private." Agreements to share water that would have been impossible among individuals emerged almost naturally when third parties were part of the problem-solving process. People kept to agreements witnessed by their neighbors.
> So normative and structural considerations reinforced each other. (Uphoff 1989b, p. 124).

How such a change occurs, what qualities of sensitivity and interper-sonal skills are essential, what sort of community conditions provide a fruitful basis for such learning, how the context affects the success of this process—these are some of the key questions for which there are few answers at present.

Conclusions

Capacity enhancement is at the heart of the development process, and the building of collective capacity among the poor is the most valuable trait of intermediary development organizations. Intermediaries are well positioned to strengthen informal and formal grassroot groups. The GSOs studied for this volume have also significantly contributed to the building of MSOs, that is, higher-level membership or popular organizations. Some exhibit a remarkable ability to shift behavioral patterns from individual and self-centered motivation to cooperation and from helplessness to purposeful action. The accomplishment of concrete joint tasks was seen to lead to more demanding and complex endeavors, thereby creating a positive dynamic that Hirschman has called "social energy."

It was shown that the best GSOs transfer to grassroots groups the confidence and ability to deal effectively with the outside environment and to acquire skills for managing their own resources along with techniques that make the collective process more democratic. The community participation literature counsels that this outcome is highly specific to the particular community in question. However, this study suggests that once set in motion, the learning process about collective experience transcends particular local organizations, which are generally not fixed or stable anyway, and can energize a whole network of fluid and overlapping informal groups of people, from which specific forms of aggregations appear, disappear, and reappear.

When the interaction between GSOs and their client groups shifts from delivering services to capacity building, this relationship, always delicate, becomes even more difficult, although more rewarding. The most successful GSOs have managed to avoid many traps that are lying in wait and to evolve a strategy of sensitive guidance or assisted self-reliance. Clearly this concept embodies a paradox in which external initiative and support are necessary for the creation and sustenance of participatory grassroots groups.[3] In other words, some top-down planning and organization are needed to enable the poor to participate from the bottom up. In spite of the pessimism of many analysts who doubt the organizational ability of the poor and are scornful of the notion that NGOs can promote true community autonomy ("it is questionable whether the voluntary sector is any more able to promote authentic participation than the state" [Midgley 1986, p. 157]), this study offers evidence for a more optimistic assessment of both capabilities—an assessment shared by social scientists who are re-evaluating the possibilities of collective action in modern democracies.[4]

Notes

1. In summarizing the experience of Development Alternatives, Inc. in rural development projects funded by the U.S. Agency for International Development, Honadle writes:

In fact it can be hypothesized that when dealing with non-dominant groups [poor people's organizations], an essential element of successful capacity building is likely to be the acquisition of control over a set of natural resources. Thus, capacity building efforts, based only on providing social services or improving management practices and procedures without an economic base, are unlikely to be sustainable. Success commonly requires a link to income-producing activity and sufficient control over the disposition of that income. (Honadle 1982)

2. Based on a decade of comparative studies at Cornell, Esman and Uphoff found that in terms of performance, the average summary scores of small base groups with several tiers of supra-local aggregations were almost twice the average for all organizations. In small organizations, there is more solidarity among members. They are better able to mobilize resources based on strong commitment and to control "free riding." Federations have advantages of economic scale, superior vertical linkages, and bargaining power (Uphoff 1989a).

3. This general finding is confirmed by the experience of Dutch rural sociology scholars identified earlier as the Leyden Group; see Grijpstra (1982.)

4. For example, based on research in Italy, Robert Putnam writes:

Social trust, norms of reciprocity, networks of civic engagement, and successful cooperation are mutually reinforcing. Effective collaborative institutions require interpersonal skills and trust, but those skills and that trust are also inculcated and reinforced by organized collaboration.

Putnam rejects the notion of gloomy public choice theorists who believe that cooperative networks weaken both economic performance and effective government (Putnam 1992, 30–31 and 35–36). See also North (1990).

7

Wider Impact: Innovation and Policy

Most of the interest in and clamor about wider impact is directed toward grassroots support organizations (GSOs), or those nongovernmental organizations (NGOs) that are run by volunteers or professionals, rather than to membership support organizations (MSOs). Yet, the very virtues of GSOs—their small size, informal nonbureaucratic style, committed attention, limited scope, and participatory microprojects—are seen as inherent obstacles to expansion. Perhaps an unstated element in the mind of some donors is that since GSOs are not representative of their clients or accountable to them, they should not be entrusted with large-scale, permanent programs. In spite of these reservations, GSOs have great potential in the wider-impact dimension.

Although factors relevant to the horizontal and vertical expansion of membership associations, such as second- and third-level cooperatives or farm labor unions, are very important, this discussion is limited to the scaling-up potential and policy relevance of GSOs, for two major reasons: First, there were only a few MSOs in the sample; second, the focus of the study was on NGOs that support the poor without formally representing them.

In the sample, there were no instances of massive scaling up, large-scale transfer of methodology, or substantial demonstration effects. In most countries the competitiveness and clannishness of the GSOs, often exacerbated by donors, are serious obstacles to joint action. However, there are some very interesting openings.

One-third of the organizations in the sample were rated high in the wider-impact dimension. Four of these exhibited networking and "cloning," two had regional impacts, two influenced legal policy, and two had government links for scaling up. One GSO (FIDENE) had both regional and networking effects, and another (PROTERRA) performed well in both land legislation and regional impact. The organizations were also rated on their *potential* for wider impact, and eleven of them were judged to have good scaling-up potential, most of it related to possibilities for regional effect or to forging more effective collaboration with the state.

Among the sample, wider impact is most perceivable by technical and institutional innovations (CACH, CEDECUM, ANAI), legislation and precedent-setting court cases (PROTERRA, FUNCOL), public-policy influence (UNIDAD, FIDENE), and networking and cloning (IPRU, INDES).

Innovation

Intermediary organizations can achieve a broader impact through innovative programs that can be replicated or adopted on a larger scale. How innovative are the organizations in the sample? Have their innovations led to broader impacts? Although the innovativeness of NGOs in general has been called into question (Tendler 1982b), it has also been argued that smaller, less structured organizations are more suitable for testing new ideas and methodologies (Uphoff 1986; Gow et al. 1979). This appears to hold true for a number of organizations in the sample such as ANAI, CEDECUM, and PROTERRA, but some of the larger GSOs have also shown a capacity for innovative behavior, such as CACH in Costa Rica, FMDR in Mexico, and CIPCA, the largest GSO in Peru.

A common thread running through the problem-solving approaches of these innovators is a dynamic internal culture that encourages experimentation and risk taking. Innovation in these cases is rarely spontaneous. The ability to create new technologies, methodologies, and institutions means detailed knowledge of the subject and careful identification of intervention points. As an example, after finding that government mishandling of paperwork was causing intolerable delays in issuing legal titles to property, Instituto Tecnológico Agrario Proterra (PROTERRA) lawyers developed innovative ways to streamline the titling process, thus allowing the relevant agencies that adopted the new methods to work more expeditiously. The strategy was based on PROTERRA's detailed knowledge of the legal complications and official procedures involved.

The innovative activities of intermediaries are seldom documented or researched. Thus, the links between research, promotion, and learning become tenuous. Donors have regularly supported GSO research, but such research is externally rather than internally oriented. Among the sample, there were no cases of research aimed at analyzing the organization's own methodological and technical approaches. This lack seriously limits the refinement, adaptation, and wider diffusion of innovations as these evolve. Even Centro de Educación y Tecnología (CET), an organization with a separate research unit and whose main business is to generate and diffuse alternative technologies, does almost no research on how its own technological packages are adopted (or not) in practice or on how best to modify the packages.

Most of the sample organizations have been innovative and experimental by developing unique solutions to small problems, but the heart of the issue is whether these small-scale experiments have a real potential to be expanded to reach larger numbers of beneficiaries and can further influence macropolicies. In the process of implementing an integrated beekeeping program, Fundación para el Desarrollo Nacional (FDN) has evolved a system of moving hives to areas where flowers are more abundant at alternate seasons (transhumance). This technique is now being replicated in other areas of the country. Centro Agrícola Cantonal de Hojancha (CACH) in Costa Rica has invented a system of handling tree seedlings without bulky plastic containers. This system allows the transport of tens of thousands of seedlings, first by truck, then by horse, from the drop-off point to the distant and mountainous planting sites of farmers. Thus, CACH may have solved a major problem of many reforestation projects, where it was almost impossible to organize the planting of large numbers of trees on dispersed farms using conventional nursery technololgy (Murray 1984). CACH has also successfully grown transplanted seedlings without shade and water, with a 90 percent survival rate. Many such innovations with diffusion potential are unrecorded and unrewarded by donors.

Perhaps an exception to this obscurity is Centro de Investigación y Desarrollo de la Educación (CIDE's) well-documented innovative methodology of adult education, which has been adopted by various training institutions not only in Chile but elsewhere. The main reason for CIDE's ability to diffuse innovations is that CIDE is the hub of a research network on population education, and information dissemination is one of its main purposes. In other cases, when operating GSOs (as distinct from research GSOs) stumble upon or evolve interesting techniques, it seems to be the responsibility of donors to provide extra funds for their documentation and dissemination or, better yet, the creation of networks where these functions can become institutionalized. The experience of large-scale NGO programs in Asia led Tendler to conclude that experiments that might lead to reproducible innovations should be done in an environment where the institutional capacity for replication is already in place—a rather tall order. Alternatively, she suggests that project leaders have links to power centers that can open doors to broader institutional networks—a requirement that fits the Latin American cases discussed here rather well (Tendler 1989).

The work of GSOs often gives rise to even less obvious or visible innovations than the technologies and methodologies discussed above. These are referred to here as *institutional innovations*. The term refers either to changes in the legal and customary framework, such as combinations of incentives and disincentives that regulate behavior, or to the specific organizational forms in which new types of behavior (in this case, collective behavior) are embodied. For example, GSOs that have taken up the difficult task of promoting group formation among unorganized populations (for example, ANAI in Costa Rica or ORD in St. Vincent) have consciously or unconsciously evolved new systems and codes of behavior in which cooperation, as opposed to selfish individualism, is encouraged and socially legitimized, and where "free riding" by members is made more difficult. (Uphoff's [1992] on the extraordinary and unexpected shift of attitudes and behavior of Sri Lankan irrigators toward cooperative water management analyzes this process.) A more general point is that virtually all the groups in the sample that exhibit promising participatory forms of local organization are informal rather than formally constituted base groups. Surely there are very important lessons in discovering what sort of informal groups work well under what circumstances and how they could eventually evolve into formal organizations, at least to the extent that they could operate under the extraordinarily rigid Latin American legal system.

Sometimes the innovation consists of securing for informal groups the right to obtain credit, sign contracts, conduct businesses, and so on. Under the repressive laws of the Chilean military, SADECSA, a small farm association, could not expand the membership of its base communities. Yet, with the help of sympathetic GSO professionals, the association evolved a system in which campesinos outside the formal membership rolls could also benefit from the organization.

Unfortunately, this sort of knowledge remains unanalyzed and undocumented. Donors could provide more incentives and resources for such work and encourage the many research-oriented GSOs to shift from their tendency to demonstrate the failings of the social system to careful evaluation of social experiments and study of the institutional innovations implicit in the operations of their action-oriented colleagues. Chambers (1983) has pointed out that practitioners do not have the time or the inclination and often lack the skills to reflect on and evaluate their development work. Academics, on the other hand, tend to be too far removed from the real field of action and not sensitive to the practical problems facing practitioners. In order to breach this divide, hybrid professionals (intellectual practitioners or pragmatic academics) would have to be created or some other way of ensuring a meaningful exchange would have to be devised. In any case, the issue is relevant to Latin American GSOs. For example, Murray points out that the path-breaking tree planting technology developed by CACH staff could be followed up by field observations on the growth and survival rates of trees at a very modest cost, so that the economic feasibility of the techniques would be verified and disseminated. But somehow this essential work has fallen between the cracks: CACH is narrowly concerned about its own members, the Forest Service is not in the habit of picking up someone else's field experiments, and donors do not even know about such potential spillovers unless outside evaluators point them out (Murray 1984, 71–2).

Yet another aspect of institutional innovation that is exhibited by some of the organizations is the formation of public-private combinations. These are especially widespread in Costa Rica, where it is common to encounter nongovernmental bodies with public-sector participation, such as the regional agricultural development centers, to which government agromomists and extension workers are seconded. But this type of collaboration can also occur in specific sectoral dimensions of a GSO. For example, Centro de Investigación y Promoción del Campesino (CIPCA) in northern Peru is recognized by the Ministry of Education as an official educational institution, and part of CIPCA's staff is paid out of that agency's budget. These arrangements acquire special significance for countries where greater complementarity between private and government-provided services is considered desirable.

Public-Sector Linkages and Policy

Many GSOs justify their existence by an antigovernmental stance, but their relations with government agencies are closer and better than might be expected given their rhetoric. Most of the high performers are clearly adept at identifying, cultivating, maintaining, and institutionalizing relationships with the public sector, although these tend to be of an informal and ad hoc nature. Operationally, the most important and helpful linkages appear to be at the local and regional levels, typically involving branches of state agencies, local universities, and municipal authorities.

Bebbington reports a case of an Ecuadorian GSO that cofinances projects with the local agricultural agencies, "inviting" public sector into activities for which the GSO has the primary administrative responsibility. It then uses the leverage of its financial contribution to ensure peasant participation in project management, even in the planning of research and extension approaches:

> Beyond this, the goal is to show state field staff that it is possible to work closely with the rural poor. The NGO's idea is that once convinced, these staff will pressure from within the public sector agency for a wider use of these methods in other projects . . . such local, often informal collaborations are far more common and far more successful than formalized agreements between central offices that run into political and administrative barriers. (Bebbington 1990a, 20)

The more successful GSOs and MSOs invariably have links to powerful people in politics, the church, business, finance, or government, partly because many of the leaders of these organizations have had previous public-sector experience. Support from people in power is especially important when the organization moves into areas of conflict, when it touches upon entrenched interests—often creating an institutional crisis—or when it expands beyond a few isolated communities and begins to look less innocuous.

In repressive regimes, GSOs are often forced to negotiate with unfriendly public agencies to assure the continued viability of their member groups. They find and mobilize allies, bolster the claims to legitimacy of their constituents, and contribute to the upward channeling of local claims. This appears to be true even of GSOs and MSOs that have a strong antigovernment stance and would not accept funds from the state, partly on principle and partly for fear of losing their independence and credibility. But for many others, if the political situation opens up, some partnership and complementarity with the state become possible or even necessary. Thus, being able to identify common or mutually compatible objectives and complementary resources is an indispensable skill.

In more open regimes, GSOs normally have close links with regional and national political figures whose influence is important in resolving bottlenecks, arranging for credit, obtaining permits, and, in some cases, even lobbying for policies and legislation favorable to their constituencies. The Centros Agrícolas Cantonales in Costa Rica, which have both private and government representation on their boards and get regular budgetary support from the Ministry of Agriculture, exemplify such links.

Some GSOs have links to specialized technical research and educational institutions, both public and private, to keep up-to-date on the results of research and to obtain technical information needed by their clients. Asociación de los Nuevos Alquimistas (ANAI) in Costa Rica, working in agroforestry, and CET in Chile, working in organic farming, are examples of technological networking. Centro de Desarrollo para el Campesinado y del Poblador Urbano-Marginal (CEDECUM) has established a working relationship with the International Potato Center (CIP) and the National Potato Program to strengthen its seed-improvement scheme.

A number of older, more established GSOs and MSOs that operate in more congenial macroenvironments—such as the cases from Costa Rica and some examples from Brazil after the *abertura,* or political liberalization—see their long-term role as linking the poor to the mainstream service structure. Although they are occasionally surrogates for what should be a public function, they argue that their essential role is to extend and complement the reach of government agencies, to make the public sector more responsive to local needs, and to teach the poor how to deal more effectively with the government and the market.

Thus, linkages with government programs can become a valuable asset. GSOs can reorient bureaucracies once local people are organized and are shown to be effective clients of state services and "respectable" partners of officials. Bebbington, who has studied NGO-state links in agricultural technology generation and diffusion in several Latin American countries, thinks that GSOs have an important role in generating innovations in field-implementation methods. Their grassroots orientation, microknowledge, and financial flexibility allow them to run risks (innovation necessarily implies risk) and enter into partnerships with the state by assuming the cost of experimentation and reducing the risk to the state. In the process, they can introduce innovations that the state would otherwise not develop (Bebbington, personal communication, June 1991).

It is hard to capture the precise impact of such catalytic effects, but they are real and potentially important. Interviews conducted by the research team repeatedly showed that whenever GSO promoters and official extension agents worked in the same location, there was considerable pressure on the public agencies to perform better. Also, the effect of complementarity should not be overlooked. Agricultural officers in remote rural locations generally lack transport, fuel, equipment, and communication facilities. Friendly GSOs often collaborate by providing some of these crucial facilities to their colleagues so they can work more effectively.

There is also evidence of noncollaboration, rivalry, ill will, and resistance to any links with government. In Peru, a GSO project director, when asked why he had not sought the help of the ministry's veterinary laboratory for the campesinos' parasite-ridden sheep, replied that the lab was far away and its staff were too busy to attend to such matters. A subsequent visit to the nearby veterinary facility disclosed that the staff was not only available to lend assistance but was eager to do so (Fite 1987). Such attitudes, not uncommon among GSO personnel, obviously are counterproductive and limit scaling-up efforts.

Closely related to public-sector linkages is the issue of policy influence. Nowadays, some NGO advocates are encouraging NGOs to move from their microconfines to influence "policy" or to effect some change in the central government's legal, economic, financial, and administrative setup. Such changes generally favor the population groups assisted by NGOs, usually the poorer, lower-class, disadvantaged sectors. Implicit in this interest is the notion that microinterventions cannot be effective when some of the crucial macrofactors are unfavorable (such as distorted or discriminatory price policies). The obverse is also true; in the rush toward structural adjustment and in unleashing the market—policies pushed by the large financial aid agencies—goverments lay a disproportionately heavy burden on the poor. Thus, "policy" impact by NGOs also comes to mean possible measures to protect and buffer the poorer sectors from the adverse effects of economic liberalization or, more generally, a push for policies in which equity goals complement growth objectives.

It should be made clear that the demand (or hope) that GSOs have more of a policy impact is somewhat misplaced: By definition, GSOs are service providers and capacity-builders among the poor; they are not in the policy business. Other types of NGOs, especially those in the research or advocacy category, are better positioned to produce outputs useful for policy or to include specific policy changes as their objectives. Thus, as might be expected, this study offers limited evidence for policy-relevant work by GSOs in the rather ambitious terms outlined above. At the same time, there is potential for achieving policy goals, perhaps by more indirect routes.

Some fields of GSO activity may be more congenial for achieving a policy impact than others. One of these clearly is in legal protection and legal reform. As discussed in Chapter 3, PROTERRA, FUNCOL, and USEMI are all in the legal business—the former in securing land tenure rights, the latter two in assuring the rights of ethnic minorities. The effect of these programs on how laws are administered is substantial and, in some cases, even includes changes in the laws themselves. Some of these legal reforms look like the institutional innovations discussed earlier in this chapter, such as streamlining land titling procedures by computerized records and resolution of conflicts by local committees. But more generally, these types of GSOs show that they can have a significant impact on the judicial system in the securing of human rights and also in better access to and fairer treatment in the provision of essential services.

Scaling-Up

For the kinds of activities that were identified in Chapter 3 as conducive to improving small-scale agriculture, there is apparently a fundamental contradiction between size and quality. Some GSO leaders believe that trying to transplant their projects into different settings is not compatible with their local knowledge-based approach to working with the poor. Their view tends to be that a better approach would be to increase coverage through a network of similar regional GSOs.

For the most part, GSOs are not under pressure from their traditional donors or beneficiaries to produce a large impact and have little incentive to do so. Many appear content to operate in a limited region, often with a very narrow focus. Others have developed reliable methods to multiply applicable elements of projects but lack the opportunity or the means for doing so.

In contrast, a number of organizations in the sample have found unexpected ways to bring about larger changes. In some instances, these less-noticed gains assumed more importance and were more impressive than the originally articulated objectives. CIPCA, for instance, has been successful in influencing government policy by first establishing a strong, permanent presence in the Department of Piura. CIPCA is considered the authority on agrarian issues in northern Peru and is regularly consulted by organizations planning development activities in that region. CIPCA has a better library than the local university, and the caliber of its research is considered much higher than that of its public-sector counterparts. Moreover, CIPCA's long-term perspective allows the organization to experiment, track changes and trends, and publish studies that are of interest to public and private agencies.

With respect to scaling up the size of intermediary NGO programs, there is yet little evidence that these organizations can use significant domestic resources without compromising their integrity or mystique, which stems from their relative independence from national politics and mainstream bureaucracy. However, some better-performing GSOs have shown that such collaboration is possible. An outstanding example is the recent trajectory of União Nordestina de Assistência a Pequeñas Organizações (UNO) in Brazil. This GSO is serving as a recipient of considerable World Bank financing channeled through the government. So far, it appears that UNO has been able to maintain both its effectiveness and autonomy (see Box 7.1). In Peru and a number of other countries, plans for decentralization offer favorable prospects for forging some sort of broader cooperation between public-sector agencies and the intermediaries. Donors (who in many cases are also anti-public sector) should be alert to opportunities to facilitate such linkages where the political situation is favorable. Donors and NGO networks may also want to let public sector agencies know that contracting with GSOs and MSOs is better than providing services in-house and that many intermediary NGOs have special skills for establishing collaborative arrangements.

However, contract relationships, whether by governments or by external aid agencies, can be damaging to the integrity of a GSO and may preempt its capacity-building qualities.[1] Brown and Korten have recently highlighted a tendency by aid agencies (and more specifically by the U.S. Agency for International Development) to look for ways to entrust NGOs with the implementation of large-scale social projects that government has proven incapable of handling. They warn the NGO sector that becoming public-sector contractors would undermine most voluntary organizations (Brown and Korten 1989). This study does not support such a sweeping judgment. Some excellent service providers have been unaffected by large-scale contracts. Others have made important contributions without substantial expansion. Thus, to realize a wider-impact potential an organization need not grow beyond its optimal size and can learn how to live with contracts.

Another way to achieve a greater impact without growing beyond an optimal size is through cloning and networking. Some attention has already been given to the catalytic effect of IPRU in Uruguay and INDES in Argentina to inspire and create new service organizations, usually of a specialized character, to offer more permanent and much more extended services than the GSOs could originally perform (Ferrin 1989). In a number of cases, GSOs have achieved a wider reach by helping membership groups to federate and expand. Examples are UNIDAD's work in nurturing community associations in Ecuador and CEDECUM's impact on the *multi-communales* in Puno, Peru.

Another way of extending impact is by forming networks of like-minded GSOs. Some donors, notably the U.S. Agency for International Development, have recently launched special initiatives to facilitate the creation of NGO networks. Multilateral agencies such as the World Bank are also interested in NGO aggregations to facilitate NGO participation in the implementation of their projects. As yet, there is understandable reluctance in GSO circles to launch integrated or coordinated initiatives, especially in the realm of financing, on the grounds of ideology and intellectual independence. But even in very loose coalitions, concerted GSO action could have important scale and policy effects, as is already evident in the increasingly common voice employed by some environmental groups.

Private Agencies Collaborating Together (PACT), a U.S.-based organization that itself is a network of various private voluntary organizations, has a program to promote NGO networks and coalitions, especially in the microenterprise field, based intially on the systematic exchange of information on common experiences. (PACT 1989 describes the initial years of two networks, ACORDE in Costa Rica and ASINDES in Guatemala.) Among the cases, only Federación de Organizaciones Voluntarias (FOV) in Costa Rica has attempted to assume a formalized networking role. But lack of donor financing for the core costs of networks has forced it to change back to a direct service-providing mode. However, FOV could not sustain a position in which it was perceived as a direct competitor to the member organizations of its own network. (See profile in Chapter 12).

The Regional Dimension

The most interesting possibility of wider impact is found in rural regional development, through organizations operating in a spatially determined socioeconomic area. The regional approach has several advantages. First, by working regionally, GSOs and MSOs gradually acquire an intimate knowledge of the socioeconomic situation of their territory and can diagnose its key poverty problems. This puts them in an extraordinary position to design programs for regionwide application and, perhaps more

Box 7.1   UNO: The Lace Makers of Iguaraci

União Nordestina de Assistência a Pequeñas Organizações (UNO), a business-inspired GSO, has evolved from an urban micro-enterprise service to a more broadly based organization working with rural and small-town-based microproducers joined together in associations. It is unique in the sample in that it now operates largely with government resources, supplied in large part by the World Bank. This has prompted Inter-American Foundation (IAF) senior representative for Brazil, Bradford Smith, to ask the following question: "Will increased pressure to expand services, while making operations more efficient, mean the sacrificing of the conscientious individualized attention which has become UNO's trademark?"

Evidence so far indicates that this has not happened. The major drawback of state financing has been the slow approval and erratic disbursement of funds. How UNO manages to maintain its autonomy is illustrated by the following story taken from Smith's project record:

> Where UNO does not always manage to escape political interference is at the local level. Much of UNO's work is done in small towns and cities where the power of the mayor is very much in evidence. Everyone, working in such settings, be they church, NGO, union, or otherwise, must at least coexist with the mayor, who, under Brazil's increasingly democratic system, is an elected official. He is often a large landholder, and/or doctor or lawyer to boot, which gives him a lot of influence over the local populace. And mayors like to inaugurate things and put their names on them. For example, the *Casa das Rendeira*, a production and meeting center for lace-makers in the town of Iguaraci, was built primarily with IAF funds, and much smaller support from the local *prefeitura* (mayor's office) and government/World Bank program, *PRORURAL*. The plaque next to the front door reads:

> CASA DE RENDEIRA DE IGUARACI
> PREFEITURA MUNICIPAL DE IGUARACI
> FRANCISCO VICENTE SOBRINHO
> Prefeito
> UNO/PRORURAL/IAF
> Governo de Estado de Pernambuco

> This plaque faithfully reflects the reality of community development efforts in the interior of Pernambuco. The efforts of tiny community groups of poor producers (in this case lace-makers) are framed within, and to a certain degree usurped by, a plethora of government bodies— the mayor's office, PRORURAL, and the State Government. UNO and IAF are credited but indistinguishable from the rest of the official bodies and acronyms. Relevantly absent from the picture is the group of lace-makers themselves. Thus, the impression given by such a plaque is symbolic of the way community action is conceived of and carried out in Brazil's Northeast—as an activity made possible by the State.

UNO's and the lace-makers' roles in this process are fascinating. In an exceedingly pragmatic fashion, UNO accepts the reality described above, and seeks to act as an intermediary and facilitator between the government and groups of micro-producers. This posture requires a great deal of vision and flexibility; an attitude that says: "Sure everyone's going to stick their name on the plaque, but this center is being run by the lace-makers them-

selves and will serve as an organizational tool, long after the official programs have come and gone." The lace-makers approach the whole situation with a tremendous amount of *jogo de cintura*, something which in
Brazilian Portuguese is roughly analogous to "finesse." For them, life in
the dry lands has always been a harsh and unfair struggle where development has been a process which has left them out. They want to earn more
money from their lace which is one of the few ways they can supplement
household income. They want a community center in which they can
work, socialize, and meet to discuss community problems. If the mayor,
PRORURAL, UNO, IAF, et al., can be used to meet these needs, then a
plaque is a small price to pay.

In summary, UNO has succeeded in becoming self-reliant in terms of
supporting itself almost entirely with local resources. That these resources
come overwhelmingly from Brazilian government sources is understandable within the context of Brazil's Northeast. UNO has been able to use
such resources in order to help communities meet their expressed needs.
In doing so, UNO has avoided partisan political interference. The main lia-
bility to UNO has been the bureaucratic snags which are inherent to the
government funding process.

---

important, to collaborate with other organizations and share their
knowledge.

The second advantage is that it is often easier to collaborate with
regional and municipal government organizations than with national or
even local agencies. Frequently a strong spirit of regional solidarity can
be used as a coalition builder and mobilizer of influential provincial per-
sonalities and local resources. The Instituto de Desarrollo Social y Promoción Humana (INDES) program in northeast Argentina, for example,
has forged a fruitful alliance with the provincial government in Chaco
province. This positive effect of regionalism can also be observed in the
FDN's work in Chiclayo. When the fieldwork was being carried out,
FDN's project director was a local notable who made promising efforts
to line up the provincial business and civic leaders to support the FDN's
rural development efforts. The importance of these regional or local linkages was confirmed by a recent study on Bangladeshi NGOs. Sanyal
(1991) found that NGO influence on local government was equally significant or more significant than at the national policy level. This finding
is relevant to many Latin American countries where decentralization
efforts are under way. Perhaps the best illustration of the regional network strategy comes from Colombia, where the IAF has fostered several
GSOs along with their satellite community groups. The regional support
organizations provide vital services to an interlinked set of base groups.
Three of these territorially linked systems are described by Ritchey-
Vance (1991): a regional artisan network in the southwest, a community
capacity-building network on the north coast, and an economic cooperative network in the eastern Andes.

The third advantage of a regional approach is that in some regions there are so many local organizations, especially where there are ethnic communities, that broad programmatic reach and collaboration among them is relatively easy. Instituto de Promoción Económico-Social del Uruguay (IPRU), has taken advantage of the territorial reach of a cooperative federation to forge a large-scale collaborative program. In a sense, the relative smallness and homogeneity of Uruguay allows that country to serve more as a "region." Unidad de Educación para el Desarrollo de Chimborazo (UNIDAD) has built an impressive network of Quechua-speaking community organizations in the Chimborazo region of Ecuador and has helped to create a regional federation of Indian communities.

The fourth advantage concerns the spillover from innovative programs and the possibility that it can affect large numbers of potential users within a region. For example, in Peru's Lambayeque Department, the effect of a beekeeping project currently being carried out by FDN is already spreading beyond the 400 original beneficiaries. The laboratory established through IAF assistance in Chiclayo is beginning to service a wide clientele to certify honey quality and to develop profitable techniques for the production of beekeeping by-products. The beekeeping program also illustrates that programs showing growth in group capacity and a wider impact are likely to be sustained. The continuation of technical research and advisory services beyond the IAF-supported project depends on the ability of the new beekeepers' association to retain a portion of the sales receipts from honey marketing which is now performed by FDN (see the profile of FDN in Chapter 11).

The final advantage is that the regional approach provides a great opportunity to multiply grassroots base groups beyond the usual project framework, as shown in some of the organizational profiles, such as UNIDAD (see Box 3.4) or CAPS (see Box 8.1), and by the Colombian and Argentine networks mentioned above. Sometimes sustainable impact depends on coordinated joint action by many groups and communities, inspired and led by either provincial *técnicos* or private-sector specialists. An interesting case in which participation and regional impact are combined was reported from Ecuador. Increased understanding by potato producers of the importance of clean seed—disease-free potatoes for the next year's planting—has resulted in a collaborative effort by seventeen communities to manage a potato seed rotation system. This could not have been accomplished at the individual community level (Bebbington 1988). It is interesting to note that a case for the strong regional presence of MSOs can be made for reasons that are exactly the reverse of the elite linkage argument made above for GSOs. According to this view, MSOs must counterbalance hostile powers that dominate regionally.[2]

The better-performing regional organizations in the study have in common well-articulated goals and strategies and a strong institutionalized identity. All have acquired sufficient legitimacy in the eyes of donors, grassroots groups, and the professional community within their countries so that they need not spend scarce energies on gaining acceptance (Martinez-Nogeira 1984). Their internal strengths also derive from having resolved—at least to some extent—the ever-present tensions and ambiguities that characterize the life of GSOs and MSOs.

There are many opportunities for GSOs to make a larger impact than the limits of their grassroots support projects would seem to indicate. Growth is one thing, influence is another. With more generous and steadier funding, many GSOs could grow. Even if the funds came from the government, they could grow without necessarily losing their independence and vitality, as is often feared. However, growth exacts a price. Diseconomies, managerial overload, and diffusion of activities often accompany too rapid growth. Larger GSOs can lobby more effectively and can mobilize public and private resources better, but there is a definite loss in participation and capacity building with increased size. Some of these dangers can be reduced by decentralizing and by granting considerable autonomy and flexibility to regional offices or subprograms. But the key lesson is that wider impact can be made without individual GSOs becoming too large.

Successful decentralization was observed in the very large UNO program in Brazil and also in the regionalized structure of FMDR in Mexico. But FDN in Peru missed a great opportunity to develop the promising linkages proposed by its project director in Chiclayo because its centralized management, fearful of losing control, tightened the reins, causing the departure of the local director as well as his successor.

A regional or territorial approach permits an unusually effective combination of vertical and horizontal linkages: GSOs can dig in and acquire an intimate knowledge of the poverty problems within a region and of key points of intervention. At the same time, they can collaborate and build coalitions with local agencies, foster intergroup activities, and build second-level membership associations.

Understanding how poverty problems at the local level are affected by the macrocontext and searching for pragmatic solutions through microprojects can bring an organization to the point where it can formulate viable policy proposals. For example, PROTERRA's success in land legislation was an outcome of securing land titles for ex-collective members. It is precisely the lack of this "field connectedness" that limits the utility of the urban-based think tank-type NGOs. Good microwork can lead to—and may be necessary for—sound macropolicy initiatives.

Note

1. Under the newly democratic Chilean regime, AGRARIA was awarded contracts by the state extension agency, INDAP. While this arrangement has given

AGRARIA much greater scope for technical diffusion and has enabled it to more than double its staff, the administrative burdens associated with inflexible contract provisions has constrained its pursuit of social promition and capacity building (Aguirre 1991).

2. The elite confrontation, rather than co-optation, argument is based on the experience of the Mexican *ejido* federations.

> Rural democratization depends on the emergence and consolidation of economic power. Since rural elites often concentrate power regionally, rural mass organizations must also concentrate power at the regional level in order to become effective counterweights. (Fox 1989, p. 15)

8

Organizational Attributes of Strong Performers

In the previous five chapters the performance of the thirty GSOs and MSOs was examined by applying the criteria established at the beginning of this book. These discussions often alluded to the internal strengths and weaknesses of the different kinds of intermediaries and how capacity at the grassroots is developed. Moving back to take a wider view, this chapter considers the capacity of the support organizations themselves as a entity.

All thirty of the cases rate high in some respect, as mentioned earlier. But about a third rated high in all three major dimensions (service delivery, participation, and wider impact, which are actually three pairs of criteria). Another third rated significantly high in two of these dimensions. What organizational features are associated with good overall performance?

An answer to this question may be found by ascertaining whether correlations exist among the six disaggregated performance characteristics employed in the analysis (service delivery, poverty reach, participation, group capacity building, innovation, and policy impact), by testing a number of organizational features that might be related to performance, and by attempting an analysis of the dynamics of performance (that is, how performance is affected by change over time).

Correlations

Looking for associations among the six characteristics is important because positive associations suggest that more than one desirable outcome can be achieved simultaneously or even that progress in one direction can reinforce progress in another. Conversely, negative associations indicate the likelihood of a trade-off, suggesting that certain results can be achieved only by neglecting other desirable outcomes, or even that to be a good performer in one direction means heavier costs in other areas.

Table 8.1 shows the correlations encountered among the characteristics. The sample is not random enough and the numbers in each category

Table 8.1   Correlations among the performance indicators

	Service Delivery	*Poverty Reach*	*Participation*	*Capacity Building*	*Innovation*	*Policy Impact*
Service Delivery		Medium	Very high**	Medium	High*	Low
Poverty Reach			Very high**	Medium	Medium	Low
Participation				High*	Medium	Low
Capacity Building					Low	Low
Innovation						Very high**
Policy Impact						

Product-moment correlations (*n*) were used.
* Significant at .05 level.
** Highly significant at 0.1 level.

are too small to provide a rigorous statistical test of correlation. Nevertheless, there are some interesting patterns. Our confidence in these patterns was reinforced by analysis of data from Peru, in which the ratings of forty-two intermediary NGOs exhibited very similar associations (Humphreys, Carroll and Scurrah 1988).

Notable are the unexpectedly strong relationships between participation and poverty reach and between service delivery and participation. The latter refutes the notion that organizations that devote a lot of energy to fostering beneficiary participation cannot provide services as effectively as those that do not and confirms a basic tenet of the Inter-American Foundation (IAF): The involvement of the poor in all phases of development activities and their sense of ownership of the development process are essential elements in the appropriateness, fit, implementation, and eventual sustainability of activities undertaken by NGOs. Assuming the right direction of causality, it also seems to confirm a central hypothesis of this study: Delivering beneficial services can be a prerequisite to eliciting participation where little or no collective experience exists. This is especially true if beneficiaries voluntarily contribute time and labor. It is also not surprising that there is a high association between participation and capacity building. The two concepts are closely related and normally go together as traits of GSOs and MSOs. As already discussed, a participatory style is a necessary, but not sufficient, precondition for capacity building.

Less predictable is the very strong synergy between participation and poverty reach. This suggests either that the poorer target populations are relatively more "organizable," perhaps because of their traditional village or ethnic cohesion, or that those intermediaries that prefer to work with the relatively poorer groups are by their very nature more participatory.

It is also interesting that service delivery is associated to some extent with all the other indicators except policy impact. This once again appears to confirm this study's findings that if GSOs or MSOs are not good at generating concrete economic and social benefits, they cannot hope to achieve other aims which are often more complex and distant. Or, looking at it another way, there is less conflict than some critics have alleged between the bread-and-butter types of basic services and the loftier aims espoused by the IAF and many other donors.

Conflict, or trade-off, becomes more evident, however, if one disaggregates organizations that see their mission mainly as service delivery rather than capacity building or empowerment. These are the classic service-provider GSOs and MSOs. Twelve in the sample fall into this category. Four are "retailers," four are "aggregators," and four are "advocates," according to the modified typology presented in Chapter 6 (Figure 6.1). All twelve exhibit a negative association between service delivery and group capacity building, and the eight that make up the aggregators and retailers together also show a negative—though not as strong—correlation between service and poverty. (The four advocates all received top ratings in both service delivery and poverty reach.) What this means is that the organizations in the sample fall into two contrasting groups based on the importance they place on the service function. About 40 percent see their main mission as serving the base, and the remaining 60 percent consider service as a means to other goals.

The low association between policy impact and all the other characteristics (except its twin, innovation) simply means that scaling up and policy influence are more independent than the other variables. This could mean that policy impact hinges more on special characteristics such as leadership, vision, or government receptivity than on traits that contribute to effective service delivery. As discussed in Chapter 2, the GSOs and MSOs were rated rather low on actual policy impact, but the ratings improved for potential policy impact. This analysis leads to the hypothesis that many kinds of GSOs and MSOs (perhaps more than one would have thought) are capable of making a wider impact and are not actually fettered by the microlimitations generally attributed to them by their admirers and critics alike.

Organizational Features of Performance

This section, which examines a number of organizational features such as size, level of formality, relationships with governmental entities, and so on, is based not only on the thirty cases in this study but also on the results of a Peruvian GSO study that examined forty-two intermediaries (Humphreys, Carroll, and Scurrah 1988).

GSOs versus MSOs

It must be pointed out that GSOs as a group significantly outperform MSOs, as confirmed by the ratings presented in Chapter 2. This is rather paradoxical. Although consensual decisionmaking and accountability to the base membership are conceptually the strong points of MSOs, in most of our cases these advantages did not translate into solid organizational effectiveness. The very formality of the MSOs in the sample as well as their origin in and control by state agencies have made them more bureaucratic, hierarchical, and inflexible than GSOs. Most of the MSOs can be thought of as having "low-trust" interpersonal relations. A low-trust organization is characterized by expectations of reciprocity through a precisely balanced exchange in the short run, careful calculations of costs and anticipated benefits of any concessions, and minimal dependency on the others' discretion, with a resulting tendency for suspicion and the invoking of sanctions against default of obligations (Galjart 1982). GSOs, on the other hand, are characterized by "high-trust" relationships in which members share strongly held values, bear toward one another a diffuse sense of long-term obligation, offer one another spontaneous support without calculation of costs or anticipated benefits, communicate freely and honestly, and give one another the benefit of any doubt that may arise with respect to goodwill or motivation.

Regarding formal versus informal beneficiary participation in decisionmaking and operations, the interviews indicated that high-scoring GSOs valued beneficiary influence on their decisionmaking processes. Yet the cases show that formal representation by beneficiaries on a GSO's own governing board did not improve performance; an informal participatory style was more effective. It is clear that an open, collegial management style, which builds confidence and trust among beneficiaries and support organizations, is a key organizational quality. In the sample of GSOs, beneficiary participation in and of itself did not seem to be essential to effective service delivery or policy impact, but it is probably fair to say that the sustainability of service flows and the ability to take advantage of improved policies depends highly on beneficiary involvement and improved capacity at the grassroots level.

Features Unrelated to Performance

Some organizational features seemed to have little, if any, impact on GSO or MSO performance. Size, in terms of number of staff, is one example. Smaller organizations, such as SADECSA and ANTISUYO with fewer than ten staff members, performed as well as or better than some of the largest, such as CIPCA or FMDR with over a hundred staff members.

Private-sector linkages also proved to be only weakly associated with performance ratings. This apparent lack of connection with the business world reflects, on the one hand, the public-service orientation of most GSOs and MSOs and, on the other, the competition that cooperatives and microenterprises represent to established business interests.

In contrast, relationships with other nongovernmental agencies, national and regional, served to enhance the impact of the efforts of GSOs and MSOs. Those that were members of NGO associations or networks outperformed those that had little or no relation with other NGOs.

Organizational Strategies and Approaches

Turning to organizational features that appear to contribute to strong performance, the degree of organization of beneficiary groups proved to be important. GSOs and MSOs performed better when dealing with more or less structured client groups than with unorganized ones. The exception are organizations serving land reform collectives in Peru and Chile. Still, there is a question about the direction of causality: Is the relative organizational level of beneficiaries a precondition or a result of the GSO's group capacity building?

The findings of this study indicate that organizations implementing a limited number of tightly connected projects performed better than those undertaking loosely connected or unconnected clusters of projects. The synergy created by closely related project interventions enhances the overall impact of GSO and MSO efforts.

Similarly, the cases show that a well-defined territorial scope generates better results than a spatially dispersed structure. The "region" in question varies in size: It can range from a couple of provinces in northeastern Argentina (INDES) to a relatively circumscribed river valley on the Peruvian coast (PROTERRA), but it always means a geographic or territorial unit with certain unifying features within which GSO or MSO programs can assume the necessary coherence, relevance, and potential scale. Generally, such a regional space coincides or is part of an administrative or political unit as well, which gives the organizations opportunities to tap into regional public and private networks and even to mobilize regional pressure on national authorities. The strength of these linkages and the decentralization of authority correlate closely to performance. Those GSOs and MSOs that have regular contacts and collaboration with ministries, universities, and other government agencies, especially at the regional or decentralized levels, scored higher in performance than did those with tenuous or no contact with the public sector.

A GSO's perception of the role of external donor funding is also associated with its overall level of effectiveness. The better performers preferred institutional rather than specific project financing. They also preferred that funds be employed to deepen and extend already existing services rather than to initiate new activities, as the weaker performers did.

In general, the findings lend support to the hypothesis that the best institutional model for intermediary organizations in inegalitarian settings entails vertical extension of key functions supported by brokerage roles that facilitate horizontal cooperation (Peterson 1982).

Financial Health

A solid financial position is a basic requisite of good performance for GSOs and MSOs. What are the elements of financial health in intermediary NGOs? For GSOs it means having a diversified portfolio of donor resources assuring a steady flow of funds, especially for core costs. GSOs that are partially enterprises must generate enough income through revenues to cover operating expenses plus, strictly speaking, amortization and depreciation.

The same applies to MSOs, which in the sample are all cooperative-style quasi-businesses. Centro Agrícola Cantonal de Hojancha (CACH), which runs its operations as a business service, was at the time of the field survey 70 percent self-sufficient. But this unusually high degree of cost recovery comes at a price: Most of CACH's services are unaffordable by the region's poorer households. For example, the average cost of planting one hectare with valuable tree species is around $500. Almost half the farmers in the area cannot afford to make an investment that will not yield cash returns for a number of years.

MSOs that also engage in social services whose cost cannot be directly recovered (such as the Costa Rican cooperative unions) may be able to cross-subsidize if the revenues from the business end are sufficiently buoyant, but in most cases there is some subsidy from outside public or private sources. Socially oriented business, like cooperatives, are under constant tension between their profitmaking and equity-promoting selves. This schizophrenia has been eloquently analyzed by Tendler (1983b). According to Tendler, co-op federations are essentially businesses with an exclusive membership. The fact that they often benefit poorer members or even nonmembers is explained partly by the social norms that co-op leaders must respect or by the co-ops' need to obtain supplies from (or sell to) a much wider clientele than its membership (spillover benefits). In neither case is altruistic motivation involved.

At any rate, what matters most in the case of these MSOs is financial viability without too great a grant element. If this cannot be achieved, the organization is in trouble. Its capacity to offer services to the members is seriously impaired and it may go bankrupt, as happened with many of the Peruvian and some of the Costa Rican cooperatives.

Several older cooperatives that have survived rough times still labor under the burden of huge past debts, even if their current books are balanced. These co-op debts are as much the fault of the lenders as the borrowers and can be retired only if the lenders bear the lion's share of the losses.

To be sure, the financial health of MSOs is not only a function of their own management but is significantly affected by external factors, such as price or trade policies, the severity of competition, and so on. There can also be a favorable external environment, as in Costa Rica, where co-ops are given various kinds of preferential treatment and subsidies. However, the state not only supports, it also frequently meddles. So an organization may not be to blame for financial problems when the state withdraws previous concessions or restricts the freedom of MSOs to maneuver and manage themselves. If the state regards co-ops as a socially desirable form of organization, it needs to offer sensitive, sustained support of the same sort described in previous chapters as the basis for sound GSO-MSO relationships. Perhaps Uruguay, where IPRU and its spin-offs have enjoyed this sort of environment is a good illustration of a healthy situation, where support is extended without coddling or domination.

To be financially sound, GSOs must at a minimum be able to cover their core costs. However, it is not clear what should be considered core costs. ANAI maintains an experimental forest plantation and nursery; some GSOs have radio stations. Are the costs of running these things to be counted as "core"? What about long-term commitments, such as debt service? In this discussion, core costs are limited to the salaries of management (board members are usually volunteers) and a few essential technical and administrative staff and the costs of running the central office. In the sample, these core costs averaged about one-fifth of the total annual expenditure. In small organizations like SADECSA or ANAI, core costs may go as high as one-third; in large ones with extensive field programs such as UNO or FMDR, they may be as low as one-tenth.

Most donor assistance goes to finance projects—which means the cost of *new* activities. In the development business, this is commonly called the "additionality principle" and is derived from the way external aid agencies extend project funding to governments. In such transactions the aid agency assumes (often erroneously) that salaries and other recurrent expenditures will continue to be paid from regular government budgets. Some agencies may insist that such budgets be increased and specifically earmarked for the project they are funding. This serves to demonstrate to their governing boards that the aid contributions are truly "additional."

Most donors to NGOs are reluctant to cover any of the core costs related to the projects they finance; they hope that someone else will pick up these costs. They fear that adding core expenses will make service delivery less cost-efficient, and they do not want to leave themselves open to the criticism that too few of their aid dollars are actually reaching the poor. As discussed earlier, this attitude is self-defeating and turns out to be false economy. Someone has to bear the full costs of service delivery. The promotional and developmental costs of innovations, linkages, and capacity building—all desired by donors—are seldom included in project budgets. Highly regarded intermediaries excel precisely in these aspects.

Donors often fail to appreciate the more mundane but essential costs of the project cycle: adequate planning, preinvestment work, program management, and supervision. Intermediaries are seldom given the resources to perform these functions that are so essential for successful project outcomes. Donors are sometimes under the illusion that they themselves can perform these functions. (The realization that much of the preproject work and the supervision cannot be carried out from Washington has prompted the Inter-American Foundation to institute an in-country support service capacity.)

It is somewhat curious that none of these scruples about core costs seem to apply to consulting firms (or even to "NGO contractors"), through which much of the development business is conducted (Brown and Korten 1989). Such contractors are accustomed to receive substantial overhead fees in addition to actual salaries and other project costs, often amounting to a three- or fourfold multiplier of the salary component.

Uncertainty over core funds impairs the capacity of intermediary organizations. In the sample, multiyear assurance of core staff salaries is closely related to overall performance. For example, a significant portion of the salaries for CIPCA's top management is assured through either the Jesuit Order or the Ministry of Education. In FIDENE, the local university pays for a number of the professionals who devote the major part of their time to FIDENE's action program. If there is uncertainty about where these funds will come from, leaders (especially of GSOs) have to spend too much time raising funds and writing proposals and have difficulty retaining their key staff members. Worse yet, these leaders are forced to take on personal consultancies or business obligations, which further cuts into the time and energy they can devote to their own organizations.

Motivation and Leadership

The question of whether it is better to have a competent staff or a committed staff was discussed previously, and it was concluded that both are essential. It was also documented that this improbable combination has actually been achieved by a good number of the highly rated intermediary organizations and that these attributes may be acquired in any order. However, the motivation one observes in the best intermediary organizations, especially at the field operation level, cannot be explained by either competence or commitment. The staff salaries paid by GSOs and MSOs do not differ much from government pay scales and are less than those prevailing in the private business sector; job security is low; fringe benefits are thin or absent; the hours are long and working conditions in the interior are often rough. Why do the staffs of these organizations work so hard? Why is sensitive, helpful behavior toward the poor a norm rather than an exception?

Beyond recruitment practices that are more selective (and self-selective) than elsewhere, a large part of the answer lies in the socialization of the staffs. A pervading sense of mission is widely diffused throughout each organization so that behavior consistent with the guiding vision, although not necessarily codified in established guidelines, is constantly reinforced. Uphoff (1992) has called such behavior a manifestation of "social energy" in an elaboration of Hirschman's (1984) original formulation, and has identified its components as "ideals, ideas, and friendship," each producing a positive sum output. It should be pointed out that such mutually reinforcing relationships exist not only among the staff but also between the staff and the beneficiaries. Job satisfaction is maximized when the work of the staff is appreciated and when staff members enjoy a good reputation among their clients. The sense of self-worth of the cadre is also enhanced by the considerable freedom given to them in the field, a freedom that carries with it an increased sense of responsibility. Speaking of his relationship with generally suspicious native communities, a *promotor* in southern Chile said, "I have their trust [*confianza*], even if we disagree and I must tell them things they do not want to hear."

The internal organization of virtually all the GSOs and MSOs is less hierarchical and more collegial than one encounters in government and business. Social distances are minimized and the usual bureaucratic culture of "salute the seniors and boss the juniors" gives way to a more interactive and informal style. Loyalty is based less on the usual forms of reciprocity (expecting and dispensing favors) and more on shared values and a sense of purpose articulated by the leaders.

These feelings of loyalty are put to the test when there is a change in leadership or when a split appears at the top. When Tejada, the charismatic leader of CEDECUM in Puno, Peru, had a row with his Lima-based, more conservative board-member colleagues, the rank and file of the staff backed him up. When he was finally forced out, much of CEDECUM's staff resigned in protest. A continual internal debate about means and ends is healthy, but an ideological split can cause serious problems. In some of FMDR's regional divisions in Mexico, the field agents or *promotores* have become gradually more radicalized in the sense of identifying with the poorer peasantry and more vocal campesino organizations. This has brought the agents into conflict with the FMDR's more conservative businessmen directors. PURISCAL in Costa Rica embodies two visions, a hard-line economic orientation and a "soft" community development perspective. The effectiveness of these organizations, as long as they remain torn into different directions, is impaired. If internal divisions over ideology or strategy become too acute, the intermediary organization may divide into more homogeneous parts. It was observed that although such a split may cause temporary setbacks, it is eventually a healthy development. It consolidates shared values and loyalty in each of the successor groups around the new constellation of leaders. It may also allow each successor organization to focus on a unitary task (see the PROTERRA profile in Chapter 11).

The idea that strong leadership is linked to higher overall performance is controversial within the IAF and elsewhere, where GSOs or MSOs led by dominant individuals are viewed with some concern about internal democracy and external give-and-take. Yet the evidence clearly points to the importance of inspired central leadership, at least in the early years of an organization's establishment and consolidation. In this process, the main leader need not be the founder; sometimes the second or third leader becomes the key. What is needed is a strong personality with enough commitment and drive to give the organization a central focus and, equally important, external legitimacy and alliances. These traits help an organization overcome crises and weather adversities, experiences that eventually help make a GSO or MSO a good general performer.

Innovation is often a function of experienced and imaginative leadership. Strong central leaders and managers or a small team of ideologically committed professionals appear to have played an important role in the establishment and later development of the sample GSOs and MSOs. However, in some organizations, lack of depth of leadership creates an ongoing problem of orderly succession and continuity.

Innovation requires an organization to live with uncertainty and take risks, to engage in long-term planning, and to consider the possibility of failure at least initially as a learning experience. Some routine, specialized organizations have been known to transform themselves into innovative ones. It is interesting to compare two national development foundations, FMDR in Mexico and FDN in the Dominican Republic (this FDN is not one of the thirty cases). The former has continued with its original functions, but the latter has been able to diversify and spin off several promising affiliates.

Organizational Dilemmas

One of the most salient issues that emerges from this book is that, in an ambiance pervaded by ambiguity and tension, the thirty organizations in the sample seem to have succeeded in managing inherent conflict or bringing their main opposing forces into a workable equilibrium. Some of these conflicts are well documented in evaluations of IAF intermediaries. Studies of FUNDE (Tendler et al. 1984), FMDR (Diskin et al. 1987),

UNO (Tendler 1983a), IPRU-INDES (Martinez-Nogeira 1984), and five women's organizations (Yudelman 1987) describe features of each organization that allow positive and negative elements to coexist. These retrospective, after-the-fact assessments had a longer time frame than was available to the authors of *They Know How* (IAF 1976), the IAF's earlier attempt at self-evaluation and articulation of its mission. The assessments clearly show that the organizations face not only numerous internal tensions in setting and carrying out their purposes but also dilemmas inherent in their relationship with the outside world—their clients and donors.

As mentioned earlier, many intermediaries have difficulty trying to balance their roles as generalists versus specialists.[1] Generalist GSOs and MSOs try to respond to the multiple needs of their beneficiaries. This is especially true of those intermediaries that have a regional scope or those operating in areas where the coverage of government services is very thin (such as CIPCA in northern Peru or FIDENE in southwestern Brazil). Specialized intermediaries focus their attention on distinct service sectors but tend to neglect organizational strengthening and capacity building.

It is preferable for intermediaries to have a clearly defined central focus around which several types of activities can be clustered and gradually to acquire specialized professional competence in some fields (for example, communications or commodity processing). However, gaining such professional competence may become a problem if highly trained but poorly socialized staffs need to be integrated into the organization. Such professionals also have many alternative, better remunerated opportunities and are less likely to forgo the rewards associated with their skills.

MSOs that arise as a result of the alliance or federation of primary groups face different dilemmas. They can act as a secretariat for coordination or lobbying, they can offer technical or financial services to their members, or they can become implementers and operators of programs at a level where economies of scale are favorable. Each role offers certain advantages and disadvantages. Restrictions on how much highly trained professionals can be paid are even more strict for MSOs than for GSOs. Volunteer MSO board members (who represent base member organizations and are not high-status outsiders like those that might be found on GSO boards) and assemblies are reluctant to approve compensation levels for hired managers and technicians that are too far above their own standards.

One of the inherent problems of all intermediary organizations (and perhaps all NGOs) is the long-term career development of their staffs. The strong appeal of a shared mission, described earlier, is likely to weaken eventually, with job security and career advancement plus family-related motivations pulling people in other directions. Managing staff turnover and socializing new recruits are problems experienced by mature organizations.

The cases show that these ambiguities and conflicts may be embodied within a single program, such as credit or technology generation. For instance, the FUNDE and FMDR reports incisively illustrate the conflict inherent in providing credit (with good repayment percentages) and alleviating poverty. A "tough," financially sound credit program that achieves sustainable increases in productivity and high repayment rates is inherently more suitable for the "upper poor," or those with assets, experience, and managerial ability. (Whether "poverty lending" following the Grameen Bank's unique experience [discussed in Chapter 4] can alter this conclusion remains to be seen.)

In another case, de Janvry (1983) points out the conflict between inward-oriented strategies such as the organic gardening programs of CET and more long-term market-oriented solutions. In Chile's open cash economy, for example, projects based on self-provisioning and using one's labor for improved subsistence can be only a temporary solution to recession, exacerbated by repression. (These issues are discussed more extensively in Chapter 3.)

Some GSOs and MSOs are by origin and preference small, autonomous, and social; others are larger, highly linked, and economic or technical. Some want to be specialized, others do not. More generally, however, GSOs and MSOs deal with organizational dilemmas or conflicts in one of three ways: trade-off, compromise, or synergy. The trade-off option is a conscious choice by the organization to pursue an alternative path; organizations that opt for compromise follow coexisting but not interacting strategies; and the synergy option means searching for an appropriate combination of mutually reinforcing strategies.

The strongest GSOs and MSOs in the sample are able to take the two latter options. For example, to cope with tension between serving the relatively weak versus maintaining financial viability, URCOOPAPA chose compromise as the solution and decided to extend its services to medium-scale farmers. Although this expanded the resource base, it also brought together two types of farmers with different needs and probably different interests. In another instance, synergy was ANAI's strategy when the organization combined agroforestry technology with precooperative group formation. In this arrangement service delivery reinforced capacity building and vice versa.

The better-performing GSOs and MSOs in the sample do not seem to conform to the value of narrow specialization and bare-boned task specificity, sometimes identified as necessary for NGO effectiveness.[2] Although a clear focus and a lean organization are important factors in conditioning performance, accommodation to conflicting pressures and adaptation to dilemmas are more common features of successful GSOs and MSOs.

The Dynamic Dimension

Another aspect of organizational analysis deals more explicitly with the life cycles of intermediaries, that is, how they change and evolve over time. Organizational dynamics can reveal changes in goals, tasks, scope, or capacity as a function of external and internal factors in a constantly moving setting. Montgomery suggests that it is "best to learn from a dynamic institutional process than attempt to replicate a static, finished model" (Montgomery 1988). An improved understanding of the stages and phases of the development of GSOs and MSOs might also help donor agencies identify where the organization is in its evolution, with an end to providing timely and appropriate assistance.

Setting well-defined goals and strategies and allocating sufficient resources to achieve those goals clearly affect organizational effectiveness. Some GSOs and MSOs have been able to articulate clear goals consistently, but others have been burdened by unclear objectives. This lack of clarity is often the consequence of trying to do too much. Some older organizations have not been able to shift to a new central focus when the original goals that once provided their raison d'être are no longer valid or relevant. One could describe these as organizations in search of their destiny. This seems to be particularly true of institutions originally set up or promoted by governments.[3] These may lose their original legitimacy and focus when political circumstances change. At any rate, the cases in the sample are consistent with Paul's findings (1982) drawn from other contexts, in which the program performance of service organizations is associated with the ability to shift from an initially narrow goal or service to sequential diversification and phasing of interventions. (The opposite sequence has been seen in some of the "social" GSOs that succeeded in focusing and consolidating after a fuzzy beginning.)

A central goal may also be obscured by initial failure. This is illustrated best by the URCOOPAPA case (see Chapter 12). When something does not work, it may be a long time before inertia can be overcome and the unpromising activity replaced by other, more manageable tasks, as happened in the case of PURISCAL. However, it is to the credit of a number of organizations in the sample that they have been able to shift gears and adjust their strategies, even if it took some time and additional resources.[4] Lack of clear objectives and strategy leads to lowered organizational capacity, but, as suggested, intelligent compromise and synergy can subsequently increase that capacity.

It is possible that GSOs and MSOs do not follow a predictable sequence of development, although within certain types of institutions (such as marketing or credit cooperatives, consumer support), there are some patterns. The case studies illustrate that the evolution of these organizations is characterized by highs and lows, by conflict and uncertainty. The reasons for these swings are complex. They range from political opportunity, macroeconomic conditions, and natural disasters to leadership, internal management, and availability of donor funding.

The forty-two Peruvian cases and the thirty examined here reveal that GSOs and MSOs that varied or adjusted their goals and strategies over time did better than those that branched out and adopted completely new goals and techniques. These studies observed an interesting trend toward convergence of approaches within both the better-performing technical/economic and social/educational GSOs and MSOs. High overall scores are associated with a group of organizations that started out with very strong social inspiration but later tempered it (or channelled it) by adopting a more practical orientation and concentrating on satisfying specific beneficiary needs. CAPS in Guatemala, for example, shifted from an emphasis on popular education to the provision of production credit (see Box 8.1). Another group of organizations started out initially with a strong entrepreneurial/business orientation, heavy with technical and economic features, but later tempered it with greater social consciousness and sensitivity toward poverty issues and political-economic considerations.

GSOs and MSOs that moved from the social/educational realm toward a more production-oriented approach performed better than those moving in the opposite direction. This is consistent with Leonard's hypothesis, which holds that socially committed organizations can more readily acquire competence than the other way around (Leonard 1982a). On the other hand, within projects, strategies that begin with technical assistance and economic/productive activities proved to have more substantial and long-lasting impact than those that begin with training and organizational and pure community development activities.

How GSOs and MSOs diversify and grow without excessive bureaucratization and loss of sensitivity is another key issue of organizational dynamics. CAMPOCOOP's earlier history suggests that too rapid an expansion into new areas without attention to internal capacity can be disastrous. CIDE has managed to grow while maintaining an informal atmosphere and a participatory spirit using a decentralized structure (the creation of relatively autonomous projects). However, the increased number of projects and staff have strained the organization's consensual decisionmaking style. Like many other GSOs, CIDE has an executive council that is supposed to be responsible for decisionmaking and internal coordination. The case study found, however, that the council's functions are not clearly defined, that it is burdened with too many details that should be decentralized, and that it lacks power to carry out its decisions. Other larger organizations in the sample, such as FMDR and CIPCA, also have these problems. The necessity to delegate responsibility, especially during heavy work-load periods, puts a strain on the informal collegial style practiced earlier when the organizations were smaller. Evidence from both the Peruvian study and the thirty cases suggests that GSOs and MSOs that significantly expanded the range of beneficiaries did not perform as well as those that varied their services or methods to the same type of clientele.

As the needs of beneficiaries expand, so must the capacity of the organization to continually meet those demands. The Organization for Rural Development (ORD), which operates in isolated areas of the Caribbean island of St. Vincent, provides an exemplary illustration of organizational evolution. As the capacity of ORD's client farmers moved increasingly from subsistence to more market-oriented production, ORD responded by gradually improving staff members' expertise in increasingly sophisticated production and marketing systems. At the same time, the organization evolved from a highly centralized administrative structure to a more decentralized, regional administration. This change improved the organization's ability to respond to expanding needs and allowed more staff and beneficiary participation in decisionmaking and operations.

In more mature organizations, the problem is not so much to form new groups for collective action but to maintain and give new life to existing groups. One alternative is the PURISCAL model, where a completely new and much desired activity was superimposed on a rather dormant set of local groups. This galvanized them into action and encouraged them to devise other good programs. Another possible model is the new HORTICOOP, in which the old cooperatives now have to share power with management and compete with individuals for services. The cooperatives will have to either revitalize or disappear. This is drastic medicine, but it works.

In the case of SADECSA, different strategies have been used for different activities. Initially, SADECSA formed to help member societies maintain legal rights to their land. Now that the societies have greatly reduced their risk of losing the land and are engaged in production beyond the subsistence level, the strategy has shifted to an emphasis on income growth. Another more recent shift has been from providing assistance exclusively to male heads of households to integrating the family in all activities.

From a historic perspective, current strategies do not reflect either the past or the future in the life cycle of a GSO or MSO. Older organizations such as URCOOPAPA and CAMPOCOOP were probably more concerned with capacity building from the start, and, in fact, CAMPOCOOP might return to that strategy once the political environment in Chile shifts. In contrast, ANAI will have to become more oriented to income growth in the future as its nursery groups gear up for diversified tree crop production. What this means, and what the ORD example illustrates, is that different organizational capacities may be needed by GSOs and MSOs at different times in their life cycles. Donors might be able to

Box 8.1   CAPS: From Popular Education to Production Credit

Centro de Autoformación Para Promotores Sociales (CAPS) had its origin in 1967 as an organizational unit of the University of Rafael Landival, a Catholic institution. It now works in seven of the twenty-three departments of Guatemala attending Indian villages that are mostly isolated and bypassed by other development programs. The average landholding of its beneficiaries is approximately one acre.

CAPS is an example of a facilitator GSO that started out in nonformal education, community development, and organizational assistance and gradually took on a more economic/technical role stressing credit. After the devastating earthquake of 1976, community leaders and CAPS-trained promoters expressed interest in credit schemes. It is important to note that the villagers asked that CAPS offer credit—it was not a preference of CAPS, but a response to the local communities. Beginning with only US$47,000, CAPS made seventy-five village loans in its first five years of lending.

In 1981, in the face of severe government repression in the countryside and a deteriorating economy, CAPS augmented the fledgling credit program for low-income farmers with the help of the IAF. The IAF grant supported twenty-five group loans which generated forty-five projects not only in agriculture and livestock but also in small rural crafts and businesses. The loans required no collateral. The repayment rate has been an excellent 90 percent. The loans benefited thirty-six communities and over 1,200 families. Communities must express interest in the program, invest their own labor, and pay a fee for the training course before the loans are granted.

CAPS is particularly careful not to allow its credit program to promote a local elite. It has avoided this common problem through restrictions. For example, loans may not be used for hired labor and may not exceed the amount required for one person's work. In addition, CAPS is sensitive to the problem of creating dependency relationships through the credit program. Extensionists are trained to reduce their contact and advice to communities as the projects become more viable. Moreover, communities are encouraged to seek assistance from other development organizations and social service agencies.

It is notable that by taking up credit CAPS did not diminish its educational and organizational efforts. In fact, the credit program complements and strengthens the education program. Promoters have incorporated credit into their community development efforts. However, CAPS, like many other GSOs, considers credit as a means to community development, not as an end in itself. In sequencing its promotional approach, CAPS likes to place credit last, that is, at the culmination of intensive awareness training, group formation, and the accomplishment of tasks that are not dependent on external inputs. However, in practice this sequence does not always work. Credit (with other assistance in economic activities) now often serves as an entry point on which community solidarity can be built. Clearly this combination requires a group credit scheme, which is the basis of CAPS lending.

One great strength of the group credit program is the high quality of CAPS's extensionist/promoter field staff. CAPS was the first in Guatemala to make use of indigenous extensionists. Most extensionists are campesinos who speak the Indian languages. CAPS promoters are not formally tied to CAPS after their training. In fact, many of them go on to fill leadership positions in other community grassroots organizations. This has created an informal yet wide network. Through networks with other NGOs (erected with CAPS sponsorship), many of the innovations of CAPS are widely accepted and used.

In spite of long periods of repressive military regimes, the organization has maintained working relationships with government agencies. CAPS views the long-term implications of its credit program as preparing its client groups for dealing more effectively with state or commercial credit. By putting pressure on official agencies such as BANDESA, the main source of agricultural credit in Guatemala, CAPS seeks to make them more effective and responsive. This pressure has already resulted in more timely release of funds before the planting season.

It is also noteworthy that CAPS has evolved an effective management style and a rigorous lending process, unusual in a GSO of social welfare origins. Through the revolving credit program, CAPS has opened up the possibility of becoming more self-reliant financially.

CAPS has instituted a series of procedures that are perhaps unique for such a GSO in their detail and stringency for the cycle of application, approval, disbursement, and monitoring of credit funds:

- A group that wishes to apply for a loan must complete what is in effect a community study, describing the economic base of the community and the needs that justify the loan. A detailed financial cost/benefit study is also done, documenting the profits that can be expected to accrue to participants in the project.
- Every project is reviewed and approved or rejected by the central council, consisting of the executive director, the administrative director, the coordinator of extensionists, and the accountant. The rejection rate may be as high as 33 percent, though rejected proposals may be revised and resubmitted.
- The village committee members make a trip into Guatemala City (at their own expense) to participate in the formal signing of the agreement. This requirement, as well as the earlier community study, is maintained as an educational device and to instill in project participants a sense of the seriousness of the matter.
- The extensionist must also be present for the signing of the agreement. He or she becomes cosigner of the loan and is made to feel responsible for its timely recuperation.
- After signing the loan agreement, which carefully specifies the interest rate and amortization schedule, the committee is given a check for the purchase of materials. This check is issued in the name of the company or store from which the inputs will be purchased. The borrowers never receive cash.
- Installments are repaid to the central office—a procedure that appears to meet with the approval of the village committees. The committees are urged to convert their cash to a check in a municipal bank but find pleasure in delivering a large bundle of cash to CAPS.
- As part of every monthly report, the extensionist must prepare a detailed *radiografía* (x-ray) of each credit project, specifying the activities carried out in that month, the resources utilized, the achievements, the problems that arose, and the solutions that were applied. He or she briefly evaluates the project.

anticipate changing needs and perhaps help prepare their grantees for new tasks.

It is important not to lose sight of the dynamics of history and context in arriving at a notion of GSO/MSO performance. Although there are some young organizations among those with top ratings, most are older and seasoned. They have learned how to deal with donors, clients, friends, and adversaries, and they have arrived at some measure of internal coherence and external legitimacy so that they do not have to live from crisis to crisis.

However, even these seasoned and mature intermediaries are now facing new challenges as the new decade unfolds. They will have to gear up for further organizational adjustments. We have learned from the earlier chapters that their new challenges are likely to include the following:

- Maintenance of vigor and dynamism without the stimulus of the original founders and leaders;
- Expansion and management of larger workloads without loss of quality;
- Learning to collaborate with governments without loss of autonomy;
- Forging closer GSO-MSO links without tutelage and interference; and
- Networking and joining with other institutions without loss of identity.

Conclusion

GSOs and MSOs from the sample that consistently rate well in major respects are generally small (as organizations go) but large enough for functional specialization. They can be larger as long as they do not lose their collegial, informal style of operation. Over time, they have developed a clear, coherent agenda, modifying their goals and methods according to the changing needs and circumstances of both their beneficiaries and the environment in which they operate. Instead of expanding their scope of activities and range of beneficiaries, successful GSOs and MSOs generally intensify and deepen their efforts, employing a set of interconnected activities so as to create synergy or complementarity among projects. The best performers also actively seek and subsequently respond to beneficiary input, more through informal channels, such as day-to-day interaction between staff and clients, than through formal mechanisms. Although they have mastered the art of listening and responding without dominating, they do offer sensitive guidance. They tend to operate on a regional rather than local or national scope. By employing a spatially coherent strategy, they take advantage of opportunities to form beneficial linkages with decentralized public agencies and other NGOs involved in similar efforts. Linkages with national government ministries and agencies and private technology centers are seen as beneficial. Even with extensive state collaboration and resource transfers, the good performers manage to preserve a measure of independence. Functionally, they combine effective service delivery with capacity building of base-level organizations.

The good performers started either with strong social inspiration and gradually tempered it with greater professionalism *or* with an entrepreneurial or technical orientation and gradually acquired greater social awareness. The top organizations are generally able to weather various crises and overcome serious conflicts. They almost invariably get going and develop under strong inspired leadership, but over time, the top staff rotate as the original leaders leave. Finally, the best-performing GSOs and MSOs usually can count on some degree of financial security for their core support.

To rise to the challenges of this decade appears to be a very tall order. It will not only tax the ingenuity and dynamic capacity of intermediary NGOs but will also call forth new types of thinking and new modes of support from their sponsors and donors. The next chapter addresses the question of what donors might do to help bring out the best in the intermediary organizations they sponsor.

Notes

1. This discussion is inspired by David Brown's report on support organizations in Asia. He uses the term *support organization* to designate so-called apex organizations that support other NGOs, rather than in the sense that support organization is used in this book. The inherent tensions Brown identifies within apex NGOs are also largely applicable to individual grassroots-oriented NGOs (Society for Participatory Research in Asia 1990).

2. This contradicts Tendler's earlier study (1982b) but is supported by the analysis of Esman and Uphoff (1984), based on a large sample of cases.

3. These government-initiated NGOs evoke different reactions from the critics. Montgomery clearly is not bothered by public-sector origins or linkages and favors "bringing both government and business leaders into the act" (Carroll and Montgomery 1987, p. 38). NGO purists warn that the formation of government-organized NGOs (GONGOs)

> seldom reflects a spontaneous expression of shared value commitment, and participation is often less than voluntary. The motives of forming such organizations may be positive, and they may serve useful social functions, but they are less likely . . . to serve as consequential agents for social innovation. (Brown and Korten 1989, p. 222)

4. In some cases, opportunistic organizational behavior is masquerading as experimentation or innovation. Funds are accepted for projects favored by certain donors in fields where the organization has little experience or comparative advantage. (This was the case in the push for export promotion in Costa Rica and Peru by the U.S. Agency for International Development.)

9

Donors and Their Clients

Donor Attitudes

Donor attitudes and policies can make a big difference in the way intermediary nongovernmental organizations (NGOs) in general and grassroots support organizations (GSOs) in particular perform. Although donors supply the financial lifeblood for GSOs, the way they do business with their grantees is often counterproductive and inhibits the development of the GSO's potential. This chapter examines some of the donor attitudes and perceptions that inhibit good performance and suggests a number of actions donors could take to bring out the best traits in the intermediary organizations they support. The chapter focuses on GSOs because they account for the bulk of donor financing, yet they continue to provoke controversy. Membership support organizations (MSOs), as representative intermediaries, are generally accepted as permanent institutions worthy of sustained support. The legitimacy of GSOs is not as firmly established, and they are often regarded as expendable.

Certain types of organizations are especially worthy of support, and certain traits and practices of these organizations are worthy of developing further. The thirty cases examined for this book show that even the "best" GSOs do not perform well enough in certain dimensions, but they have the potential to perform better. They should be able to reach more and poorer constituencies and to make a more sustainable and significant impact—a view voiced increasingly by commentators on the NGO scene. They also should be able to do more in capacity-building and empowerment—their essential tasks. But fewer commentators complain about these latter shortcomings, perhaps because they assume that most NGOs are already doing all they can, or they do not realize the potential of intermediary organizations, especially of GSOs, in this regard.

Critical analyses of NGO performance come mostly from scholars and lately from the NGOs themselves, but hardly ever from donors, even though donors are perhaps in the best position to exercise constructive and informed criticism. One reason for this silence may be the mutual dependency relationship between donors and their principal clients. This relationship limits the number of policy changes donors might be prepared to make. All donors have to perform in a manner that their own boards and funding sources find satisfactory if they want to stay in business. The NGOs need the donors' money, and the donors need the NGOs so that money can be disbursed and visible progress can be reported. In this operational, rather than philosophical, sense, NGO donors are not too different from more conventional external aid organizations.[1]

Clearly a donor's attitude is crucial in helping to nurture a GSO from an often precarious beginning through difficult periods, and eventually to the sort of mature, experienced organization described in this book. A donor must be cautious in the first place not to contribute to organizational schizophrenia by offering grants for programs not central to the GSO's agenda. It is also largely up to the donor to encourage the GSOs it supports to act more like development organizations, less like consulting firms. In order to do this, an investment has to be made in reinforcing the GSO's own institutional and organizational capacity. This is not simply a question of funding, but of timing, risk taking, strategic planning, and, above all, continuity.

The Inter-American Foundation (IAF), as a donor, has played a very important role in the early period of the organizations discussed in this book, when their promise was more evident than their track record or actual capacity. Subsequently, the IAF has also helped a number of these organizations overcome internal or external troubles.

Client Scorecard

Although the IAF has been an unusually bold risk taker and has displayed great sensitivity and flexibility in funding strategy, its attitude toward GSOs has been infused with some ambiguity. This ambiguity is also shared by many other donors that value participation and empowerment. Therefore, the comments about the IAF in the following pages are of interest to and relevant for other Northern agencies that finance developmental NGOs in the South.

One of the questions that gave rise to this study is how organizations like the IAF can deal effectively with intermediary organizations, those designated here as GSOs and MSOs. The IAF posed this question because support organizations presented it with a dilemma: Although GSOs and MSOs often played a useful role in fulfilling the foundation's purposes, these grantees were not the "genuine grassroots." By giving them grants, the IAF was in a sense bypassing the poor and undermining its self-promoted image of "direct to the poor" (the title of an IAF publication; Annis and Hakim 1988). In addition to favoring the base, donors like the IAF tend to feel more enthusiastic about intermediary-level (nonbase) organizations in which the membership has a formal voice, or MSOs, than about GSOs that are not formally accountable to the people they support.

The thirty cases, which represent a set of intermediary organizations with which the IAF has had satisfactory working relations, reveal that GSOs have special strengths and advantages, and MSOs have special weaknesses and disadvantages. On the whole, GSOs have outperformed the MSOs. Of the twenty-three GSOs in the sample, ten were judged to be outstanding and thirteen very good.

Investing $20 million in the twenty-three GSOs was a good decision for the IAF, although there is little quantitative evidence to support this judgment. By investing as it did, the IAF reached poorer and less organized households than would have been possible through MSOs. The money made a much bigger impact than if it had been split into 500 individual grants to base groups. Not only have more poor families benefited directly and indirectly, but also, as all the organizational histories show, the grassroots groups assisted by the GSOs, the GSOs themselves, and other organizations they inspired have all grown in effectiveness.

It must be pointed out, however, that despite this positive overall judgment, these GSOs do not escape criticism. Virtually all the serious evaluation reports reviewed in the course of the research for this book identified multiple weaknesses in these highly rated organizations. The most frequent criticisms were unclear objectives, insufficient diagnosis of the optimal approaches to poverty alleviation, and lack of attention to sustainability and to viable models of participatory local organization.

But as important as this overall assessment are the following observations:

- The great majority of the GSOs excel in precisely those areas that the IAF values: participation, capacity building, and self-management. And with respect to group capacity building and wider reach, they have a substantial unrealized potential.
- MSOs and GSOs should not be seen as alternatives—each has its role. The former can be complementary to and supportive of the latter as the mode of assistance changes with the maturing of the membership organizations.
- In some cases, the GSOs supported by the IAF have had important catalytic effects by spawning a whole network of support organizations that together are having a significant influence on a whole sector or region.
- The apparent dilemma of having to choose between financing base groups and financing intermediaries may turn out to be an artificial dichotomy. After all, the base groups reached through GSOs are no less the IAF's grantees than those financed directly. Furthermore, as the IAF realizes, it is not

possible to make many small, quality grants and supervise and backstop them with its own operational staff. This is why in recent years the in-country support (ICS) system was installed, often through national GSOs. (The ICS is a device to enhance the IAF's field effectiveness without enlarging and permanently outposting core staff. The IAF contracts with a national organization in each major country to provide project backstopping and monitoring services to its grantees.)

IAF's criteria for intermediaries appear to mirror the image the IAF has of itself. A GSO, to merit support, must be savvy but modest, respectful, responsive, hands-off, and internally collegiate and have a flexible management style with devolved responsibility.

However, the IAF, like other donors, has had some difficulty acknowledging the role of GSOs as committed but independent allies, friends, and brokers capable of providing valuable links to outside knowledge centers and financial, economic, and legal institutions, while safeguarding the very integrity and viability of the representative local organizations themselves. These are the roles that the sample GSOs have performed so well, as documented throughout this book.

Myths of Grassroots Development

One of the most appealing features of the IAF is its ability to preach and to practice participatory microdevelopment without losing faith in its mandate, yet remain open and accessible to questioning and debate. However, rhetoric and the need to project a public image sometimes get in the way of in-house learning and prevent greater contributions to development practice.

Two themes appear to have infused all of the IAF's work. The first is the high value that is universally attached to self-initiated, autonomous choice and self-responsibility for the success of development activities, along with faith in the inherent ability of the poor to rise to the occasion when given the opportunity. This belief structure has given rise to an almost obsessive preoccupation with a hands-off, noninterfering stance as an antidote to dependency, tutelage, or manipulation by "outsiders."

The second and somewhat less pervasive theme is that this process of unleashing creative energies must be accomplished through poor people's own organizations, or grassroots groups. Hence the IAF's constant search for groups that embody the ideal of ownership by their members and in which benefits and responsibilities are widely shared. The faith, in this case, is extended from the individuals to the group engaged in collective action. When people are stimulated and inspired they are capable of engaging in altruistic, other-oriented cooperative behavior on a sustained basis, again assuming that they are not coerced, directed, or co-opted by outside forces. Given these two themes, it is no wonder that GSOs are suspect, even though they are also needed and often appreciated.

These strongly held premises (along with some others, such as affinity with native Indian cultures and distaste for big-stick U.S. policies for Latin America) have given the IAF staff a constant source of inspiration, pride, and commitment and have sustained it in difficult times.

These values also incorporate some myths, not only about internal reinforcement but about the IAF's public image as well. However, maintaining such myths exacts a price, in terms of both operational performance and learning and diffusion of developmental knowledge, an often-stressed objective of the IAF. What are these myths, and what is their relevance to the issue of GSOs?[2]

The first is the "spontaneous combustion" myth. According to this myth, organizations can come into being and flower from within through natural processes, unadulterated by action from without, a sort of "immaculate conception." Perhaps a spark (a project) is all that is required to set off an evolutionary chain reaction. Interference is damaging. As an article of faith, this is a noble concept, but as an operational principle, it has limitations. It undervalues the vigorous promotion needed to create sustainable grassroots organizations and the nurturing support needed to help them grow, mature, and multiply. This support is precisely the role of the GSOs. Given Latin American social history, the fear of domination, paternalism, and co-optation is real, but sympathetic alliances, stimuli, teaching, protection, and prodding must not be downgraded. They are essential elements in the organizational flowering process.

The "lone ranger" myth celebrates rugged independence or, in IAF parlance, autonomy. More autonomy and its reciprocal, less dependence, are desirable, but an obsession with both social and economic independence is counterproductive. Greater self-reliance of both individuals and small groups is a most worthy goal. Growth in awareness, self-worth, pride, and confidence as a result of accomplishing successful grassroots projects is well documented in IAF literature (Wasserstrom 1985), but development implies interdependence, not autarchy. The aim of egalitarian development efforts is not to produce isolation but to facilitate a more balanced interdependence, in which the weaker participants can be on a par with the stronger as both producers and consumers. The best GSOs take on this facilitation role, as was documented earlier.

A recent contribution by Linda Stone, an anthropologist working in Nepal, reinforces this point. She finds that the notions of self-reliance and independence in community development have meaning primarily for Western developers whose cultural values stress individuality and equality, but not for Nepalese villagers who perceive their world as operating through personal relations and hierarchical linkages. Villagers perceive development as something that comes from the outside, with which they need to establish meaningful connections. She writes,

> Rather than encourage an attitude of "independence" on the part of village communities, a development strategy based on the idea of interdependence between villagers and their government development agencies and institutions or between villagers and "outsiders" generally would be more realistic and appropriate. (Stone 1989, p. 212)

The third myth involves the "egalitarian community," a notion that is always disclaimed or strongly qualified by experienced researchers, but that nonetheless has a damaging effect. Sometimes the group with which the IAF works is relatively inclusive and democratic, but it is more common for base groups to be exclusive and internally unequal. This internal stratification is well documented even in indigenous traditional communities, which, in the Andes and Mesoamerica, are favorites among the IAF's grantees.[3] Worse yet, it is clear that the process of economic development, far from narrowing inequalities, tends to widen them. The IAF's staff is skilled at weeding out applicant groups that are the creation or wards of opportunistic leaders and at assuring an acceptable level of commonality and lack of elitism within the groups that it sponsors. However, a measure of inequality both in participation and in benefit distribution is a fact of life, as is factionalism, clientelism, and vulnerability to external manipulation by hostile powers. Sympathetic GSOs can play important stabilizing roles in such situations. They can frequently hold down or help eliminate corruption, mediate in disputes, or reinforce democratic leadership. The best GSOs act as neutral, trusted advisers and can deflect disruptive internal or external forces.

The "small is beautiful" myth has also lost some of its earlier appeal, but aspects of it still create blind spots. Although the value of the IAFs microapproach has never been questioned, and it quite properly remains as its trademark, a noticeable evolution is taking place toward larger systems and "policy relevance." This issue poses a real dilemma for the IAF, because its comparative advantage is in microdevelopment. The relevance of GSOs in bridging the micro/macro gap is obvious. The patient examination of the local scene enabled PROTERRA lawyers not only to resolve individual cases but also to lobby successfully for new land tenure procedures at the central level and to achieve new legislation. It was the intimate, hands-on knowledge of the rural economy in Rio Grande do Sul that enabled FIDENE to design strategies to diversify the soybean-dominated farming structure. The lesson is not that small is beautiful but that through the microreality, one can tackle macroissues and, conversely, that the correctness, costs, and benefits of policy reform show up best in the microsetting.

The fifth myth, called "fringes of poverty," is the opposite of the "tarmac" proclivity of aid agencies identified eloquently by Robert Chambers in his seminal book *Rural Development: Putting the Last First* (1983). According to this view, development agencies, both foreign and domestic, tend to look no further than the edge of the paved road to find their clients, who, not surprisingly, turn out not to be the poorest at all. The IAF and others whose commitment runs deep often fall into the opposite trap (this is true of some GSOs as well): They seek out special, isolated poverty pockets or make common cause with remote tribes or special constituencies. Although there is usually no doubt that these people are needy and sometimes suffer from special forms of oppression and isolation, this approach carries two dangers. One is that it is easy to lose perspective about what is more important. A project that attacks *mainstream poverty* or at least a slice of it can have a demonstration effect or policy impact on many other similar cases and for that reason is more important than attending to nonreproducible cases that may be attractive anthropologically but have limited impact. The other danger is that, by becoming advocates for a very narrow class of the poor, one tends to lose sight of broader interests, of rival tribes or downstream water users, of conflicting claims over scarce natural resources, of long-term versus short-term benefits, and, finally, of the "public interest." This is not at all an argument against strong commitment to the causes of the forgotten and the oppressed. It is just a reminder that not all causes are equally strategic. The cases also indicate that GSOs working with very special clientele not only tend to bypass the bulk of the poor but also gravitate toward welfare approaches. These are also the GSOs and their donors that have the greatest reservations about establishing links with public agencies.

The last myth is the "happy campesino." The dark-skinned peasant brandishing his tools and his female counterpart with her hand loom or market cart appearing on the cover of *Grassroots Development*, the IAF journal, symbolize the IAF's dedication to the genuine Latin American underdog who rises through his own and his group's efforts, thereby becoming empowered. There is nothing wrong with this imagery. It enhances the IAF's public image, just as similar photographs in the brochures and annual reports of other aid agencies convey the human side of development.

The problem with the ubiquitous image of the happy campesino is not what it conveys but what it does not convey. Seldom represented are other heroes of grassroots development: the activist priest defying local authorities, the dedicated lawyer or agronomist, the socially responsible businessperson, the upper-class volunteers, and the intellectuals and educators who are the founders, directors, and staff members of GSOs that stand behind the campesino man and woman. Perhaps it is time to acknowledge IAF's partnership with the GSOs and to legitimize the GSOs as targets for organizational strengthening. In recent years, many Latin American GSOs have increasingly stressed their independent agendas and their organizational autonomy (Padrón 1987; Arbab 1988). This should not deter donors from seeking to establish partnership relations, based on mutual understanding and respect.

The IAF's support of GSOs is yielding an important but largely unrecognized benefit: increasing the number and involvement of socially committed and skilled Latin American intellectuals and professionals. Leading staff members of GSOs are becoming influential beyond their own organizations as they move back and forth in the realm of government, politics, business, and universities. Their hands-on experience, acquired while working directly with poor groups and microprojects, is salutary to both the academically inclined who are likely to have radical or theoretical backgrounds and to practitioners who tend to come from more conservative and technocratic origins. Enhancing the capability of committed and skilled professionals to deal constructively with poverty, even though they are not themselves from the poorer social groups, appears to be a very wise investment. Also, in a wider social context, such alliances across traditional class boundaries can be beneficial.

The "happy campesino" myth carries another drawback, once again in what it does not convey. It gives the impression of harmony, of cooperation, of community. It masks the real world of conflict, rivalry, and tension, a harsh world in which the IAF's projects and client organizations operate. As noted above, grassroots groups in particular must tilt with outside forces and also confront the realities inherent in their own structure. How institutional development occurs in these circumstances and how outside support agents, the GSOs, and the IAF deal not only with a common enemy (landlords, middlemen, illegitimate states) but also with internal weaknesses (factionalism and corruption) is the stuff of operational research.

Why the Fuss about Group Capacity?

In reacting to a draft of this book, several readers asked, "Why all the fuss about group capacity? It's not the only way—sometimes it is the individual and sometimes it is the group." In a sense, they are right. Group capacity cannot grow without individual learning by members and leaders. The ultimate effectiveness of a group can best be appreciated through the enhanced welfare of its members. Also, some of the highly valued GSOs and MSOs perform services that do not necessarily or directly involve groups (legal advice, enterprise credit). But grassroots development means joint or group action conceptually and practically, and the essence of the IAF's aims is also accomplished through groups of common or ordinary people. Meehan, in his thoughtful 1978 book on the IAF, identifies the local or primary organization as "social capital" and hence the key to the IAF's work. The IAF's mission, according to Meehan, is to help people develop organizations and learn how to use them. The independent evaluation group in its 1984 report, states it rather well:

> Whether a grant goes directly to a base group or gets there indirectly through an intermediary, the Foundation sees itself as fostering institution-building by the poor. A functioning institution, in turn, provides the group of poor people with a basis for helping themselves and for seeking public services. (Weintraub 1984)

What has been called group capacity building throughout this study is therefore the crux of the institution-building process. It is curious that this conscious, cumulative, and difficult process is not adequately articulated, studied, and recorded at the IAF, which among donors is perhaps in the best position to provide such documentation. Although prospective grantees are carefully scrutinized, subsequent progress and performance are reported in terms of project outcomes (as is customary in virtually all external aid agencies) rather than in terms of organizational outcomes. Perhaps this is a consequence of one of the myths discussed earlier, the "spontaneous combustion" syndrome. In line with this thinking, the project itself is seen as the necessary spark or catalyst to bring an organization into being on its own or to strengthen an existing one. No further buildup or nurturing is needed; indeed, such outside efforts are perceived as interference in the self-organization process. Sharon Holt (1991) encountered this same attitude in her study on village banking. Sponsoring agencies and the village bank model itself assumed that participatory local organizations were self-regulating, and supervision was viewed as a threat to community independence. This led to frequent financial mismanagement. It was later found that supervisory services such as semiannual audits did not jeopardize the village banks' autonomy. This passive and, as argued in this book, idealistic and naive vision is not strictly followed in practice. Brian Smith interviewed a representative sample of IAF staffers and obtained the following scores for their ranking of agency goals (the eight respondents ranked each item on a scale of one to six):

Goal	Score
Building community-run institutions and networks operated primarily by the poor	37
Empowerment of the poor to challenge and change dominant political and economic structures	36
Improving skills and problem-solving capacities	36
Enhancing recipient bargaining power vis-à-vis local merchants, credit institutions, government agencies, and so on	34
Increasing income and/or employment	25
Immediate alleviation of suffering	4*

Source: Brian Smith, "U.S.-Canadian Non-Profit Organizations and International Development," Working Paper 70, (New Haven, CT: Yale University Program on Non-Profit Organizations, 1983), p. 127.
* Half of the respondents refused to rank this goal, considering it inappropriate to their work.

Collective action and institutional power, rather than service or individual economic or social improvement, are seen overwhelmingly as the IAF's purpose. It is also notable that three of the four top-rated priorities are concerned with active group-capacity enhancement.

A strong emphasis on group capacity building, although not in line with the IAF's mythology, is nonetheless substantially endorsed by its representatives who are at the cutting edge of the agency's operations. The author interviewed twelve of these representatives and asked them to rank the performance criteria. Group capacity building was definitely the top choice, with virtually all the respondents rating it first, second, or third in importance. More predictably, its twin, participation, was second choice, with service delivery a close third. For those who see the concept of small-group capacity as too restrictive, the work on MSOs in this volume offers a broader horizon: A multitier system of membership organizations allows for the development of two types of capacities, individually among the members and collectively at the federation level.

Suggestions for Donor Policies

This section offers some specific suggestions for donors. These are addressed primarily to those donors who see NGOs as intrinsically valuable, such as the IAF and most of the European bilateral agencies, rather than to those who view them instrumentally, that is, as channels for credit, health services, and other assistance. The latter stance is more typical of multilateral financial aid institutions and large bilateral agencies.

Terminology and Identification

GSOs and MSOs as intermediary organizations are sufficiently distinct from donor-supported base groups, from each other, and from other NGOs to merit separate treatment. The records kept on these groups should clearly reflect the distinct nature of supra-local development organizations. In donor reports, each grant is a distinct project, classified only by country and sector. There is no recognition of the functional difference between a marketing project carried out by a group of farm women at a local market, a co-op federation, and a facilitator-type GSO. A recent evaluation of the African Development Foundation employed a sample of twelve projects, eight of which were operated by GSOs. These are correctly identified in the text of the report as "intermediary organizations," but in the evaluation they are treated the same way as grassroots groups (Office of Technology Assessment 1988).

It is assumed that experienced donors can sort out the opportunistic and often unscrupulous grant seekers from the genuinely committed, serious GSOs. Brown and Korten (1989) comment:

As the availability of public funding for NGO activities increases, so too do reports of retired bureaucrats, unemployed local touts, and other opportunity-seeking individuials rushing to form NGOs to qualify for funding. These organizations are formed more as an entrepreneurial response to market or political opportunities than on the basis of value commitments. (p. 24)

In practice, of course, there is always a mix of motivations. Certainly, IAF representatives who are thoroughly familiar with their territories and are supported by their in-country service colleagues are skilled in this weeding-out task. But not many donors are able to adequately appraise organizations as opposed to project proposals.

More problematic is the correct identification of a GSO's predominant orientation or niche and hence the judgment of its potential. Perhaps the typologies offered in this volume can be helpful in classifying NGOs in general and GSOs in particular so that their comparative advantages and disadvantages and their suitability for different programs or modes of operation will be more clearly understood and communicated.

Creating "Partnerships"

Operationally, it makes sense to select GSOs with a proven track record and future potential and to work with them intensively over a long time. In fact, the IAF has been doing this over the years with some GSOs, but rather haphazardly. The recently created partnership grant system, in which longer-term institutional objectives rather than short-term projects are the basis for grants, may also be useful in strengthening the organizational capacity of GSOs and should be used more consistently.

It should be more widely recognized that GSOs (often called "outsiders" in this study) play a highly important support role even after their initial promotional activities are accomplished. There is an unfortunate tendency to view the role of GSOs as strictly temporary, until more "genuine," member-based organizations can take over. Even after the emergence of local and associated membership groups that they have helped to nurture, GSOs need not "fade away," but might merit donor support to complement and reinforce membership organizations in areas where the latter are weak or vulnerable. And their continued role in taking up the development process with a new set of clients is perhaps more important. Even within regions, the relatively small scale of location-bound GSOs seems to offer plenty of scope for client rotation. However, several GSO leaders have pointed out that they face additional costs when seeking out new clients to organize. Donors have often perpetuated dependency and lack of broader coverage by refusing to provide for these extra up-front organizational expenses and by failing to offer incentives to GSOs for disengagement.[4] This study has stressed the complementarity between GSOs and MSOs and the tendency of this relationship to shift at different stages of grassroots organizational development.

Donors need to do some creative thinking and experimenting on how the financing of membership associations (at both the base and intermediate levels) can be combined with grants to GSOs. Several instances of cluster funding on a regional basis have been reported here among the thirty cases (CEDECUM, UNIDAD), but this practice is not yet widespread. Part of the either/or mentality of donors can be explained by the necessity of having a single organization responsible and accountable for funds and performance. Also, many independent-minded GSOs would object if their financing tied them to other actors over which they had no control, or limited them to a contractor/consultant role. Yet it is precisely this insularity that needs to be modified, even if it means that decisions about the kinds of services or assistance that membership organizations want and are willing to pay for would gradually shift from GSOs to MSOs, as the latter mature.

There is also the question whether membership organizations, once they receive development funding directly from donors rather than through GSOs, would accept or even pay for technical assistance in managerial, technical, or organizational matters from GSOs if it did not come with funding. It may very well be that this issue will lead to more differentiation and specialization among GSOs: Some would continue to take responsibility for base organizing and outreach, others would offer training and management support, and others would be transformed into permanent service institutions.

Institutional Support

For especially creative GSOs, donor support sustained over a sufficiently long period of time would provide a way to ensure institutional stability. Similarly, a willingness on the part of donors to convert project support into institutional support, where warranted, should contribute to easing the withdrawal pains in the GSO as it winds down one project and turns to another. This recommendation is reinforced by the Organization for Economic Cooperation and Development (OECD) in a recent report by the chairman of the Development Assistance Committee, which keeps track of and evaluates international development assistance.[5] European funders are more likely to provide longer-term institutional support than U.S. donors. However, this steadier commitment is often based on religious or political sympathies and may be accompanied by fuzzier goal definitions and reduced accountability for program outcomes. The argument for longer and more institutional support is certainly not to be confused with a carte blanche approach. It is *not* suggested that the project format be abandoned. In fact, many GSOs would benefit from better planning, strict financing accountability, and tracking progress through the project cycle. The argument is for more flexible arrangements in which any one project can become part of a program or a development sequence. Donors could also make institutional support dependent on more active client rotation and organizational outreach.

Projects should be tailored to the organizational evolution of the GSO. In many cases this is already being done by IAF representatives who are intimately familiar with their countries and clients, but it should be adequately documented for the purpose of learning and evaluation. Sustained donor support would also contribute to making GSOs more poverty oriented. Short-term projects often push GSOs to work with more accessible clients who already have some capacity and hence can assure a quicker payoff. A longer planning horizon makes it possible for GSOs to devote the preinvestment time and energy necessary to work with poorer and less organized beneficiaries.

Program financing implies a new type of relationship between GSOs and donors. This generally means not only a shift from projects to programs and toward institutional core support, but also a continual dialogue about objectives and strategies, rather than simply a specification of outputs and targets. Some donors are not equipped to carry on analytical or monitoring functions of this intensity and may have to acquire more in-country capability.

It has been also suggested that most donors are reluctant to continue financing any one GSO's projects for too many years to discourage dependence, with the result that an organization—often just when it begins to show significant results—may lose an important donor. This tendency is also reinforced by the constant search for new NGOs and by the pursuit of the development fashion of the day. Some donors also feel that their clients should be kept "on their toes" and not allowed to become complacent and lose creativity as a result of financial comfort. One way donors can make longer-term commitments without appearing to coddle GSOs is by helping to establish endowment funds, such as the one operating in Colombia by the Fundación para la Educación Superior (Arbab 1988).

Donors should not be reluctant to cofinance promising GSOs. Among the sample GSOs, some rely heavily on the IAF and many others receive grants from other sources, which should be seen as a positive attribute. Within a regional framework, the possibilities for fruitful cooperation with other donors multiply. In the same vein, GSOs in countries with sympathetic regimes should be encouraged to collaborate with government agencies, especially at the municipal and regional level, so that their work can affect public programs and their heavy dependence on external funds can be reduced.

However, the insistence of many donors that GSOs become fully self-sufficient may not be realistic. Perhaps MSOs, because they are often able to obtain income from member-supported activities and are viewed as more permanent, can become more financially independent than service and advocacy GSOs that cannot charge sufficient fees to recover their costs. (See the case of CACH in Chapter 12. About three-fourths of all operating costs are covered by the sale of services.) It is quite appropriate for donors to encourage and assist GSOs to gradually develop revenue sources and to collect fees for their services when it becomes possible. However, as Brown and Korten so aptly state:

> The task of the catalyst Voluntary Organization is to build self-reliant sustainable institutions that are accountable to the people, rather than to become self-reliant and sustainable itself. The concern of the donor, therefore, should not be with whether the catalyst organization is itself becoming financially self-reliant so much as with whether it is effectively developing self-reliant, self-sustaining organizations and structures." (1989, p. 12)

The opportunities for financing base groups in areas of GSO influence should not be seen as a substitute for further grants to the GSO. Projects should be designed so that they have a specific goal or terminal point when the GSO can either switch to a different assistance mode or go on to a different client group. At any rate, a given project should be part of a longer-term institutional relationship with the GSO.

Projects should be designed with specific reporting requirements based on criteria for building beneficiary capacity. Longer-term commitments, moral or contractual, will not impair donor supervision or grantee accountability if the arrangement is well phased and provides for periodic reviews and adjustment. What is important is to maximize the capability of the "worthy" GSOs to develop their full potential in an atmosphere of greater security and in which GSO leaders are less preoccupied by fund-raising and routine reporting.

Extending Promising Approaches

Donors should resist the temptation to push GSOs prematurely into new activities or new areas. (Donors may be doing this because they want to be able to report on "fresh" approaches and use new publicity opportunities or because they have lost interest in existing areas and beneficiary populations that have already received some grants.) The reward system of donors should be adjusted to favor building on the accumulated experience and growing expertise of GSOs, taking advantage of the initial capacity acquired by beneficiary groups and deepening and extending promising approaches. At any rate, when to dig in and when to shift gears should be a constant dialogue between GSOs and their donors.

Among the promising services that lend themselves exceptionally well to GSOs and MSOs are preventive community health care in the social field, nonfarm rural self-employment in the economic realm, and low-risk, low-input technology. There is enough accumulated experience to warrant a much more massive application of such programs. As to new approaches, GSOs and MSOs might move into the area of creating more wage employment for the rural and small-town poor, especially in labor-intensive infrastructure construction, by making it possible for community groups to undertake self-contracting.

One of the most promising ways to optimize the potential of GSOs is to develop a regional or territorial approach. Among the sample, GSOs with an established regional base exhibited an enormous potential for wide and sustained impact, without the danger of excessive bureaucratization. A regional approach is also most appropriate in countries embarked on decentralization. This not only opens up new avenues of collaboration with regional planning or action agencies, but presents opportunities for popular organizations to participate in new local sources of decisionmaking at the municipal level.

With a regional strategy, a donor may work with one GSO and a network of base groups or even with several complementary GSOs operating in the same region. However, a regional strategy is especially demanding and entails not only longer than customary donor support but also heavier than usual front-end costs.

Through trial and error, the IAF has developed a very interesting regionalized funding system in Colombia. Actually a three-tiered network arrangement, it is anchored by a strong support institution of regional scope (a GSO), but funding is also extended to grassroots groups and federations of grassroot groups (MSOs) in the same area. Ritchey-Vance (1991) describes this sytem as a "spider," with the support institution as the main body at the center, grassroots organizations at the extremities, and a dense web of connecting threads between.[6] This excellent model brings together a number of the suggestions made in this chapter.

Diagnostic studies combined with pilot approaches to find strategically significant and reproducible approaches have high priority, as do techniques for diffusion and communication. Among the highly rated GSOs, Centro de Investigación y Promoción del Campesino (CIPCA) in Peru was criticized by an evaluation team for not living up to its regional potential, but the three European donors were also admonished to shift their grant patterns to help CIPCA in this task (CIPCA 1987). Other evaluations also stress the need for donors to get engaged in evolving a regionally sustainable longer-term strategy.

One way to minimize the perceived negative impression (on the outside board or public) of making repeated and substantial grants to the same organization may be to stress that these grants really benefit different grassroots groups, which are assisted by a given intermediary. Indeed, some projects may be structured so that a portion of the grant is channeled directly to the beneficiaries, while another portion goes to the GSO, as in the Colombian case cited above. In general, donors accustomed to working with base groups should seriously consider not funding any primary community group unless it is linked to an outside support organization.

Capacity-Building Action and Learning

Enhancement of group capacity is judged to be the essence of GSO performance. Another useful term is local organizational development. Ten years ago, the IAF equated organization with social capital and saw it as a key to human improvement. It was suggested then that the focus of the IAF's learning effort should be on organizational development.[7] The case profiles suggest that access to resources and services does not necessarily enhance the capacity of base groups, even if the projects clearly respond to local initiatives. Some GSOs lack the technical and organizational skills and incentives needed to effectively assist in *local organizational development*. The case profiles also reveal that no one has analyzed what organizational forms are desirable and appropriate in various social and economic settings and what kind of outside assistance is suitable to each type. The assumption is, of course, that although there are no universally applicable models, certain patterns with good possibilities of application under similar circumstances can be identified.

This assumption is not unique to Latin America. A recent review of Asian NGO experiences in seven countries concluded:

> There is a lack of clear understanding of, and consensus on, the optimum approaches to group formation that reinforces group cohesion and sustainability. Simple examples are whether the group should be homogeneous (by sex, social stratification, or occupation) or heterogeneous (covering an entire village or district); whether the official structure should be used; and whether the NGO should offer specific help or wait until the community decides its own needs. The NGOs in the Asia study adopted very different approaches to these issues, usually claiming, with little empirical support, the superiority of one approach over another. (Bowden 1990, p. 145)

As mentioned earlier, successes in capacity building are seldom documented and evaluated so that people both in and outside the organization can learn from experience. It is therefore proposed that the notion of group capacity enhancement should occupy a central place in the research and learning agenda of development-oriented funders.

GSOs should be encouraged to keep detailed notes on their group promotion efforts. Articulate leaders of base groups should be asked to share in periodic reevaluations of the programs they find most useful. Joint efforts between scholars and practitioners in capacity building research should be supported. The IAF Fellowship Program, a great potential learning resource, especially at the doctoral level, could more firmly target organizational development and grassroots capacity building as preferred themes for dissertation grants.

Donors and GSOs together would do well to explore the effectiveness of training and informal education experiences that can best contribute to the kind of capacity building described in this book. In this sense, training (or better yet "capacitation") has two dimensions: training for fieldworkers, promoters, and the GSO's own staff, and training for the leaders and members of the participating population. Most training programs are too short and superficial, their content is either too technical or too philosophical, and they are not suitable for massive adaptation or incorporation into formal education programs. Among the cases, FIDENE offers the best example of an educational/action system anchored at a regional university. Other examples are Agua del Pueblo, which has used its experiences with Guatemalan water supply projects to develop a full-fledged two-year course to prepare rural sanitation technicians. Another is the efforts of the Fundación para la Aplicación y la Enseñanza de la Ciencias (FUNDAEC) in Colombia to introduce a whole new curriculum at the Rural University in Cali based not only on notions of social change but also on concrete problem solving (Arbab 1988).

It is discouraging to observe that the research carried out by GSOs themselves has little to do with the assessment of their own programs. A number of very competent GSOs combine research with action programs. However, almost invariably, the research and action components are quite separate with research seen as having an output unrelated to programmatic guidance. (See Chapter 13 for profiles of CET and CIDE.) Donors can reorient GSO research toward more action relevance and even insist on participatory evaluations of the GSO's own programs. In future research grants to GSOs, priority should be given to studies related to factors that influence participatory microdevelopment. Such research could enrich periodic self-evaluations. In general, donors should encourage self-reflection and the exchange of experiences among GSOs about financial and technical issues and the effectiveness of their institution-building strategies. Donors and grantees should work together to find out how self-help capabilities have been sustained and review how the lessons learned have been incorporated into the GSO's current method of operations (Bowden 1990).

Increasing Organizational Capacity

Much more needs to be done to help increase the administrative and managerial capacity of promising GSOs. Perhaps if donors offered longer-term core support, the resulting stability would enhance the value of training. Yet, capacity building requires more than the usual short-term courses in accounting, finance, or fund-raising. Most social-activist

GSOs increasingly need "hard" management skills in planning, budgeting, and financial and information control. Technical, business-inspired GSOs also need skills for grassroots organizing and institutional development. Management training designed for business or for the public sector may not be appropriate, and such training is certainly not sufficient for training in grassroots development.[8] Proper training should involve strengthening the peculiar constellation of features that enable an organization to achieve a desirable balance between effectiveness and commitment. This means that the needed "professionalism" should not occur at the expense of maintaining an internal value consensus that defines and energizes GSOs.

One way that donors can enhance the organizational capacity of GSOs is by developing and funding "tertiary support institutions" that service GSOs on a regular basis. The effectiveness of such apex or service entities depends to a great extent on the willingness of GSOs to collaborate and on donor policies that support less dispersion, fragmentation, and competition. Providing incentives for collaboration among GSOs with similar interests is also highly desirable for achieving a stronger policy impact.

The Macroeconomics of GSOs

Many of the more mature GSOs are currently struggling to redefine their future role and are facing the need for strategic planning. Donors should assist GSOs in this process, which must inevitably address the prospect of scarce resources, the question of priorities and rationing, the issue of scale, and the ever-present dilemma of the proper balance between welfare and development.

If their money came from domestic philanthropy, GSOs could, with a clear conscience, go to places and do things in whatever way the donor's wishes or their own preferences dictated. And if MSOs relied solely on the financial contributions of their own members, they too could do whatever their membership wanted, without fretting about moral or socioeconomic priorities. But as already discussed, virtually all the resources are external and noncontinuous. As countries become less repressive and more pluralistic, some of the presently available external aid may dry up altogether. The concepts of need and special interest alone, whether internally or externally defined, will not be enough of a guidepost to strategic planning. Some combination of need plus potential and need plus general interest must be constructed, which again brings up the debate around the *estrato promovible* (see Chapter 4), or the potential for economic and social capitalization.

This debate is likely to become exacerbated by the current retrenchment of most Latin American governments. Because of their heavy debts and the pressure of structural-adjustment policies required by the major external finance agencies, they are less willing to fund social programs and pay attention to poverty issues. In this situation, the danger is that governments will be only too happy to have NGOs take over the responsibility for routine nonreimbursable services, where the state is unable to provide even minimal coverage. Brian Smith articulates this danger in even more dramatic political terms. He concludes that governments allow indigenous GSOs (led by idealists and politically disaffected groups from the middle classes) to operate partly as "gap fillers" to provide low-income groups with services and partly as pacifiers to make the recipients more acquiescent to the existing order (Smith 1990, pp. 277–78). This is a trap for foreign donors and serves no developmental ends. This book has argued that GSOs should help their clients to graduate, acquire sustainable management capabilities, and stimulate or pressure the state for improved public services. But if the state abandons its responsibility to foreign-financed NGOs, there is no place to graduate to, no public service to sensitize or make more accountable.

A similar dilemma exists for cost recovery. In the sample, only a small portion of the costs of services was recovered from their users. However, evidence from other GSOs shows that beneficiaries can and do pay for services such as health, water, land titling, or marketing if they are assured of good quality and a reliable supply. In fact, economists like to claim that the real test of the value of service is the willingness to pay for it. The macroissue here is that intermediary NGOs cannot be expected to charge realistic user fees when the state offers the same facilities free of charge. The fact is that free or subsidized services are often appropriated by the better-off and, in practice, are unavailable to or unsuitable for the poor.

Another trap lies in the mobilization of free labor. Governments and large external aid agencies are more than happy to reduce their costs by using beneficiary labor rather than commercial contractors. Although voluntary work on projects of direct interest to beneficiaries is a standard and legitimate feature of community development endeavors, extracting unremunerated labor for infrastructure construction beyond the exclusive use of the household or consensual social unit is neither realistic nor ethical. "Why should the poor be required to construct their own schools and clinics while the wealthier sections of society have access to state provisions?" asks Midgley (1986, p. 158). One solution would be to institutionalize self-contracting within community groups, which could remunerate their poorest members who are least able to provide free labor.

Putting it more positively, resource-scarce situations should be taken as an opportunity for donors to negotiate with governments that are interested in significant GSO coverage of social services. Instead of simply requiring the usual counterpart contributions to current costs, the governments may be asked to provide regular capitalization to an endowment fund to be used exclusively by GSOs and to provide tax incentives for private contributions for the same purpose. Policies favorable to cost recovery across the board can also be negotiated. For donors that do not deal directly with governments (such as the IAF), the choices are narrower. They can help in the formation of networks and consortia that can do more massive fund-raising. They can themselves attempt some capitalization and assist in revenue-generating schemes.[9] And, of course, they can encourage their GSO clients in various ways to seek collaborative arrangements with sympathetic government entities.

Another positive feature of the Latin American macroscene is the opportunity offered to the GSO sector by the current wave of redemocratization. Although some donors may be tempted to reduce their support to GSOs in countries where the state has become more pluralistic and more concerned with equity, others could see much greater opportunities in a partnership between government and the NGO sector in general. In a study on Latin American rural development prospects, de Janvry et al. (1988) pointed out that the old concept of integrated rural development could be replaced by a combination of public programs and decentralized grassroots initiatives. Large integrated rural development projects had enormous difficulty mobilizing and coordinating the work of a host of public agencies, each with its own traditions. Furthermore, projects located far from the central political process were unable to hold public attention and sustain budgeting support. De Janvry's public-private alliance might alleviate these problems. On the other hand, as the case studies have shown, grassroots initiatives, no matter how competent, are often of limited effectiveness because of an inappropriate macroeconomic context and the lack of public-sector support in technology, credits, infrastructure, and other public goods.

If the newly democratized countries can begin to fulfill their public functions by providing a sectoral and institutional framework favorable to peasants and to rural areas and if popular and grassroots organizations continue to legitimate and sustain rural development efforts, the stage may be set for a fruitful partnership between public and private initiatives. One of the greatest challenges to donors is to nudge both GSOs and their governments toward such a symbiotic program mode.

Notes

1. The tension that affects the performance of intermediary NGOs is well documented by Alliband, based on his experience with Indian and other Asian NGOs, but it is equally applicable to Latin America. Alliband observes that the pressures exerted by the ultimate givers of resources who contribute to donor agencies and by the ultimate takers, the poor recipients, create a major structural tension that constantly affects donor-intermediary relationships. Donor agencies pressure indigenous intermediary organization (usually GSOs) to show documentable success in the short run, so that they can assure the flow of continuous funds from their contributors. At the same time, GSOs face pressure from their

clientele to dispense assistance. Since there are relatively few communities or villages where demonstrable results can be obtained quickly, clients can often hold GSOs hostage in terms of how much change they must display in exchange for a given resource contribution. Once this aspect of the voluntary organizations' program is understood, it helps clarify some of the less-than-ideal decisions that donor representatives and GSO managers are making (Alliband 1983, p. 82).

2. The six myths are a takeoff on an oft-quoted paper *Learning from Failure,* issued in the early years of the IAF (Toth and Cotter 1978). The "Lawrence of Arabia syndrome" warns about projects built around a strong central figure; the "Pollyanna syndrome" underestimates the managerial skills needed to sustain self-managed, autonomous enterprises; the "messiah syndrome" warns against elitist promoters or zealots; cases in which outside assistance is needed to induce local commitment and cooperation are attributed to the "artificial insemination syndrome"; finally, the "Dr. Strangelove syndrome" represents instances in which projects serve as vehicles of social engineering promoted by outsiders. It is notable that all of these warnings imply a profound mistrust of intermediaries (the "administrative elite") and place virtually unlimited faith in the poor's capacity for democratic self-organization and consensual management.

3. See especially Alberti and Mayer 1974; Lehmann 1982; Fonseca and Mayer 1988. Fonseca writes about the internal differentiation of the Andean indigenous communities:

> The peasant communities are not egalitarian societies, integrated or homogeneous, as until now the officials of the various governmental agencies charged with integration of the *campesino* into the national society continue to imagine.

Fonseca goes on to cite Mario Vasquez, one of the original team members of the famous Cornell-Peru experiment in "guided" community development. Vasquez concluded that, in Vicos, the ex-hacienda whose name became identified with the literature on this project, there were three types of households: the rich with eleven to fifteen head of cattle, the medium-income households with eight animals, and the poor who possessed only a few sheep and were forced to migrate to make ends meet. Which groups participate and benefit from community development projects?

4. This aspect was not adequately studied. Local IAF monitors sometimes complained that some GSOs tend to prolong their assistance beyond what is optimal. It seems easier to formulate donor projects for known clienteles and settings than to start in completely new areas and with unfamiliar groups.

5. "In order to preserve the autonomy, integrity, and distinctiveness of NGOs, some donors have adjusted their cofinancing procedures, originally based on matching grants, by introducing more flexible and long-term arrangements such as block grants, multi-year funding, revolving funds, and credit guarantees. It is generally agreed that in the future donors should proceed in this direction and promote the financing of multi-year programs which enhance long-term planning and coordination rather than rely on the more traditional fragmented project support." (OECD 1989)

6. Ritchey-Vance (1991) reports that in Colombia the IAF has gradually come to terms with the dilemma described earlier in this book about donors needing intermediary GSOs but being reluctant to divert funds away from the grassroots to pay for core and overhead expenses of GSOs. As long as GSOs build capacity and foster autonomy of base groups,

the Foundation has become more willing to provide long-term core support for intermediaries at the same time that it makes short-term grants to the grassroots organizations they promote. (p. 68)

7. "The central focus of the IAF learning effort can be defined quite accurately within the context of organizational development and performance." (Meehan 1978, p. 74)

8. This point is especially well illustrated by the case of Instituto Centro-Americano de Administración de Empresas (INCAE), one of the most prestigious management training organizations in Latin America. The IAF granted INCAE $1.5 million for three years (one of its largest grants) for management training for leaders of microenterprises, cooperatives, and other NGOs. A recent evaluation concluded that the INCAE training effort for GSO-type nonprofit organizations was inadequate because INCAE did not have faculty specialized in socioeconomic development to complement its business and public administration expertise and because it lacked field experience and teaching materials on practical local grassroots problems. The evaluator especially urged INCAE to acquire capability in methods of organizational nurturing in grassroots development programs (Lassen 1989).

9. For example, the IAF helped the Fundación para la Educación (FES), a Colombian GSO, establish a permanent capitalization fund. FES has evolved into a sort of a self-financing national foundation that offers financial as well as technical and administrative support to other Colombian NGOs. It manages a variety of permanent endowment funds and has been highly innovative in multiplying the value of national and international donations. FES administers several IAF grants, and its own contributions over the life of each grant are capitalized into an endowment fund. This arrangement has made it possible to cover 60 percent of the operating costs of the beneficiary organizations from six to nine years beyond the termination of the IAF grants (Ritchey-Vance 1991).

10

Concluding Interpretations of Performance

During the past twenty years a significant collection of new social actors, nongovernmental organizations (NGOs), has arisen in Latin America in support of grassroots development. The most important kind are those that work directly with the poor—called grassroots support organizations (GSOs). This phenomenon occurred in Latin America somewhat later than in Southeast Asia, but earlier than in Sub-Saharan Africa. However, in all three developing regions GSOs have evolved along similar lines and with the following rather unusual common characteristics:

1. They moved into "free spaces" left by state and market failure to reach and serve the interests of the poor. This was made possible by external funding from donors that wanted to bypass governments. As a result, GSOs expanded even into repressive environments.
2. Most GSOs are not formally accountable to their clients. Nevertheless, they have become more successful than formal representative organizations in benefiting relatively poorer groups, in achieving greater participation of their beneficiaries, and in making their work more policy relevant.
3. They have expanded the organization of poor people beyond the traditional class-based or occupational membership organizations, such as peasant cooperatives and labor unions. GSOs sponsor informal grassroots groups for people who have never before had any real voice (for example, women, the landless, ethnic communties).

In the meantime, the evolution of representative membership groups —membership support organizations (MSOs)—proceeded more slowly. In Latin America the old type of farmer and worker associations have been suffering from both internal weaknesses, such as a widening gap between leaders and members and lack of professionalism, and external problems, such as poor linkages and state manipulation. Only recently have most MSO turned from protest and politics to more pragmatic and sustainable development strategies in which the buildup of a productive base is combined with access to specific services. This shift is likely to increase the level of participation and loyalty of their members. Greater internal strength, in turn, can increase their ability to formulate clearer policy proposals and may lead, in alliance with GSOs, to more effective pressure for national policy changes.

It is evident from the previous chapters of this book that the two kinds of intermediate NGOs should be considered complementary rather than competitive. Although the evolution of a mutually beneficial relationship is delicate and difficult, GSOs can be immensely helpful to MSOs in providing sympathetic nonpartisan assistance with specific developmental problems and in enhancing their internal as well as external capacity. In turn, MSOs can confer on GSOs a greater measure of legitimacy and justification to acquire a firmer domestic financial base and even to enable them to build more solid bridges to the state without jeopardizing their integrity.

This book has dealt with developmental NGOs in Latin America that work directly and face-to-face with poorer communities in providing services and performing functions of intermediation. These functions involve vertical linkages, connecting people and institutions at different levels through upward and downward flows of resources and information. Performance, then, is associated with the quality of these linkages. The participatory elements in the work of these intermediary NGOs, which many see as their distinctive advantage, introduce some horizontality into the intermediation function. Solidarity or cooperative group formation becomes an important component of the NGO agenda, not only for effective management of resources but also for equity and sustainability. Performance depends on the way in which vertical and horizontal linkages are combined.

This chapter offers some concluding thoughts on two interpretations of the performance characteristics of intermediary NGOs: a divergent or segmented view and a convergent or synergetic view.

Divergence

An original aim of this study was to understand intermediary NGOs, to explain what they do well and how they could perform even better. The analysis involved classifying and disaggregating the sample organizations in various ways. This process led to a series of subclasses or segments of the organizational landscape, each with its special set of advantages in rural poverty alleviation. One set of grassroots support organizations (GSOs) excels in providing social services, often called basic human needs or entitlements. Dramatic illustrations of the effectiveness of such social-service GSOs can be found in worldwide experience in the self-help housing area (Turner 1988) and in the field of rural water supply, as featured in a retrospective article on the United Nations Water Decade in *Grassroots Development* (Douglas 1990). This is also the group of organizations with superior scaling-up potential.

The problems that arise for these organizations revolve around minimum standards, cost-effectiveness, affordability, and cost recovery. The community development elements in social-service delivery help to reduce the burden of pure "giving" by the promotion of self-provisioning, or reliance on the beneficiaries' energies for coproducing these services. In a similar vein, such GSOs establish important linkages with the state for the coproduction of complementary services that the private sector cannot provide.

In contrast, another segment of GSOs excels in the promotion of productive activities, in many ways a more complicated and failure-prone field of endeavor. Instead of enhancing the consumption of basic necessities, here the business end of the household economy is enhanced. This orientation raises the bothersome issue of the degree of viability of small enterprises and how far the poor can become entrepreneurs rather than workers. (Remarkably, there are no GSOs that promote wage employment.) As in the social fields, the necessity of lowering costs and promoting sustainability propels production-oriented GSOs toward self-employment strategies in which family labor is mobilized for the small enterprise beyond its opportunity cost. Another dilemma here is whether the aim is a tolerable level of subsistence on the one hand or accumulation and growth on the other. It is also in the realm of productive strategies that group-based collective microeconomic forms of organization become important, whether on the grounds of economies of scale, benefit distribution, or market power. Consequently, it is here that second-level membership support organizations (MSOs) arise to coexist and interact with GSOs.

Another segment of GSOs are the group capacity builders. While some try to form base groups from scratch and search for "organizable" clients, most work with base groups already incorporated in some form of local organization. The uphill task of GSOs here is complicated by the fact that most of the existing formally recognized base groups (many created by previous government sponsorship) are exclusive and not particularly democratic. This has often led GSOs to stress informal groups.

The final segment of GSOs are specialized intermediary institutions with a narrow and highly focused agenda, catering to a special niche of service or clientele. One could even argue that the future belongs to such specialized GSOs rather than to those that still maintain an "integrated" view of development assistance. For donors or governments this means looking to different NGOs to provide elements of a complex assistance package, relying on one specializing in technology, on another in finance, and on still another in community organization, leadership training, or legal services. In fact, several of the multipurpose GSOs in the study have become unifunctional or have even broken up into segments of their former selves that have become independent organizations. PRO-TERRA, for example, is now focusing only on legal work, having spawned another GSO dedicated to agricultural extension. Some of the catalytic GSOs like IPRU in Uruguay have given rise to a whole cluster of specialized institutions whose tasks and hence performance standards are less multidimensional and more straightforward than the classic GSOs.

The entry of large financial aid agencies into the NGO donor community has highlighted the divergence of GSOs and sharpened the difference between those that provide socioeconomic services and those that consider themselves mainly capacity builders or innovators. The World Bank, the regional development banks, and the large bilateral aid agencies want to involve NGOs for effective service delivery (shelter, credit, health care, and so on) and rapid disbursement of project funds. They also want assurance that funds will be spent and handled honestly and that a sense of "ownership" promoted by such NGOs among the beneficiaries will contribute to sustainability or project results. A greater role for NGOs in the provision of public services is also seen by these donors as part of the desired privatization of the state.

How are these increased pressures (and opportunities) to serve as subcontractors of the government affecting GSOs? Much really depends on the political context. In countries such as Bolivia and Costa Rica, where GSOs are comfortable with the government, mutually satisfactory arrangements can be worked out; in countries where mutual distrust and even hostility prevail, such as Guatemala or Haiti, there are more serious barriers to large-scale international funding via the state.

This difference is clearly documented in the extraordinary success of the rapidly implemented Bolivian Emergency Social Fund (ESF) and the long negotiations and acrimonious disagreements that held up the approval of the Guatemalan Social Investment Fund (SIF), both designed to give NGOs access to external loan funds (PACT 1990).

In intellectual circles it is feared that to the extent GSOs become subcontractors or parastatals, they will lose many of their virtues, especially flexibility, informality, originality, and innovation. Others contend that large-scale collaboration with governments and external financial agencies will cause GSOs to "lose their soul"—that is, abandon their mission of working toward an "alternative" development paradigm.

The evidence from the research for this book points to different conclusions. There are GSOs that do not appear to lose their valuable traits when they take on large-scale jobs mediated by government. The same may be said for some MSOs with a strong social commitment. True, scaling up places great strains on their organizations. With such quantum leaps in scale they can no longer be as informal and flexible as before, but they can remain poverty oriented and participatory.

Other service deliverers cannot be said to have lost their souls because they never really had souls, in the sense that they never strived to empower their beneficiaries. These are the competent, businesslike nonprofit contractors that work mainly in microenterprise development but also in social infrastructure. Considering how important it is to have private alternatives to public services, why not let these organizations, which are outside the capacity-building domain anyway, evolve into full-fledged consulting firms and contract businesses? Why pretend that they are (or should be) like the others, whose social commitment and empowerment orientation we celebrate?

Perhaps donors and intellectuals who write about NGOs are doing a disservice to the very causes they pursue by insisting on scrambling the roles described here. Many GSOs are now searching for a better definition and self-understanding. If the segmented view argued above is accepted, then GSOs should be advised against mixing visions and strategies that are better left unmixed.[1]

The segmented interpretation, however illuminating, may easily lead to a confirmation of trade-offs (which have been the staple description of NGO advantages and disadvantages) and even to an acceptance of the somewhat pessimistic view that NGO strengths inherently mirror weaknesses, so that progress in one direction necessarily involves sacrifices in other dimensions—a sort of zero-sum game.

Convergence

In thinking about performance, especially in light of the evidence from the highest rated organizations, a certain convergence of capabilities—even some synergy—along different dimensions of performance may be perceived. In this sense, progress in one direction may enhance progress in another. At the very least, it seems that there is less contradiction than was thought possible in the capability of these organizations to meet several of the criteria simultaneously or sequentially. Three sets of dichotomies illustrate this idea.

According to the first dichotomy, GSOs are either service providers or social-change agents. Good performance in servicing relates to reaching poorer, inaccessible populations in culturally appropriate ways and to matching the service to community needs. The main direction of the action is down, toward the beneficiaries. The role of the social-change agent implies advocacy, mobilization, consciousness-raising, and empowerment. The predominant flow of energy is up from the grassroots.

In case after case, the bridge between these positions is local capacity building. The only way service provision can become a sustainable and cumulative process is if the recipients learn to manage their resources, deal more effectively with the government and the market, and develop community-based institutions of their own. Effectiveness in the social-change role, on the other side, depends on a solid core of tangible benefits around which community mobilization can take place. The dynamic process that is called "incremental capacity building" in this study is precisely a progression of service and organizational reinforcements leading to cumulative group capacity. The case studies provide evidence that social commitment and professional competence not only can be found within the same organization but can reinforce each other. Furthermore, if advocacy succeeds in changing the status of the poor and their access to resources such as land, credit, or education, there has to be a stronger, more capable local institutional structure to take advantage of these new opportunities.

The second dichotomy concerns the GSO's relationship to the establishment. Either GSOs are committed to "alternative" development, in which case they oppose both the state and the market and seek to reinforce the "autonomy" of their client groups and reduce their dependence on outside power holders and market entanglements, or they are brokers and mediators that strive to link the beneficiaries to mainstream development. The former are seen as inherently small scale, and the latter have scaling-up and policy potential.

Again, the evidence of the case studies shows that in practice, independence and autonomy are relative. Reduction of purchased inputs and better self-provisioning make sense but are not equivalent to autarchy. Self-sufficiency proves to be utopian, especially among peasant producers who nowadays are almost invariably in the market economy. Even organizations celebrated for their indigenous governance and native enterprise use their capacity to negotiate with and manipulate the state and the market to their perceived advantage. The time- and labor-intensive operational style of participatory GSOs is often compatible with achieving wider applicability and policy reach; it is not necessary for individual GSOs to grow to unmanageable size in order to have a more massive impact. Networking and coalition building are fruitful activities. There is also some evidence that acceptance of resources from governments or external finance agencies does not necessarily cause GSOs to lose their identity or integrity, as long as donors learn how to adjust their operational style to the peculiar capabilities of the GSOs and do not treat them simply as service contractors. The most serious reorientation of GSO relations with the government is taking place in those countries that are redemocratizing after periods of repressive regimes. The tendency of GSO leaders to move back and forth between NGO and public agency posts has a very salutary effect on the possibilities for collaboration and complementarity. Even in the case of GSOs that definitely do not want to accept government funds or commissions, there is a healthy tendency to work on technical and institutional innovations that can have wide applicability, especially at the regional level. It is also at the subnational level that the most fruitful collaboration with public- and private-sector agencies is observable.

The third dichotomy has to do with the social status and relative preparation of GSO beneficiary populations. The sample GSOs, especially the ones with a productive technical orientation, tend to work with the not-so-poor who display some economic viability. Even in the social realm, IAF-supported GSOs assist groups that are self-selected, able to make convincing applications for assistance, and have some previous track record of joint endeavors. Working with clients who can readily absorb assistance and show results within a short time is typical of GSOs whose donors operate in the project mode. Even though the relative income level of such clients is considerably below that of comparable government programs, they have something in common with traditional aid efforts: They rely on existing capacity to build development momentum.

Such an approach is disdained by the opposite camp, where favoring the upper-middle poor is equated with "kulakism" in the economic realm and with widening disparities in the social field. Thus, the poverty purists seek out the most disadvantaged and isolated groups—the landless, women workers, migrant labor, the handicapped. GSOs operating with these groups have a strong welfare-relief tradition. But the important point is that they are working generally with unorganized social groups that possess poor development linkages. Such groups have potential only, not existing capacity.

This book has pointed out that capacity-building processes have not generally been accorded sufficient attention by donors. Nonetheless, the profiles of the IAF-supported organizations show that, over time, grassroots capacity, as embodied in more effective member-based local and intermediary organizations, has been built up in what were often initially rather unpromising circumstances. In the IAF literature, a number of these cases are celebrated as examples of competent and democratic self-empowerment. What is not clear and not documented is how this capacity was acquired in the first place. The hypothesis of this research is that outside forces and change agents, like GSOs, have played crucial roles in stimulating and nurturing this capacity-building process and that, in terms of investment in social energy, the present state of organizational capital embodies a sunk cost, which is not borne by those who can now successfully invest in this previously constructed capacity.

A recent review of the World Bank's experience with NGOs offers support for this idea. It found that World Bank projects with NGO involvement were most successful when they were built on preexisting experiences. Although organizational capacity was not explicitly identified, the examples used were all based on cooperative and collective development organizations that had established themselves earlier and had acquired both the internal cohesion and external legitimacy stressed so strongly in this study as the twin requisites for organizational capacity.

The World Bank report sums it up: "Good projects rarely begin at the time of first disbursement" (Salmen and Eaves 1989).

In conclusion, the best GSOs have a special ability to elicit this latent capacity and viability, not only in individuals but in grassroots organizations. In this sense they prepare the ground for the later linking of such groups (often of the really poor and least promising) with mainstream development agencies, the commercial/financial world, and the political system. Hirschman (1984) thought that the social energy of collective action has its origin in previous radical acts or reactions to aggression. This explanation can now be extended by observing that the conversion of this initial energy to a development resource—a network of organizational capacities—can best be accomplished with outside independent and sympathetic assistance and with a support structure that provides both vertical power linkages and horizontal networks of civil engagement.

Thus, the microwork of the top GSOs—their patient, intensive efforts to combine small amounts of resources with large doses of promotion and education, to match internal cohesion with external linkages, and their ability to offer to the as yet "unviable" some experience that dispels isolation and mutual distrust—should be seen as helping to lay the foundation for future grassroots-based development. This special trait is the essence of their performance.

This trait also gives a final clue to the title of the first chapter, "Tending the Grassroots." "Tending" comes as close as any word in describing the relationship between grassroots organizations and the NGOs that support them. It implies a complex relationship between unequal partners in which one, the "tender," provides sympathetic assistance to the other, uncompensated in the commercial sense but embodying reciprocity, especially in the form of a growing trust and a growing capacity for self-improvement by the "tendee." This is neither an easy nor an unambiguous relationship. The tender, no matter how altruistic, must be prepared for misunderstanding and even resentment. Although this book has dealt with "tending" as a relationship between organizations and people within a given country, this same relationship across nations is what international development assistance should embody. Much international aid fails because it is offered and sought for self-serving reasons that have nothing to do with development. Clearly, the attitude as well as the act of tending that this book has struggled to articulate is not only morally correct but ultimately the most effective.

Note

1. The author is grateful to Anthony Bebbington for this formulation.

II

Case Studies

11

Profiles from Peru

Country Context

The emergence of intermediary nongovernmental organizations (NGOs) in Peru can be explained by three sets of circumstances. The first is the historic extreme economic, social, cultural, and spatial inequality of the poor as well as the Indians who, even in the process of losing their ethnic identity, are, as a class, the most disadvantaged and impoverished. NGOs have traditionally worked with indigenous communities, mostly speakers of native languages in the Sierra. During the last decades native communities have evolved their own federations (MSOs) both in the Sierra and in the Peruvian Amazon. For example, CEDECUM has as its clients *multi-comunales*, or community associations, of indigenous people.

The second circumstance arises from the efforts of the agrarian reform of the early 1970s. These reforms were accompanied by massive state-inspired campesino organizations, mainly designed for the reform beneficiaries as member-managed production and service cooperatives, but also for aggregating smallholders not directly affected by the land distribution. The scale of those MSOs tended to be very large, and their technical and administrative requirements were complex. By the end of the 1970s there were over forty *centrales* or second-level agroprocessing and service federations. Central 3 de Octubre (CENTRAL) is one example. Other such MSOs were the agroindustrial complexes illustrated in the PROTERRA case by CALEPS, designed to serve the new owners of the expropriated estates. The withdrawal of state support from these new enterprises, beginning with the post-Velasco regimes, and their internal weaknesses gave rise to a precipitous decomposition of these nonparticipatory and financially precarious new membership organizations. The resultant agrarian crisis, however, opened up opportunities for a whole host of GSOs concerned with either the salvaging and recasting of what remained of the reform cooperatives or the defense and development of smallholders who were cast adrift as a result of the fragmentation of the reform enterprises. Two of the cases exemplify these types of GSOs: CIPCA, working in the northern coastal area, and PROTERRA, active in the central coastal region trying to solve tenure problems and fill the technical vacuum left in the wake of land subdivision.

The third set of contextual factors for NGO activity in Peru encompasses the very rapid growth of the coastal cities, especially but not exclusively Lima; accelerated migration into squatter settlements from the Sierra ("urban campesinos"); and a loss of ethnic identity and subsistence income, resulting in increased proletarianization. A new brand of GSOs has emerged to support the informal sector in the towns as well as help diversify what is left of the rural economy. FDN, one of the profiles, falls in the latter category.

It is estimated that in the mid-1980s the number of Peruvian GSOs reached 350. Many had their origin in the social activism of the church and the liberation theology of the 1960s; other were founded by university-based intellectuals. A third source of organizers and staffers was the government. The earlier administration of Belaunde Terry (1963–68) initiated a large-scale community development program, Cooperación Popular, which involved the voluntary service of university students in rural communities. The Velasco regime established Sistema Nacional de Movilización Social (SINAMOS) which recruited a large number of young professionals for grassroots promotion in support of the reform programs. When the Velasco period ended, the state institutions responsible for the reforms were dismantled, and their staffs were dismissed. Many such ex-officials became founders of GSOs registered under various forms of civic associations, and thus were able to take advantage of their previous experience in the pursuit of social causes.

Radical leftists originally opposed NGOs by considering their staffs as ineffectual liberal reformers who were only delaying the revolution. But by the late 1980s a more pragmatic attitude prevailed in left-wing intellectual circles, with the consequence that many former critics joined GSOs in order to provide concrete solutions to the problems of the poor. As a result of all these influences, most Peruvian GSOs belong ideologically to various shades of the left but without party affiliation. A minority are ideologically center-right, mostly those working with individual microenterprises in the informal sector with financing by the U.S. Agency for International Development (USAID) and technical assistance from U.S.-based private voluntary organizations.

In Peru, intermediate NGOs have an opportunity to establish a strong regional and territorial presence as a result of increasing regionalist sentiment and recurrent state efforts at decentralization and granting greater provincial autonomy. CIPCA, CEDECUM, and PROTERRA are GSOs that have excelled in making a regionally significant impact. However, at the start of the 1990s, the work of Peruvian GSOs with an extensive field presence in the countryside is endangered by the threat of terrorist activity.

These recent trends and the special circumstances that gave rise to the vital NGO sector in Peru are illustrated in the five organizational profiles that follow.

CEDECUM: Effective Regional Promotion but Over-Dependence on a Single Leader

Puno: A Mecca for Development Projects

The Department of Puno is one of the poorest departments in all of Peru. Its inhabitants are largely Aymara and Quechua speakers living in small isolated villages without adequate access to health, education, and transportation services. Most of the Aymaras, who live along the shores of Lake Titicaca south of the city of Puno, are subsistence farmers who supplement their mixed crop and livestock production with petty trading, migrant labor, fishing, and other activities. Alternate years of drought and flooding, combined with increasing pressures on scarce communal lands, have aggravated the already fragile economy of the region and have forced many to migrate to the coastal cities.

Historically, Puno has attracted many development projects sponsored by the government, large international aid agencies, international private voluntary organizations, and Peruvian nongovernmental organizations. As one development observer noted, Puno has had more development projects than any other department in the country. Typically, government and international donor projects have assisted communities through large-scale infrastructure projects in housing, irrigation, road building, and electrification. The execution of these projects was facilitated by the existence in Puno of one of Peru's most effective regional development corporations, CORPUNO. On the other hand, the work of private and nongovernmental development agencies has tended to focus more on issues of basic needs, social promotion, organization, and training. These private agencies work largely in isolation and do not often attempt to coordinate with government. Within this group, there is a tremendous diversity in ideology, methodology, and strategy. Some are clearly directive organizations displaying strong political and religious overtones.

The Birth of CEDECUM

Inserted in this institutional mosaic of state, international, and private entities was the Centro de Desarrollo para el Campesinado y del Poblador Urbano-Marginal (CEDECUM), a young, competent team of agronomists, social workers, and veterinarians. CEDECUM pursued an integrated microregional development approach that highlighted seven types of action: (1) organization and management, (2) crop production, (3) livestock production, (4) storage and processing, (5) marketing, (6) natural resource management, and (7) women's activities.

CEDECUM was originally created to accompany an irrigation project sponsored jointly by the Peruvian government and USAID by providing production and income-related support to small farmers who were to benefit from the irrigation works. However, CEDECUM was soon forced to rethink its role and strategy when the government suspended work on the irrigation program. At the same time, a person who had had differences with CEDECUM's leadership in the past was appointed director of the regional development agency (CORPUNO), thus complicating CEDECUM's plans to serve as an effective link between local government and farmers' groups.

Despite these complications, Manuel Tejada, the charismatic director of CEDECUM and former director of the National Planning Institute in Puno, conceived an independent role for his organization and went ahead with a small pilot project based on the original irrigation plan but with a microregional focus. The strategy was to offer assistance to peasant communities, not in a predetermined pattern, but at the client's request, and to carry out specific activities in a collaborative manner. The microregional focus was seen useful for both technical and organizational reasons. A reasonably homogeneous area offered economies of scale of applicable technologies (for example, potato varieties, and bulk marketing), but also provided scope for linking peasant organizations to the existing decentralized government network. In less than a year and a half, the scope of the project grew from twelve communities to sixty-five and from one *multi-comunal* to three. (A *multi-comunal* is a second-level organization of peasant communities.) The total project area encompassed over 5,000 Aymara families. Although staff were to have handled the increased workload, CEDECUM's eagerness to respond to the *multi-comunales* brought on rapid changes within the organization itself.

CEDECUM's Mode of Operation

Encouraging Beneficiary Interest and Action. CEDECUM's approach was influenced by Tejada's vision of a series of strong Aymara organizations that would actively participate in the design of and decisionmaking for projects affecting their communities. Because many of the large rural infrastructure projects had strictly technical goals, they often lacked the mechanisms to encourage beneficiary interest and action. Within the microregion of Ilave-Juli, CEDECUM targeted three *multi-comunales*, through which it channeled all technical and managerial assistance. CEDECUM worked hard to establish an open, nonimposing relationship between staff and the leaderships of the *multi-comunales*, with each party signing an agreement to accept certain responsibilities and decisions during the course of the project. Each *multi-comunal* was responsible for selecting the communities that received more direct assistance from CEDECUM staff, as well as the activities that would be carried out.

Fostering Relationships between the Multi-Comunales and Other Public and Private Agencies. CEDECUM did not expect to maintain its relationship with the *multi-comunales* indefinitely. Rather, it saw itself as a catalyst that spurred ideas and experimentation and fomented relationships between the *multi-comunales* and other public and private entities. The staff maintained that it was critical for leaders to learn to plan and negotiate actively with such agencies, not simply to accept what was offered to them. Although the objective appeared sound, leaders were not always anxious to assume more responsibility in their organizations. This led to tension among leaders and technicians at certain stages. However, it did not adversely affect relations.

Providing Instruction and Support. The staff divided themselves into three multidisciplinary teams that provided instruction and support to a series of specially created committees at the community and *multi-comunal* levels. In addition to working in their areas of expertise, staff were expected to act as social promotors and researchers. All staff were fluent Aymara speakers, and courses and meetings were conducted in Aymara to promote peasant discussion and participation.

During the week, each team lived together in a selected community of the *multi-comunal* to provide intensive support to community and *multi-comunal* activities. The three teams came together regularly in CEDECUM's Puno office to exchange information and strategize for future activities. Despite the difficult living and working conditions, Tejada managed to create an internal organizational climate that both attracted and sustained a dedicated group of young university graduates.

Using the Resources of Other Technical Assistance Organizations. As part of its overall strategy in working at the microregional level, CEDECUM tried to avoid duplicating services already provided by local government, educational institutions, technological centers, and private voluntary organizations. Because CEDECUM's resources were limited, it developed a series of formal and informal agreements with other organizations to mobilize dormant human or material resources and to provide supplementary technical assistance to projects already under way in the *multi-comunales.* Its best experiences were with CESPAC (a training agency that employed audiovisual methods), the National University of Puno, and technological institutes.

Striving to Reach the Poorest of the Poor. Unlike some other development entities, CEDECUM pushed itself to reach the poorest within the beneficiary communities. Staff were extremely sensitive to relationships and conflicts within the communities, especially when they prevented poorer campesinos from participating or receiving benefits. To a certain extent CEDECUM's technique of forming special committees in the communities and in the *multi-comunales* helped widen opportunities for participation and leadership, yet there continued to be problems with leaders who failed to share information with the general membership. The experience of working closely with traditional organizations taught CEDECUM staff that despite outward appearances of homogeneity, member families were not on an equal footing within their communities. Alliances and powerful individuals could either obstruct or facilitate the distribution of benefits and resources. Thus, CEDECUM, as a sympathetic outsider, tried to serve as a positive influence with leaders to assure the equitable distribution of project benefits and to encourage leaders to act on behalf of the entire community.

Promoting Crop Diversification. Because of the harsh climatic conditions and the less than promising crop returns of the project's early years, technicians felt that developing alternatives for small farmers was the best strategy. By diversifying crop production, improving livestock herds, and introducing processing activities, CEDECUM technicians hoped to build in an extra measure of protection from unpredictable climatic and market conditions. One bright spot was the processing of potatoes into *chuño blanco* and *chuño negro* and *charqui*-making. These products, based on age-old sun-drying techniques, commanded good prices at the market. Technicians were enthusiastic about pursuing ideas that would allow campesinos to retain more of the profit from their primary production activities—whether from simple processing activities, storage, special marketing arrangements, or a combination of these.

The Crisis at CEDECUM

At the time of the case study (in mid-1987) the organization was under stress on a variety of fronts. CEDECUM was attempting to consolidate its work in the three *multi-comunales*, especially in the areas of organization and administration, which tended to be weakest. Although Tejada was firm about not taking on new commitments, CEDECUM was already finding itself stretched too thin. Crop and livestock technical assistance appeared to be most wanted by beneficiaries, yet there were problems with getting the agricultural committees to function properly. As a result, the staff often spent more of their time ironing out organizational problems than on imparting technical knowledge. Technicians also noted that they did not have enough time for applied research projects, especially involving traditional Aymara practices like crop selection, processing, and livestock care. CEDECUM was interested in promoting more communication and activity among the three *multi-comunales* so that they might help one another and build up sufficient scale to secure future projects and services from the government on a regular basis. However, disagreements and conflicts between local leaders made this job difficult.

Another issue was sustainability. From the beginning, CEDECUM looked around for ways to self-finance portions of its own work and to establish its institutional future beyond the existing project. The leadership was enthusiastic about developing a number of potential income-generating activities, many of them centered around the idea of selling services to both member and nonmember farmers in the area. CEDECUM needed to pursue these ideas to diminish its own economic vulnerability and to establish a more permanent and independent presence in the Department of Puno. Prospects for government collaboration increased after CORPUNO's director, who was unsympathetic to CEDECUM, was replaced. Yet all these issues required time and steady outside support to resolve, and at this point CEDECUM's internal structure cracked.

In 1987, Tejada resigned after a dispute with the two other voting members of CEDECUM's governing board, both of whom resided in Lima. The loss of Tejada demonstrated how much CEDECUM's success was dependent on his leadership and the strategies and orientations he devised. The technical team he had formed, though competent and motivated, was unable to persuade CEDECUM's new directors of the validity of the strategies and methodologies designed by Tejada.

After a period of debilitating conflict between the new leadership, which futilely attempted to devise and impose new directions (more conventional and less participatory), and the field team, which was effective in presenting resistance but not in providing an acceptable alternative leadership from within its own ranks, the institution deteriorated to the point where the IAF decided to terminate its support.

However, since that time CEDECUM has once again regained its operating capacity, largely as a result of the alliance forged between the field staff and the community leadership.

Lessons Learned

CEDECUM illustrates some of the dilemmas that seem to be inherent in well-performing GSOs. Innovative strategies that involve combining technical competence with grassroots organizational skills and the sensitive guidance evolved by CEDECUM require strong personal leadership. But reliance on a single leader, without the gradual building up of alternatives, can exact a heavy price in risking institutional breakdown. The process for leadership succession within a framework of continuity and consistency needs to be addressed from the start. In the CEDECUM case, unlike in most others, the organization started with a board whose members did not share the same philosophical and strategic vision. The two Lima-based board members had the legal majority and, even though their involvement with or understanding of the project may have been minimal, in a situation of conflict they had the votes necessary to impose their will.

CENTRAL: Cooperative Service against Heavy Odds

The Agrarian Reform Sector

The Central de Cooperativas Agrarias de Producción "3 de Octubre" (CENTRAL) is typical of a type of organization that was once important in Peru's rural institutional landscape. As part of the land reform of the mid-1970s, forty-three second-level federations or *centrales* were formed to serve rural producer cooperatives and to connect them with the numerous state agencies providing resources, agricultural research, and support services. Specifically, the *centrales* were responsible for purchasing and distributing production inputs, marketing, and agroprocessing cooperative production and obtaining credit and financing on behalf of the cooperatives. The "3 de Octubre" was one of the *centrales* that remained active and, despite a host of internal and external problems, successfully performed some of the key functions originally envisaged for these second-level membership organizations.

By the late 1980s, twenty years after the promulgation of agrarian reform, political leaders, campesino organizations, government officials, and academics were embroiled in an emotional debate over what to do with what remained of the cooperative forms of rural organization. The large-scale collective enterprises, created from the expropriation and restructuring of the large private estates, were disintegrating rapidly. Of the 627 original cooperatives, 278 had changed their organizational form, usually by subdividing, nearly half of them without government sanction. Those remaining continued to function as rural worker cooperatives, but their future was increasingly uncertain.

Although the administration of Alan García Pérez repeatedly declared its interest in the reactivation of the reform sector, little if anything was done to stem the de facto subdivisions of the rural workers' cooperatives. In the coastal enterprises, where the unauthorized breakups had started, it is estimated that by 1987, two years after García's election, 40 percent of cooperative lands had been subdivided. In northern Peru the situation was even more critical: According to campesino leaders, every remaining cooperative was seriously considering some sort of reorganization or subdivision, yet the Ministry of Agriculture had still not presented criteria or procedures for the cooperatives to follow.

Functions and Structure

CENTRAL was created in 1974 to bring together seven large-scale cotton-producing cooperatives located in the Central Piura Valley. By 1987, only four of these cooperatives remained affiliated, representing about 850 peasant families. The others had broken down into smaller cooperatives or had subdivided the land into family-sized plots. Although some tried to remain affiliated in their new subdivided form, internal dissension among members, conflicts with CENTRAL leaders, and pressure on leaders from private suppliers to purchase inputs created a tense climate between the new struggling cooperatives and CENTRAL

The IAF supported CENTRAL with two grants starting in 1982, primarily for recapitalization, but also for key staff salaries and operational costs at critical periods in the agricultural cycle. The financial status of CENTRAL continued to be unsteady. The profit margin from nitrate and urea sales (the most important inputs sold through CENTRAL) was only a couple of percentage points, and the base cooperatives were suffering from deficient harvests due to a drought. If CENTRAL could have continued to import fertilizers on its own the profit margin would have been much higher.

CENTRAL was structured like the other *centrales*. An administrative council of elected representatives from the four cooperatives was responsible for running the organization. An oversight committee reviewed the actions of the hired staff and the council, and specially created committees handled more specific tasks such as education and marketing. CENTRAL owned a building in Piura that housed the purchase and marketing operations. There were three sales staff and three support staff. Member cooperatives were supposed to make regular financial contributions to pay for the administrative expenses. However, due to the depressed economic situation of the cooperatives, these contributions had dwindled substantially.

A handful of the most energetic and conscientious base cooperative leaders sat on the administrative council of CENTRAL. In some periods, leaders were replaced for mismanagement of funds and self-serving behavior. Conversely, there was also insightful, forceful action as in the case of José Carreno.

Carreno was able to win the commitment of the base cooperatives to CENTRAL by confronting cooperative leaders and administrators who had *amarres* (personal under-the-counter deals) with large, private suppliers. Also CENTRAL gained prestige among the members for a number of its extraordinary services, including emergency funds and supplies provided during the floods of 1982–83 and school supplies purchased for the children of cooperative members.

Achieving Original Goals. More important, in later years CENTRAL became the type of organization originally intended. It set out to become a capable purchaser and seller of agricultural inputs not only to member cooperatives but also to other nonaffiliated cooperatives and independent small farmers in the region. In 1986, CENTRAL leaders and staff were successful in getting all but one of the member cooperatives to purchase their fertilizers through CENTRAL. In that same year, CENTRAL began importing about 1,000 tons of fertilizer directly from Holland.

Interestingly, some of CENTRAL's most loyal customers were the non-affiliated cooperatives from other valleys that no longer had active *centrales* and other independent small- and medium-scale farmers that had no associative structures. Sixty percent of fertilizer sales were to member cooperatives, and the rest were to nonmember cooperatives and individuals. Member cooperatives paid slightly lower prices and could purchase inputs on credit, and because CENTRAL ran a lean operation, prices for nonmembers were generally competitive with those of larger commercial suppliers. Although CENTRAL earned only a modest percentage, its presence in the market had increased the alternatives available to peasants and had kept prices down, even though it probably accounted for no more than about 20 percent of the total fertilizer sales in the region.

Articulating Campesino Demands. Apart from its service objective, CENTRAL was an important mechanism for transmitting campesino demands to local government officials and to national-level campesino organizations and government ministries. In the late 1980s a regional coordinating committee of the remaining *centrales* was formed to push for campesino participation on the regional decisionmaking boards of key public agencies, such as the Agrarian Bank, Empresa Nacional de Comercialización de Insumos (ENCI), and the Ministry of Agriculture. CENTRAL was also instrumental in convincing the ENCI office in Lima to replace the local representative for failing to follow policy directives in the sale of agricultural inputs to cooperative organizations.

The fate of CENTRAL was tied to the four member cooperatives. These cooperatives had resisted subdivision because they had certain characteristics in common. They were primarily engaged in highly mechanized, capital-intensive cotton production that permitted economies of scale. Second, three of the four cooperatives did not have access to irrigation. These tougher production conditions, which required joint management of scarce resources such as water, had led to a higher level of solidarity within the cooperatives. In the three other major valleys in the Department of Piura—all irrigated areas—more of the cooperatives had subdivided.

CENTRAL's role as an articulator of peasant concerns could be traced to the dynamics of a hostile operating environment and the presence of strong, conscientious leaders. The lack of a clear government policy, collusive action by private commercial interests, and the inefficient, often hostile response of local public agencies to campesino requests had mobilized a small group of determined and articulate leaders to consolidate CENTRAL's economic position in order to control critical production inputs better. Finally, the leaders of the base cooperatives were conscious of the difficulties and consequences of subdivision. Although they acknowledged the fact that some form of internal restructuring was inevitable within each of the cooperatives, they also saw the value of maintaining their own higher-level service and negotiating entities.

Erosion of Support for the Cooperative Structure

Although unique in many aspects, namely for its ability to maintain its footing with the competition for a considerable time, CENTRAL also typified the weaknesses and dysfunctions that had been undermining the reform-created cooperative structures. The future of CENTRAL was closely tied to the changes taking place within the base cooperatives. It was difficult to predict whether these cooperatives, once subdivided, would remain loyal clients. It would certainly depend on whether the leaders of the base cooperatives would continue to show interest and support CENTRAL, or whether they would decide to go their own way.

Regionally, although CENTRAL was successful in providing services for its member cooperatives, it did no more than delay the disintegration of rural production cooperatives that was occurring along the entire Peruvian coast, and especially in Piura. However, CENTRAL and other federations elsewhere that managed to function well could provide a model for a new economic support structure, even if the landholdings of most of the land-reform beneficiaries became individualized. The legal form of the new input and marketing organization might change, but it could continue to furnish the same services to a small farmer membership.

CIPCA: A Regional Link Between the "Formal" Peru and the "Real" Peru

The Need for CIPCA

With its roots in the agrarian reform movement in northern Peru, the Centro de Investigación y Promoción del Campesino (CIPCA) has accompanied land-reform beneficiaries in their struggle to build and manage autonomous, productive enterprises since the early 1970s. A group of Jesuits and laypersons experienced in popular education in both rural and urban settings created CIPCA in 1972. Its own literature refers to the time of the organization's birth as "during the heat of the agrarian reform."

In 1969, the military regime of Juan Velasco Alvarado introduced agrarian reform legislation that was to radically transform the structures and relationships that characterized agricultural production in Peru. The main objective was to break up the large landholdings and, in particular, the large agroindustrial farms in the north by expropriating the estates and then reorganizing them into enterprises to be owned and worked by the former laborers.

Before reform, which advanced much faster in the coastal areas than in the rest of the country, the irrigated valleys surrounding Piura were occupied by large privately owned cotton and sugar estates. Production was capital intensive and highly mechanized, requiring only temporary periods of hired labor. These estates were the most modernized and best capitalized in the Peruvian agricultural sector. The Piura Valley was also one of the areas where agrarian reform created the most conflict. When the estates were transformed into cooperatives and productive enterprises, there was a great deal of optimism that they could serve as the model for other valleys.

To bolster the new enterprises, the state provided the cooperatives with credit and technical and administrative assistance. Within a short time, however, it became clear that the workers—theoretically the owners of these enterprises—were unprepared to assume responsibility for their management. To worsen matters, the state maintained tight control over the cooperatives through the collection of the agrarian debt and its pricing policies for agricultural supplies and the marketing of products. Eventually the state's role resembled one of "surplus extractor" rather than one of support and coordination.

Alarmed by the lack of institutions to assist with the restructuring of the agricultural sector and the campesinos' lack of management experience, CIPCA's founders decided to upgrade the quality of human resources among co-op members. They started with a small program of adult literacy.

The Multiple Roles of CIPCA

Among the private regionally based development agencies in Peru, CIPCA was the largest, best known, and most active in providing direct technical assistance and support to a wide range of peasant groups. It was unique because of the multiple roles it performed, acting as social promoter, communicator, technical specialist, coordinator, articulator of beneficiary needs, researcher, documenter, and policy adviser. The inability of government agencies to provide citizens with basic services and the distance separating educational institutions from the "popular sector" enabled CIPCA to extend its programs and influence and establish a regional domain. Although CIPCA was widely recognized as the key development institution of the North, it did not attempt to replace the actions of local government agencies and educational institutions.

CIPCA staff were exceptionally aware of their role as change agents and of the fine line between supporting beneficiary groups and creating dependency relationships. A common thread in all projects and programs was popular education, which used participatory techniques to encourage the exchange of knowledge and experiences among beneficiaries and staff. Over its fifteen-year history CIPCA undertook programs of literacy, mathematics and accounting, administration, agricultural technology, mechanics, health, and participatory research. Each activity addressed a specific weakness or need while seeking to develop practical skills so that beneficiaries could manage their own organizations.

The members and leaders of the land-reform cooperatives, primarily those living in the irrigated river valleys surrounding Piura, occupied the center of CIPCA's thinking and actions for nearly its entire institutional life. Although there were no records on the number of beneficiaries assisted, in 1981 it was estimated that over 40,000 inhabitants of the region had participated in its programs and that 70 percent of the cooperative leaders in the department had taken courses taught by CIPCA promoters in administration, math, and literacy.

After 1981, when the neo-liberal economic policies of the government of Fernando Belaunde Terry abandoned the struggling cooperative sector, CIPCA began to reanalyze its exclusive relationship with production-oriented organizations. CIPCA leaders felt that the organization had mistakenly overemphasized production organizations when it should have been working with a diversity of groups, including more traditional forms of community organization. To expand its reach, CIPCA launched a series of studies concerning health issues and the roles of women that eventually evolved into longer-term projects. These projects became successful examples of CIPCA's shift to working with poorer segments at the community level, reaching those who had never benefited from the reform programs of earlier years.

CIPCA's Organizational Structure

Organizationally, CIPCA was guided by a board of religious and lay persons. Beneath the board was a *consejo*, which included the director and a small group of elected and selected staff who together made operational decisions. Beneficiaries did not formally participate in those decisions, but they did have a say at the community and project levels. Three main units organized activity: one brought together the four field teams; a second covered the technical committees and the demonstration farm; and a third covered the radio program, documentation center, and publications and research sections. In all, CIPCA employed about a hundred full-time staff from a variety of technical and social disciplines—forty at headquarters and the rest as field staff. The staff displayed professional competence, but perhaps more important was their deep commitment to CIPCA's beneficiaries and their high level of social awareness. The rigorous pace kept by staff combined with tough living and working conditions tended to discourage those who were any less than highly motivated and dedicated.

A Model for the Breakup of the Cooperatives

For the staff who had worked with the cooperatives from the beginning, the dramatic decline of the reform sector and the troubled situation of the remaining campesino institutions was discouraging. CIPCA had been created to help the cooperatives develop their organizational capacity.

Instead, the staff found themselves helping the cooperatives prepare plans for the breakup of their organizations and the subdivision of their lands—a last effort to help struggling members find a workable and rational production arrangement.

As part of CIPCA's mandate to develop models that could reach beyond isolated or immediate results for limited groups of campesinos, the staff collaborated with local government agencies in a pilot study for the subdivision of one large cooperative. Through this study CIPCA hoped to build a methodology acceptable to the government that could be used by other cooperatives wishing to subdivide. The study, which was carried out at the request and expense of the cooperative, involved CIPCA technicians and officials from the Ministry of Agriculture, the Agrarian Bank, and INCOOP (a central parastatal organization providing credit and technical assistance to co-ops throughout the country). The experiences of cooperatives that had already split up and subdivided their lands revealed how vulnerable individual campesinos were to private intermediaries, and to unscrupulous administrators.

Collaboration with the Public Sector

CIPCA's reputation and ability to have an impact on development decisions and policies in the Department of Piura were largely due to its strategy of developing mutually beneficial working relationships with key regional agencies of the public sector. Early on, CIPCA negotiated an agreement with the Ministry of Education in which CIPCA was recognized as an educational institution, with the salaries of twenty of its teachers paid by the ministry. This agreement, reached in 1974, was still active by the late 1980s. CIPCA was one of a few such organizations to maintain government support for its programs.

CIPCA received from the Ministry of Agriculture twenty hectares of untilled land for a demonstration farm that doubled as a training and applied research center. The staff gave occasional lectures at the National University of Piura, conducted joint research projects, and encouraged students to use the extensive documentation center. In the community of Catacaos, the largest *comunidad campesina* in Peru (over 100,000 inhabitants), CIPCA worked with local leaders and the Ministry of Health in a health-care delivery system.

CIPCA's Adaptability

CIPCA was able to adapt to ever-changing contextual situations that alternately supported and undermined its strategies. Despite oscillating policies and rhetoric in the political and economic spheres—which forced institutional shifts in focus, client groups, and strategy—CIPCA withstood the external threats and maintained its vitality and pragmatism. Such adjustments confirmed its willingness and ability to learn from past experiences, digest criticism, and move on to more promising activities and clientele.

Other support organizations often appear to have a transitory role, but CIPCA represented a unique example of one that had developed a permanent role at the regional level. It was considered the authority on issues involving the land-reform sector in the Department of Piura. Government officials regularly consulted and collaborated with CIPCA, which helped to legitimize the organization among bureaucrats. Campesino organizations and communities continually sought CIPCA's advice, which consolidated its position in the popular sector.

In a region where neither public agencies nor political parties were capable of helping the poor adjust to an increasingly difficult economic reality, organizations like CIPCA were the mechanisms by which the "formal" Peru and the "real" Peru communicated.

FDN: An Academic Consulting Firm for Small-Scale Farmers

The Fundación para el Desarrollo Nacional (FDN) is generally regarded as a successful example of an indigenous developmental NGO. It has wide support among external donors and a solid reputation within Peru. In some ways the FDN is an organization that reflects Peruvian reality, but in other ways it is very unusual.

Early History of the FDN

The origin and early history of the FDN were linked to three major factors: (1) the opportunity offered by USAID and its Iowa-Peru research/training program to use young U.S.-trained Peruvian agricultural professionals to carry out studies needed in rural development planning; (2) the National Agrarian University staff's interest in engaging in remunerative professional activities that were not possible within the academic system; and (3) the disenchantment of senior public-sector officials with the excessive politicization and bureaucratization of the agrarian agencies during the 1970s and their interest in developing the emerging commercial small-farm sector, which was both a by-product and a stepchild of the agrarian reform.

These three influences were intertwined in the career of Luís Paz, founder and president of the FDN. Through his many positions in the Ministry of Agriculture and as a professor and dean at the National Agrarian University, he was closely associated with USAID/Lima and with other international agency staffs working in Peru. He envisioned a catalytic role for the FDN: to mobilize the talent of underutilized and poorly remunerated Peruvian *tecnicos* for public policy work rather than for private business. The FDN's excellent reputation, its high technical standards, and its survival are all largely attributable to the personal integrity and leadership of Paz. The flip side of such strong leadership, of course, is a centralized management style, which, as shall be seen, is essential for some purposes but a handicap for others.

How the FDN Works

In many ways the FDN resembles a consulting firm: It seeks contracts to carry out specific tasks and supports itself from the overhead, without having a longer-term association with client groups or permanence within a geographic area. For example, in 1987 the FDN had contracts for approximately US$3 million, divided among a dozen projects, half of which were studies and half action-oriented activities. The latter had about 1,000 direct beneficiaries. One of the two largest projects dealt with the promotion of nontraditional exports financed by USAID, the other focused on beekeeping in the Department of Lambayeque, supported by the Small Projects Fund of the Inter-American Development Bank and by the IAF.

Compared to other GSOs, the FDN is a relatively large organization. It has a core staff of fifteen (including five professionals) augmented by some 130 people (of which forty are professionals) contracted for specific projects.

The core recurrent budget of the FDN is about US$60,000, or US$5,000 per month. Salaries are competitive with government, but not with the private business sector. To attract top-quality people, a number of the senior consultants have been allowed to work for the FDN on a part-time basis. The core staff is highly dedicated and works extraordinary hours. If there is an FDN mystique, it is not so much an identification with poor groups or social causes, but a conviction that solid technical-economic promotion—free of ideological currents, which have beset Peru in recent years—is what campesinos want and what the country needs. More interesting, perhaps, is the FDN's practice of enabling highly trained Peruvian agricultural scientists of different persuasions to put their skills to work on practical problem solving.

The FDN's strategy is to provide technical and some financial assistance to groups of small and medium-sized farmers to solve specific problems, and in the process either improve on existing production technology or introduce new forms of economic activities. Although the FDN charges little or nothing for its technical assistance, its longer-term goal is to establish activities that will pay for themselves. The FDN's hope is that its beneficiaries will eventually manage on their own, although in practice this goal has proved to be more attainable for individual farm enterprises than for group activities such as marketing or agroprocessing.

FDN's Crisis

During the 1980s, the FDN shifted from its early focus on commissioned studies to direct action projects. Soon after, it underwent a serious internal crisis. A new university rector attempted to undermine the FDN's independence. He wanted the FDN to administer three regional research institutes and become a financial agent to secure credits and make disbursements for nontechnical purposes (for example, to hire secretaries, pay Christmas bonuses). In general, his goal was to increase the control of the National Agrarian University on the FDN's board. After an intense power struggle, during which Luís Paz opposed these demands, the rector withdrew the university from the board of directors and set up his own foundation. In the process, he took most of the ongoing contracts out of the FDN and placed them in his new organization. In the midst of negotiations on the beekeeping project he wrote letters to the Inter-American Development Bank and to the government, requesting that the bank deal with the Agrarian University in the future. However, both the National Planning Institute and the Ministry of Agriculture backed Paz —clear proof of his personal reputation and clout with the establishment. But the loss of contracts, plus the two years it took for the first Inter-American Development Bank disbursements to be made, plunged the FDN into a profound financial crisis. Staff size had to be cut in half and loans and outside work had to be arranged to carry the organization through the lean years of 1981 to 1983.

In a display of organizational tenacity, the FDN overcame this crisis. Not only did it recover and prosper, but, after the hostile rector left, relations with the Agrarian University improved with the signing of a cooperative agreement and faculty involvement in FDN projects.

The Beekeeping Project

One can get a good sense of the FDN's strengths and weaknesses as well as the atmosphere in which it operated from the story of the Lambayeque project, which came to be the FDN's "flagship" activity. The beekeeping project, initiated by an influential local senator from Chiclayo, was an attempt to provide supplementary employment and income for about 450 farm families (including about eighty landless workers). The project had three main thrusts: (1) credit in kind for hives and beekeeping equipment, (2) technical assistance and training for productive technology, and (3) marketing. The FDN displayed extraordinary capacity in implementing the credit component. Even the concerned officials from the Inter-American Development Bank admitted that the targets and timetable set by the bank contract were unreasonable (that is, 200 beneficiaries in six months). Serious obstacles to rapid implementation included a widely dispersed and heterogeneous farming population, no previous

FDN involvement in the region, severe drought, and inappropriate disbursement rules set by the bank. Yet the FDN quickly organized a field team and within two years came respectably close to reaching the original beneficiary and production targets.

By the end of 1986 (the third year) there were over 400 credit recipients, producing over 100,000 kilograms of honey from 5,500 newly established beehives. With by-products, this volume of production from beekeeping represented a wholesale value of about US$275,000 and added an average of US$400 net income to each beneficiary family. According to a baseline study commissioned by the FDN, the average family income of the beneficiaries was US$1,060. This represented a low relative poverty level, somewhat higher than the very poorest campesinos in the Sierra Sur and somewhat below those in the Sierra Norte.

At current levels of technology the beekeeping activity adds 38 percent to net family income or almost 50 percent if the opportunity cost of family labor is included. Thus the project has been highly successful in terms of generating supplementary income and employment, especially considering the indirect benefits from local artisanal production of beekeeping equipment. It is doubtful that any government agency in Peru could have done so well.

FDN's Weakness in Cooperativism

The record of the marketing component has been more mixed. Although the FDN has excelled in exploring potential demand, establishing quality control, and negotiating sales contracts with large buyers such as supermarket chains and the local branch factory of a multinational food-processing company, it has run into serious difficulties with the newly established beekeepers' association (ADAL).

ADAL, created by the FDN as part of its contractual obligation with donors, was supposed to gradually take over and manage the project. However, the FDN was totally unprepared for the militancy and confrontational style displayed by the new ADAL leadership. The FDN had little experience in cooperative development. In fact, it had deliberately stayed clear of collective land-reform enterprises. Moreover, the organization was handicapped in two ways. First, the FDN's contracts with its donors did not include any resources for cooperative promotion. Second, private traders (one of whom had previously worked with the FDN and had close relations with some members of the ADAL board) were causing trouble because they saw the FDN's active role in marketing as a threat to their interests. The ensuing struggle, with which the FDN's project coordinator in Chiclayo was unable to cope, revealed the FDN's weakness in the social and organizational aspects of development and, indeed, its basic lack of interest in group promotion and local empowerment.

Unfortunately, this attitude coincided with a parallel tendency in the

Peruvian countryside to back away from the negative experiences of land-reform production cooperatives to the point of being suspicious of *all* forms of cooperation. It is interesting to note that local elite support, deemed essential for the success of such projects, was forthcoming for honey production, which benefited the owners of nearby fruit plantations through increased pollination. But there was no elite support for the marketing component. There the interests of small beekeepers and local merchants diverged.

Trouble with Decentralization

Spread over the interior of the Lambayeque Department and programmed over several years, the beekeeping project required the establishment of a local project unit and management office in Chiclayo. The FDN had difficulty coping with a decentralized regional office. Lima wanted to maintain tight control, but the dynamics of the program called for greater local flexibility and decisionmaking. Also, once the program was well-established (and supplemented by other small farm-oriented development projects in the same area), more regional linkages and local interest groups began to develop around the Chiclayo FDN office. These linkages did not always sit well with Lima or fit with its links to the national-level administrative structure. Disputes over record-keeping, disbursement rules, and alleged nepotism and political deal-making provided further conflict. These issues forced the FDN's first and second project coordinators, together with their administrative officers, to resign within a year of each other.

The FDN's centralism was a strength in getting things done expeditiously, for quality control, and in demonstrating accountability to donors, but was a hindrance to local mobilization, coalition building, and beneficiary participation.

Opportunities for Sustained Technological Development

Donors and the FDN alike have displayed—not atypically—a project-bound mentality, which assumes that in a fixed period of time a new technological package will be absorbed and further progress will become self-sustaining. These assumptions are clearly wrong for both the production and marketing aspects of the beekeeping project. At the present levels of production, output remains far below what is technically and economically obtainable. (Honey yields are only one-third of the potential, and the income from pollen, wax, or royal jelly is negligible—income from pollen is only 10 percent of potential.) To close the gap, further research and development are needed, for which there are no funds. Also, institutional mechanisms must be in place to continue the work, but they were not when the grant period ended.

Some technologies to upgrade production were developed by the project, such as a system of "transhumance" (moving hives at certain times to areas of seasonal flowering). Solar driers for pollen were also introduced. The FDN was undecided about whether to maintain a permanent office and program in Chiclayo and had no donor incentives to do so, although, given the economies of scale and the diminishing cost per unit, the additional resources needed for continued upgrading of beekeeping would have been modest compared to the potential income gains. These considerations led the FDN to design a supplementary combined forest protection and beekeeping project that was presented to the Inter-American Development Bank. At the time of writing, approval was being held up by difficulty relations between the bank and the Peruvian government. In sum, the FDN, in spite of its strength in technological development, was constrained to leave the project far below its optimal frontier.

Marketing

Closely related to the untapped production potential was the failure of the marketing component. Honey production generates a sizable surplus, some of which can be captured by a group marketing scheme for further development (such as paying part of the salaries of beekeeping specialists, veterinarians, or lab technicians). The FDN did put the surplus it obtained from those producers who still owed on the original loans back into the business. But these funds ran out and no viable cooperative marketing scheme was built up. Honey was inevitably bought up by the local private traders, who could manipulate the market to their advantage, and there was no surplus for redistribution among the beekeepers.

FDN's Strengths and Weaknesses

It may well have been that the participants in the beekeeping project were not good candidates for a collective marketing mechanism. The families live far apart from one another, are not a homogeneous group, and had no previous organizational experience. But it is curious that the question of "organizability" was never studied or given even a fraction of the effort devoted to technical planning. It is not that the FDN is unconcerned with capacity building. Through training and demonstration the FDN strives to enhance individual entrepreneurial capacity, as do many business-oriented GSOs. But in the beekeeping project the organization focused on vertical linkages rather than on collective, horizontal ones, which in this case (as in many others) are not only socially desirable but technically indispensable.

Concerning regional impact, the beekeeping program, even if it disappears, is likely to stimulate other small-farm development initiatives in Lambayeque. One visible offshoot is a new IAF grant to the FDN for goat and sheep improvements in the same area. Other ideas have been generated by Chiclayano notables. Also, in the last phases of the grant period, staff members of the provincial university began to get involved. However, a regional institutional model in Lambayeque for a non-governmental rural support structure is only a possibility.

One might acknowledge here FDN's ability to forge mutually beneficial links with kindred public-sector organizations, especially at the regional level. Although some of these links are formalized in the customary *convenios*, most are informal collaborative arrangements or exchanges. In the absence of the kind of decentralized government envisaged in various laws (the latest of which was being initiated by the García administration when this case study was being prepared), one could expect an organization like the FDN to have a definite role in the coproduction of rural services at the regional or departmental level. However, given the increasing importance of peasant commercial agriculture in Lambayeque, the presence of FDN projects in the region is likely to energize and put pressure on public-sector agencies. The FDN also provides benefits (for example, it lobbies for official quality control of honey) through its linkages with the national agricultural policy establishment, although the FDN has not fully exploited its capacity for policy analysis nor its linkages at the macro level, preferring to concentrate on local production capacity.

There seems to be little interest among donors, the FDN, or the government in fostering long-term, institutionalized, private-public beneficiary collaboration in the region, which could continue and expand the thrust and impact of the initial project. The FDN's short-term technical consultancy mentality, its long-standing reluctance to get drawn into local politics and social conflict, and its fear of losing direct control, coupled with the donors' reluctance to commit themselves to lengthier, more risky institutional development assistance, have inhibited the full flowering and catalytic effect of an otherwise worthy project.

In spite of these critical considerations that highlight FDN's limitations, one must return to and reaffirm its strengths. As a highly competent agrotechnical support institution capable of linking micro- and macropolicy issues, it has an important role to play in Peru, especially in light of the country's traumatic struggles to find appropriate roles and models for its peasantry and the public sector's steadily eroding ability to offer even minimal services for rural development. Perhaps even more important is the FDN's capability to connect Peruvian academics and middle-class professionals to concrete problem solving in the countryside.

PROTERRA: Filling the Gap in Government Services

After returning to a democratic form of government in 1980, Peru struggled to redefine the role in its overall agricultural agenda of the large collective enterprises created during the agrarian reform period of the military years. While government officials and politicians argued about the fate of these declining enterprises, rural workers were forced to act for themselves. Like their urban counterparts, these workers came to rely on their own norms and ad hoc arrangements to resolve their problems rather than waiting for the government.

Before the agrarian reform, the Lurín Valley had been characterized by *latifundismo*—large semifeudal estates with indentured workers. The large landholdings expropriated during the regime of Juan Velasco Alvarado were first administered by government commissions and later consolidated into one large associative enterprise called CALEPS. CALEPS was created in 1976 by bringing together nineteen *predios* (pre-reform estates) totaling over 3,000 hectares. At one time, CALEPS employed 440 workers. Plagued with administrative inefficiencies and worker disagreements from the start, CALEPS was constantly reorganized, and fed yearly infusions of capital until 1981. Then, after accumulating nearly US$2 million in debts, the enterprise was declared not creditworthy. CALEPS quickly fell into organizational chaos and collapsed financially.

Agricultural Transformations

The subdivision of CALEPS mobilized the peasantry. The Instituto Tecnológico Agrario Proterra (PROTERRA), a regional organization providing technical assistance to small-scale commercial farmers, completely changed agricultural production in the Lurín Valley in a very short time. PROTERRA was part of an emerging group of competent, technically focused support organizations working with specific groups of low-income or disadvantaged peoples. The organization of production shifted toward small, intensively cultivated, family-sized plots, accompanied by the introduction of new crops such as cotton, vegetables, and fruits. Water resources also improved as a result of the better management of existing canals and wells and, according to PROTERRA's yearly surveys of harvests among a select group of beneficiaries, productivity rose steadily for most crops. PROTERRA technicians adeptly capitalized on the momentum gained from the delivery of legal titles to prod beneficiaries to experiment in other areas such as selection of crops, pesticide use, credit, and resource management.

Since the government's technical and resource support to small farmers was limited in the Lurín Valley, PROTERRA's approach was to fill in the gaps in services by either complementing the work of local government agencies or undertaking activities not covered by any public agency. But service delivery was not the only PROTERRA objective; staff pointed out that any strategy to increase small-farm production and productivity was incomplete if it was not accompanied by efforts to address the issue of security of land tenancy and increase small farmer's access to resources and services offered by the state. Thus, technicians used services as a way to satisfy the more immediate needs of beneficiaries and gain their confidence, while working on more complex issues of access and protection.

The Organization of PROTERRA

Organizationally, PROTERRA is divided into two operational divisions: The first handles legal matters from the headquarters in Lima; and the second conducts the project's agricultural extension and rural development activities from the Lurín office.

The agricultural and rural extension division provides individual technical assistance (directly and indirectly) to over 850 small producers. This includes helping beneficiaries with production plans, soil analysis, land surveys, the application of fertilizers and pesticides, and well exploration. Beneficiaries are also guided through the paperwork to apply for legal title, obtain credit, and be granted water drilling rights.

Simultaneously, the legal division supports the work of the technical staff by facilitating the processing of legal petitions, negotiating with government officials, and undertaking legal research on specific issues or problems. Legal staff also works in the policy arena developing and promoting legislation on issues ranging from the protection of agrarian reform lands, to procedures for the exploitation of frontier agricultural lands, to its proposal for creating a *cordón ecológico* (protective environmental legislation).

PROTERRA's Key Activities

As part of PROTERRA's broader effort to encourage a more rational and environmentally sound development of the river valleys that surround Lima, it has focused its legal efforts on a progressive legislative proposal to set aside the Lurín Valley and two other valleys as future productive greenbelts. PROTERRA's legal and legislative accomplishments are quite remarkable given the extremely small staff and limited funds it has for such activities. The organization's achievements illustrate the influential role support organizations can have in policy decisions at the national level.

Much of PROTERRA's legislative work has had implications reaching beyond the confines of the Lurín Valley; nevertheless its impact is often understated. For example, PROTERRA's lobbying efforts to force judges to recognize existing agrarian reform codes protected not only landreform beneficiaries in the Lurín Valley but also thousands of rural families facing potential expulsion in other departments. In the Lurín Valley, where PROTERRA targeted about 550 small farmers (members of the nine CAUs—the new cooperative structure created after the breakup of the old collective enterprises), the number of planned beneficiaries assisted was exceeded. Over 850 campesinos received ongoing and occasional technical assistance from PROTERRA staff. In the third year, the staff expanded their reach by providing services and advice to about sixty community organizations, informal groups, *comunidades campesinas*, irrigation committees, and municipalities.

In terms of promoting and improving local farmer organization, PROTERRA has been less successful. Originally, the nine CAUs formed after the CALEPS breakup were the recipient organizations through which legal and technical assistance would be channeled to members. Although PROTERRA staff continued to work with four of the stronger CAUs, this strategy was largely abandoned due to lack of member interest.

PROTERRA staff learned that after years of imposed organization and so-called worker participation, beneficiaries were less than enthusiastic about new initiatives to organize. Concluding that its efforts were being wasted, PROTERRA was forced to reevaluate its strategy of supporting organizations associated with past models of collective-production. Instead it shifted to working with community and irrigation organizations where member participation was strong. Although PROTERRA was uncertain if it had a role to play in inducing farmer organization, the staff did respond to and encourage nascent, informal groupings of beneficiaries, which tended to be task oriented and which, with time, might be nurtured into more permanent forms of organization.

By the end of the 1980s, PROTERRA was attempting to consolidate its technical assistance program in the lower valley and simultaneously initiate work with the *comunidades campesinas* of the upper valley, whose agricultural crops and practices and resource base were substantially different from their neighbors below. The team of lawyers in Lima continued to serve the legal needs of small farmers while developing and lobbying for protective environmental legislation (the *cordón ecológico*). Through these efforts PROTERRA has occupied an empty niche in environmental law.

PROTERRA initially conceived its focus to be limited to the technical and legal problems of individual producers. Although staff documented improvements in production and family incomes, the overall well-being of the family—housing, nutrition, health—did not appear to change. Thus in 1987, PROTERRA began working with community organizations, particularly women's organizations, to address educational needs and promote more family-oriented services.

One such effort has been to improve local health services. PROTERRA has succeeded in getting the government to open new rural clinics and is pressing the Ministry of Health to have them staffed full time. In addition, PROTERRA's social workers have developed local projects in nutrition, family-care, and community organizing. Other work has been done with parent organizations to introduce new educational programs at the primary and secondary levels. PROTERRA helped one parent organization establish the first national agricultural high school in the Lurín Valley.

Financial Sustainability

Like many other nonprofit organizations, PROTERRA is in fragile financial shape. This is due in part to its own lack of concern about obtaining additional funding from local and outside sources and in part to its struggle to define a long-term role for itself. The result has been excessive reliance on a single donor.

Because of accusations that PROTERRA lawyers were helping *parceleros* only so that they could later steal their lands, the organization was unwilling to charge for its services or engage in any activity that would put PROTERRA in the position of having to account for beneficiary monies. The technical team recognizes that the beneficiaries must assume a greater financial responsibility for the services they received. In addition, technical staff saw possibilities for some income-generating activities that could pay for a portion of the organization's operating costs. Although some of the organization's activities can be financed locally, others in the environmental and policy arena remain dependent on outside funding.

PROTERRA sees its chief role as spurring action and change and not necessarily as carrying out all those activities itself. By building local capacity and the necessary linkages to help beneficiaries and government agencies communicate, PROTERRA attempts to provide the elements that will ensure that activities continue after the organization withdraws.

Relations with the Government

Unusual among private development agencies in Peru, PROTERRA has sought and institutionalized a series of mutually beneficial working relationships with government agencies at the national and local levels, in part to avoid the duplication of public-sector activities, but also to improve small farmers access to critical resources and services. Through its *Operación Tabano*, PROTERRA has lobbied local-and national-level public agencies that have a direct bearing on project activities. This unusual but highly effective strategy of identifying and courting sympathetic, influential individuals in targeted agencies has been perhaps the most useful lesson for other support organizations. They have learned that it is possible to establish friendly relations with the public sector without compromising themselves.

Attention to Detail

PROTERRA's effectiveness can be traced to clear goals and a coherent plan of action, but perhaps more important is the staff's attention to detail. From their exhaustive effort to research and compile legislation concerning the agrarian reform, to familiarizing themselves with the appropriate government entities and their processes and procedures, to developing working relationships with key political figures and public officials, to working closely with small farmers in developing production plans, the staff has exhibited a talent for surmounting obstacles that few other organizations have equaled.

After the fieldwork on this case, PROTERRA split into two separate organizations: One decided to focus exclusively on the legal/environmental field, and the other continued to work on production technology, hoping to expand into the nearby valleys. The division was amicable and corresponded to the duality inherent in PROTERRA's original functions.

12

Profiles from Costa Rica

Country Context

The open democratic political system in Costa Rica is favorable to the flourishing of civic groups, and consequently there is a large domestically based nongovernmental organization (NGO) sector. A long tradition of cooperative and labor union activity has resulted in extensive and varied representative membership organizations in agriculture, industry, small business, and even among consumers.

At the same time, the government has maintained a strong social-welfare orientation, especially since the administration of José Figueres in the early 1970s. Far from preempting the role of social-service NGOs, the Costa Rican system not only has ample space for the development of the voluntary sector but, in contrast to most other countries, has engendered a number of forms of service organizations in which the private and public elements are fortuitously combined.

The lack of serious ethnic and class divisions of the sort that have plagued most of its Central American neighbors and the relatively low level of social conflict in Costa Rica, combined with a greater degree of representativeness and accessibility of the state, have given Costa Rican NGOs a relatively tame and less colorful, less confrontational character than those in many other places. This is especially noticeable among membership support organizations (MSOs), which are here less politicized and aggressive, and more inclined to negotiate and pursue bread-and-butter issues. This does not mean that Costa Rica is exempt from the poverty problems that plague the continent: Income distribution is not as equitable as commonly believed, there are needy social classes and unacceptably poor geographic areas such as the Atlantic coast, the resource-poor and inaccessible mountainous interior, and the urban periphery. As elsewhere the condition of households trapped in these places and their family components—women, children, and the handicapped—are the targets of much NGO activity. Costa Rican NGOs dealing with environmental problems are unusually strong, especially those concerned with ecologically sustainable natural resource systems. ANAI's agroforestry program is an example of this orientation, as described below.

The community development movement has been very important in Costa Rica since the early 1960s. Unlike elsewhere in Latin America, where apex institutions supporting local community-based self-help efforts have become politicized and have mostly disappeared, Costa Rica has maintained a central service organization, called Uniones Cantonales de Asociación de Desarrollo, which works with about fifty regional community federations. One of the profiles that follows, PURISCAL, is representative of this type of MSO.

Another type of MSO of regional scope is the Centros Agrícolas Cantonales, concerned with farm technology. Originally there were sixty-six such centers, at the time of our study forty were still active. They are jointly staffed and managed by farmer representatives and state agricultural agencies. CACH is an example of this type of intermediary (see the profile below).

Cooperatives are very important in Costa Rica. The cooperative movement has had a long history there and maintains many links to the international cooperative network. In the agricultural sector alone, there are some 400 co-ops with a total membership in excess of 200,000, plus a number of apex organizations and cooperative support institutions, such as INFOCOOP at the national level. Co-ops get many kinds of financial assistance, such as tax advantages, credit subsidies, lower freight charges. Although the membership in most co-ops, as well as in credit unions, tends to be from the not so poor, many co-ops offer services that are not exclusive to members and so have a spill-over effect. URCOOPAPA (profiled below) is a regional cooperative federation.

As would be expected, NGOs sponsored by businesspeople and oriented to support small-scale private entrepreneurs are congenial to the Costa Rican environment. FUCODES, profiled below, is one of the national development foundations within the Latin American network of SOLIDARIOS, promoted and supported by U.S.-based private voluntary organizations. It is a solid and competent grassroots support organization (GSO); although it does not have much of a social or policy impact.

Other trends among Costa Rican NGOs, as represented by the Federación de Organizaciones Voluntarian, are a growing interest in networking, upper-class social volunteerism, and the importance of women's issues. All of these major types of intermediary organizations are illustrated in the following profiles.

ANAI: Ecology and Development

The Project Region

The Asociación de los Nuevos Alquimistas (ANAI) is a professionally led service organization created through the efforts of a group of ecologists specializing in agroforestry. The organization is based in Talamanca, the largest but also one of the poorest and most isolated cantons in Costa Rica. Talamanca is also one of the few cantons with an ethnically mixed population. After the banana companies abandoned the area, cacao became the main cash crop. In 1979, monilia pod rot destroyed the cacao trees, thus wiping out the livelihood of most small farmers in the region. The resources of the region have also been threatened by deforestation, uncontrolled settlement, and tourist development. Other problems in the area include the loss of crops due to bad roads, poor transportation, and few marketing outlets; insufficient training and technical assistance; poor communication systems; and lack of potable water facilities, electricity, and health services. In contrast to most other areas of Costa Rica, the farmers of Talamanca have received very little help from government agencies.

ANAI belongs to the new generation of nonmembership grassroots support organizations in Costa Rica that tries to combine income generation with organizational capacity. ANAI has successfully combined ecological principles and tangible incentives with regional organizational development, stressing all the factors necessary to make the efforts self-sufficient and sustainable in the long run. So far, ANAI has had a rapid impact on both technology adoption and community organization through the device of communal nurseries. ANAI has also succeeded in creating better links between isolated peasant communities and the public-sector service agencies in Costa Rica.

ANAI's Structure

ANAI was founded in 1971 as NAISA (the New Alchemy Institute S.A.), an independent Costa Rican offspring of the New Alchemy Institute of East Falmouth, Massachusetts. It began its activities with three North American scientists and a couple of local collaborators in 1978. In 1984 it was transformed into ANAI, a nonprofit organization with legal status under the Costa Rican Law of Associations.

By 1984 ANAI had a staff of thirteen: three codirectors, five agricultural extensionists, a farm manager, an education coordinator, a community liaison officer, a researcher, and a bilingual secretary. The organization has a seven-member board of directors and a general assembly with the following membership: six campesinos, three teachers, seven agronomists, and four U.S. scientists. The leadership is very committed and effective overall. The staff participates actively in all phases of the fieldwork.

In the early 1970s, NAISA set up an experimental farm in an isolated region of Talamanca located two walking hours from the nearest road. It began functioning as an organization in support of grassroots efforts when it encouraged and helped a group of scattered people to unite and organize into a community association. As a result, in 1973 a community committee was formed, and in 1976 the Asociación Integral de Desarrollo de Gandoca and Mata de Limón—with legal status—was created. This enabled ANAI to serve as a broker and to contact foreign donor agencies for assistance. Catholic Relief Services agreed to help purchase a boat that would help the community transport consumer goods into the area and send their produce to marketing outlets through the Atlantic coast rather than on their backs through a mud track. The U.S. Agency for International Development (USAID) contributed to a pig farm project, and the Inter-American Foundation (IAF) gave a grant for aquaculture and water pumps.

The Nursery Project

ANAI embarked on a step-by-step learning process. It undertook research and marketing studies for a series of crops and cropping systems with commercial and subsistence value. In order to incorporate the experiments into the region, ANAI explored the potential of a new plant with four of its neighbors. With the financial assistance of the Dutch government, ANAI carried out a three-year crop diversification project in collaboration with one of the farmer cooperatives of the region, Cooperativa de Servicios Multiples de Talamanca, R.L. (COOPETALAMANCA). In 1983, ANAI established a student-operated nursery at the Colegio Técnico Agropecuario de Talamanca, the only high school in the area.

The nursery project, which began in 1984, has three essential components. The first is the tree nurseries, designed to produce enough seedlings to plant one hectare of fruit-bearing trees and spices and one hectare of lumber trees for each participant farmer. The second component is educational and includes written material, technical assistance, workshops, and training. The third is research, focusing on the introduction and multiplication of superior genetic material on the experimental farm, with the objective of minimizing disease risks and maximizing marketability.

ANAI provides initial planting material, basic equipment, and technical guidance; the communities provide land, labor, and management. For each nursery, a demonstration plot is set up where all the varieties of plants and trees produced by the nursery are grown in the field. Every nursery produces improved varieties of moniliasis-resistant cacao, and a few other species familiar to the farmers.

Each of the nurseries has been designed to become both technically and financially self-sufficient. In order to make its technical-assistance component sustainable, ANAI trains one member of each nursery for an entire year. This person is supported by the community during training, but later is responsible for providing free technical assistance to his or her fellow farmers.

Both subsistence and commercial crops are introduced to achieve food security and the ability to survive another major disease outbreak or a fall in prices. In addition, great stress is placed on preventing soil erosion. Broad-scale reforestation has been initiated, with the goal of assuring the long-term productivity of the entire region.

ANAI's methodology is to design projects in which improved farming techniques and skills can be learned through direct participation in all aspects of the construction, management, and maintenance of the nurseries. Material generated by the project is disseminated through monthly bulletins, technical publications, and radio. In addition to the production of printed material, individual and group training and major educational projects have been undertaken.

Once the nursery groups were in place, a number of devices were used to develop organizational capacity. A collective working conscience has been established and an informal forum created, in which the community's problems can be discussed. Within each nursery, a coordinating committee has been set up to facilitate the decisionmaking process. At the same time, members of each nursery group have been selected to represent their nurseries at the monthly meetings with ANAI. These meetings serve as a forum for making marketing decisions and for exchanging views and problems concerning the nurseries. In addition, the meetings help the different leaders get to know one another and foster understanding and cooperation among the three ethnic groups. The nursery groups have already formed the Association of Small Reforesters of Talamanca (APRETA), in order to obtain the legal status needed to become the beneficiaries of government funds channeled to those who engage in reforestation efforts.

By the end of the first year of the project, fifteen community nurseries with 330 participants were operating. Eighteen months after the project began, the number of nurseries grew to twenty-four with 670 participants. Membership in the groups ranges from six to forty-four. Groups vary in motivation, cohesiveness, and organization. Fifteen percent of the participating small-scale farmers are women, and another 15 percent are teenaged boys.

ANAI'S Networking Efforts

ANAI tries to work with already established institutions and has proved to be highly skillful in establishing linkages to government agencies, autonomous organizations in the region, research institutions, and international donors. ANAI has also performed a promotional and brokerage role, linking the established farmer groups in the area and opening channels to government institutions. A recent agreement with the Agrarian Development Institute involved land titling services and the transformation of some of the adjacent natural areas into a refuge. ANAI's leadership sees this type of networking as a contribution to the goals of developing decentralized (but coordinated) institutional capacity.

Most links have been with COOPETALAMANCA, the second cooperative in the region, and the only one with legal status at that time. COOPETALAMANCA, which affiliates 223 farmers (only half of them active), has many problems and has not reached a satisfactory functional level. Nevertheless, ANAI's diversification project was undertaken in collaboration with the cooperative, and ANAI is interested in strengthening COOPETALAMANCA's productive capacity.

ANAI has taken advantage of the resources of various private, public, and autonomous organizations and has been able to make several arrangements with them. Centro Agronómico Tropical de Investigación y Enseñanza (CATIE) has been very helpful in setting up major training programs and in helping to import genetic material. With the Asociación Bananera Nacional (ASBANA), ANAI has made arrangements to get palmito, coconut, and guanabana seeds for the nurseries. A joint program of the Ministry of Agriculture and the University of Costa Rica has given ANAI citrus seeds. The Aquaculture Division of the Ministry of Agriculture has been very helpful with fish stock and training assistance, and the Junta de Administración Portuaria de Desarrollo Económico de la Vertiente Atlántica (JAPDEVA), a regional autonomous state agency responsible for the socioeconomic development of the Atlantic coast, has provided ANAI with two full-time extensionists.

ANAI has a good diversification of funding sources, although grants and loans are received on a project-by-project basis. The organization receives no institutional support as such and has been dependent on donors for its entire operating budget since it began the projects. The organizers of ANAI do not expect their institution to become self-sufficient.

Both private and public agencies are supportive of ANAI. ANAI keeps good contacts with institutions like the Forestry Service, the Department of Wildlife, the National Park Service, the National Museum, the National Cadaster (land survey and registration office), the National Geographic Institute, the Institute for Agrarian Development, the National Learning Institute, the Tropical Science Center, and the universities in Costa Rica.

The IAF's $115,000 grant in 1985 was designed to supplement the final two years of a $1.87 million three-year USAID/Development Initiative Coalition (CINDE)–funded project. ANAI considers the IAF's assistance as paying for the unglamorous, nuts-and-bolts infrastructural elements of the project, which are so hard to fund yet essential for success. Through other grants to interlinking groups in the area, the IAF has played an important role in supporting grassroots efforts in the same region.

Issues and Lessons

What is unique about ANAI is its strategy. ANAI provides the base groups with the incentives and services needed to develop organizational capacity. But once these groups have reached a certain level, ANAI helps them move on to the next stage by providing them with new or additional services, generally through assistance from elsewhere, while taking on new infant groups. This strategy sets ANAI apart from many intermediary-type organizations that seek to perpetuate their existence.

CACH: A Public-Private Regional Service Organization

The Establishment of Regional Agricultural Centers

The Centro Agrícola Cantonal de Hojancha (CACH) is an interesting public-private organization of regional scope peculiar to the Costa Rican policy environment. It is a good example of a successful service and financial intermediary contributing to the agricultural development of the region. It is technically competent, financially sound, and has leveraged support from the government and international donors. However, CACH tends to work with the better-off farmers and offers little outreach or capacity building among the poorest rural groups.

The origins of the regional agricultural centers or Centros Agrícolas Cantonales (CACs) date back to 1907, with the creation of agricultural councils. In 1920, the councils were turned into outgrowths of the municipalities. By 1949, the government placed them under the direction of the Ministry of Agriculture and ruled that the board of directors be composed of farmers and representatives of the government, the municipality, and the church. By 1960, their objectives were clearly defined: (1) to promote popular participation, (2) to organize and strengthen base groups (cooperatives and associations), (3) to serve as a mediator between the different government agencies in the area, and (4) to coordinate their work with the Ministry of Agriculture's extension agencies. The government gave the CACs legal status in 1973, awarded them a percentage of the sugar tax in 1974, and exempted them from paying the property tax in 1979. By 1980, all CACs were allowed to receive international assistance. In 1981, they were permitted to federate regionally and confederate nationally.

Out of the sixty-two CACs established, forty still survive today, but only ten to fifteen are truly efficient and economically viable. CACH represents one of the most successful CACs in the country and is one of the largest IAF grantees in Costa Rica.

Structurally, all CACs follow an organizational pattern set by law. In reality, however, each CAC has adapted to its regional circumstances and acquired a unique character. All CACs work through projects with individuals. The productive capacity of the area determines the type of project the CACs engage in and, in turn, the type of project determines the beneficiaries. The CACs working with milk storage, for example, have ended up working with the better-off farmers who could afford not to butcher some of their cattle. On the other hand, in the sugar-cane areas, CACs can reach lower-income sugar-cane cutters. Furthermore, these CACs receive more government funds through the sugar tax.

CACH is characteristic of many CACs in the following ways:

- The services are excellent, but there is a lack of outreach and extension programs to reach the poor.
- It is adept at experimenting with and providing numerous services at once.
- Its leadership is more representative of the more established farmers in the area.
- Its fundamentally nongovernmental character frees it from the bottlenecks that hamper similar projects (like a U.S. Agency for International Development/Food and Agriculture Organization project led by government technicians in the Hojancha canton).

The Creation of CACH

In 1970, Hojancha experienced an economic crisis. The population—emigrants from the central valley—fell by 60 percent between 1971 and 1984. The first response to the crisis was to form the canton of Hojancha. In 1976 the National Municipal Development Institute (IFAM) and AITEC (an external aid PVO) conducted an integrated rural development pilot project and created CACH.

CACH has been characterized as a diversified rural business, generating income by the creative provision of multiple inputs and services to local farmers. CACH is first and foremost a socially oriented small business that struggles to cover operating costs. The core activity is a country store with several specific projects added as funds become available.

CACH's organizational structure resembles a membership association but with public-sector participation. This hybrid arrangement reflects the Costa Rican political system in which there is less antagonism between the civic sector and the state. The board of directors has eighteen members: twelve are selected by a general assembly, and six must be government officials. The board makes program decisions and hires a staff to take on operating duties. CACH has ten paid employees. The Ministry of Agriculture covers four of the staff salaries. CACH leadership is energetic, creative, and intensely committed to the development of the region.

Income-Generating Activities

CACH is a uniquely dynamic organization because of the variety of its projects. It was originally created to stop out-migration through organization, agricultural diversification, administration of agricultural services, and management of marketing services for local produce. Out of a trial-and-error process, CACH has evolved seven income-generating activities:

1. CACH sells apiculture inputs and processes and markets honey. However, apiculture in the region was recently threatened by the arrival of the African bees.
2. As part of its reforestation activities, CACH sells seedlings of valuable, fast-growing tree species.
3. CACH promotes coffee in the area and has managed to broker with the government to achieve a *zona cafetalera* status, which opens up credit for local farmers. When the new coffee growers formed their own cooperative, CACH stopped selling coffee seedlings and in turn began growing its own coffee on rented land. Now CACH is a member of the co-op.
4. CACH runs an agricultural supply store.
5. Although cattle in the area were usually raised for beef, CACH has encouraged the cattle owners to begin milking their animals. CACH provides them with receiving, cooling, and transportation services for the milk.
6. One of the earliest projects was agricultural diversification to decrease dependence on cattle and encourage farmers to plant vegetables. CACH became the local marketing intermediary and sold the vegetables to government-supported nutrition centers and schools. The project was abandoned when the public sector cut the funds for these programs.
7. With IAF support a hybrid pig project was begun.

As in other service organizations in which members have to pay for services and make other financial contributions, CACH tends to work with the less needy population of Hojancha. CACH was created to reach approximately 1,000 small farmers in the canton. Some of its activities, such as the farm input store, are widely available, but the benefits of others are restricted. The apiculture project, for example, was undertaken with a cooperative that screened its members carefully. Only eighteen cattle owners participate in the dairy project because demand fell and the milk co-op had to be restricted to dairy farmers who could produce a regular supply of milk. But other projects, such as the tree nursery and the pig-raising enterprise, benefit a wide range of clients.

. CACH has obtained loans from public and private lending institutions. AITEC was the most avid promoter of CACH, managing to link it with funders such as USAID, Private Agencies Collaborating Together (PACT), and CATIE. Like all CACs, CACH has access to technical assistance from the Ministry of Agriculture, the Land and Colonization Institute (ITCO) and the National Learning Institute (INA), and access to credit from the National Bank of Costa Rica.

One reason CACH is favored by international donor agencies is because it covers 70 percent of its operating costs. Nevertheless, its donors are pushing for CACH to become 100 percent self-sufficient. Such pressure limits CACH even further to service the lowest 40 percent of the farmers in the area and limits the possibility of taking on financially riskier ventures that could maximize the income of the poorer farmers.

In 1981, the IAF gave CACH a grant for $92,600 for three years to cover the deficit in the core institutional costs, to expand existing services, and to start the small-scale pig project. The Ministry of Agriculture and the National Forestry Directorate provided technical assistance. In 1982, the IAF granted $3,500 to send the manager of CACH to a seminar at the Instituto Centro-Americana de Administración de Empresas (INCAE)—a regional business management training institute.

In 1984 the IAF granted $235,700 over four years to expand reforestation activities. A thorough evaluation (Murray 1984) concluded that CACH had, through trial and error and by making practical adjustments on the basis of experience, come up with a path-breaking nursery technology that eliminated most logistical problems in delivering the seedlings to distant mountain farms inherent in traditional nurseries. With this grant, CACH enlarged its tree nursery and forestry extension programs and provided new services to farmers, including tree harvesting, wood processing, and finished wood product marketing. The program benefits both small and medium-scale farmers. Other national and international agencies including the Ministry of Agriculture, the Costa Rican Technological Institute, AITEC, and CATIE also contributed funds for salaries, technical assistance, and equipment. Farmers had access to a line of credit for on-farm reforestation and conservation investments established through a USAID loan to the Costa Rican government. This credit line was available to Hojancha farmers to finance many of the investment recommendations made by CACH.

Although CACH is a public-private hybrid organization, it displays some of the weaknesses of cooperatives: restricted benefit distribution, lack of aggressive promotion and outreach, and too many activities for the available managerial attention. However, CACH has some impressive advantages: It is responsive to its membership, it is in a unique position to mobilize state and private resources, and its hands-on experimental style is yielding important technical innovations. Although it can be faulted on poverty reach and larger impact, it has a significant unrealized potential in both these dimensions.

FOV: An Organization with a Dual Personality

The Federación de Organizaciones Voluntarias (FOV) was created in 1969 by sixteen Costa Rican NGOs as a coordination entity dealing with women's issues, but it subsequently began operating its own programs for women in order to attract donor funding. After a few years of playing a dual role, FOV decided to once again concentrate on coordination. In its networking role FOV offers training for volunteers and sponsors conferences, courses, and seminars. In 1986, FOV represented thirty-one member organizations.

In the late 1970s, donor agencies showed increased interest in funding women's productive projects. FOV received limited assistance as a coordinating agency, so it decided to start its own women's projects. Its first effort was a study on the needs of low-income neighborhood women. This was followed by a program based on the findings of the study. As a result, FOV created a human development program in 1977 and transformed itself into a development agency, funding its own microenterprise projects and taking an active role with baseline groups. This move entailed training urban women to set up productive solidarity groups in such fields as baking, sewing, and food preservation. At the same time, FOV continued to function as a coordination agency.

Subsequently, FOV established a rotating credit fund in the urban sector with IAF assistance, and through additional funding by a USAID-established, financial intermediary, CINDE—the Development Initiative Coalition—expanded into the rural areas. In the summer of 1986, FOV decided to return to its original coordinating role. FOV's new goals were to strengthen the private development organization sector and itself as an apex organization, possibly with the European funds destined for institutional development.

The decision to drop the development projects was made by the six-woman board of directors, who are representatives of the establishment and elected by a general assembly of affiliates. The board makes policy decisions and appoints an executive director who administers day-to-day operations. Organized along very traditional lines, representing the world of upper-class voluntarism, the board did not feel comfortable with the more professional and technical tasks required to provide credit to base groups. At the staff level there was a clear struggle between the generalists who wanted to strengthen the coordinating role and the professionals engaged in projects. The director mediated up to a point, and then the board and CINDE had the final word.

Until 1977, except for one secretary, all FOV staff was made up of volunteers. By 1986, the staff had grown to twenty-eight, with twenty-six volunteers in three departments: administration, training and social projects, and technical cooperation. In addition, FOV has five field extensionists whose expertise varies from highly skilled to average. Also, five Peace Corps volunteers have been recruited to assist in FOV's projects. Although only a few women board members have been involved with FOV since its creation, there is no single dominating figure. Yet the executive director does have enormous control over day-to-day issues and has great leverage over board decisions.

Working in Two Worlds

FOV works in two very different worlds. One world is that of the Costa Rican NGOs. Costa Rica has traditionally had a large number of charity and relief organizations, mostly made up of upper-class volunteers or religious groups. In the past decade, however, there has been a gradual move from welfare to more development-oriented activities. Some private voluntary organizations (PVOs) have moved into the social-action areas; others are experimenting with income-generating projects. A new generation of organizations is now trying to combine income-generating projects with organizational capacity building. NGOs are exempted from taxes and receive government assistance. Most funds, however, come from international donor agencies. As a coordinating agency, FOV began to federate welfare-oriented groups and has now gradually included the more economically or technically focused.

The other world of FOV is somewhat more complex: It is the world of low-income women in Costa Rica. Although many of the poorest households in Costa Rica are headed by women, jobs, credit, and services for women are scarce. Women have the highest rates of illiteracy and the lowest rates of political and cooperative participation in the country. FOV established its loan fund for women's projects at a time when such a venture was a high risk. The country was undergoing its worst crisis since 1948. Unemployment in the marginal neighborhoods where FOV wanted to work was over 40 percent. In the rural areas, not only was unemployment high, but off-farm projects for women were relatively new.

Coordinating Activities

As a coordinating agency, FOV trains volunteers, coordinates programs and services, and tries to avoid duplication of efforts. The training program includes human development, planning, organization, evaluation and proposal writing, and fund-raising. FOV began by coordinating the efforts of socially oriented NGOs concerned with women. Through the years it has begun to incorporate more economically focused NGOs working with women or men and local branches of international organizations. As a coordinating organization, FOV stresses the importance of the horizontal linkages between the various NGOs in Costa Rica and between NGOs and base-level women's groups. For example, in the canton of Puntarenas, FOV has successfully brought together two national agencies, the municipality, and two international donor groups.

FOV's members fall into two groups: the voluntary NGOs led by middle- and upper-class volunteers who offer social-welfare services and GSOs led by professionals engaged in productive projects.

FOV's Development Projects

The Human Development Program began in 1977 as a consciousness-raising program funded by the Overseas Education Fund (OEF) and USAID for low-income women. The Costa Rican Planning Office provided funds from 1981 to 1982. Inspired by the training, some women got together in groups and began their own projects. But they had insufficient access to credit, and their projects did not take off. Therefore, FOV decided it had to add credit and technical assistance to its services.

In 1982, the IAF gave FOV a grant for $70,000. Thus, with IAF funds, FOV took the first step in providing credit and technical assistance to productive projects. In 1984, CINDE awarded FOV a grant for $134,600 to start a second credit fund. One of the prerequisites was to work with rural women's groups. So FOV took its first step toward expanding into rural areas. In addition, during this time, FOV published a collection of training manuals with easy-to-read information on credit and self-management programs. Also, FOV engaged in international networking: attending seminars, sponsoring conferences, and so on.

FOV's projects were both urban and rural. There were fifteen urban projects: eleven sewing groups, two consumer stores, a basket-weaving project, and a bakery. In addition, there were eighteen rural groups in four zones, some of which had been previously organized by the Inter-American Development Bank and the Ministry of Agriculture, that engaged in off-farm production.

Initially, FOV had better success with its urban-oriented activities, as it took some time to acquire experience with productive groups and learn about the crucial role of the markets.

During the time FOV operated its project directly, FOV's networking role was weakened. In addition, in 1986, the NGO section of CINDE was converted into a separate organization—Asociación Costarricense para el Desarrollo (ACORDE). Its purpose was to expand and strengthen NGOs through timely grants and credit. The 1987 transformation of FOV reflected its fear that organizations like ACORDE will take advantage of FOV's present weakness and bypass it to deal directly with individual NGOs.

Organizational Duality

FOV's organizational problems stemmed from the split personality. By trying to play two roles at once, FOV was spreading itself too thin, which led to high administrative costs. Also, FOV's member organizations began to view the federation as just another NGO competing for national and international funds and technical assistance. FOV was threatened by a loss of its leadership position and credibility among its members.

In the early years, FOV had been dependent on dues from its affiliates, small grants from the national legislature, and fees from government agencies for its training services. The OEF was the first donor agency to provide FOV with substantial funds. The large office complex was built on land donated by the municipality with funds from the legislature and private donations as well as volunteer labor. The U.N. Voluntary Fund for Women also contributed to FOV.

CINDE played a crucial role in FOV's decision to change into a rural funder and later back into a coordinating agency. It offered to refinance the CINDE-FOV fund on the condition that a new development organization (APRODESE) be established to take on the projects. Many donors have reservations about funding a coordinating agency that works with welfare groups as well as development organizations.

FOV's origin as an organization coordinating charity groups made it difficult to shake off the welfare mentality. It also had to struggle to overcome the initial tendency to pursue enterprises that reinforce women's traditional roles (see Yudelman 1987). However FOV has a comparative advantage in lobbying for women's rights and acting as an advocate. FOV's directors are influential and are well positioned to affect public policy in behalf of women. In addition, FOV's thirty-one affiliates have prominent individuals from the private sector on their boards.

FUCODES: A National Foundation for Small-Enterprise Credit

International PVOs and the donor community have been active in promoting the creation of many indigenous organizations with similar philosophies that are often based on the same institutional model. The national development foundations (NDFs) that provide credit to small and microenterprises are a U.S. institutional invention that grew out of concern about urban unemployment, accelerated rural-to-urban migration, the explosion of squatter settlements, and the growth of the informal sector. Most NDFs belong to the Council of American Development Foundations (SOLIDARIOS) founded in 1972. As an umbrella organization, it mobilizes financial resources to fund their credit programs, with grants from PACT, USAID, the European Economic Community, and soft loans from the Inter-American Development Bank (IDB).

In the early 1970s, agricultural credit in Costa Rica was provided through the seventy-seven regional offices of the National Banking System (NBS), with small farmers receiving the lowest interest rates. From

1972 to 1977, the portfolio doubled, and credit to small farmers tripled. Nevertheless, public and international credit was still inadequate to reach the poorest, and commercial banks required sufficient collateral to cover 100 percent of the loans. Although the USAID-supported Productive Credit Guarantee Program was expected to overcome this problem, the lending costs of the official programs were still too high to serve a poorer clientele. It was in this atmosphere that the Fundación Costarricense de Desarrollo (FUCODES) began operating and found its niche in servicing the poorest farmers. FUCODES is a business-oriented NGO, one of a family of national development foundations set up by external funding to channel resources to microenterprise.

The Formation and Reorganization of FUCODES

In 1972, a group of business leaders, with the support of the Pan American Development Foundation (PADF), formed a steering committee to engage in development activities. The group's first efforts were to import hospital equipment made available to them through PADF. With PADF's institutional support, FUCODES was created first as an information association. It later received legal status as a national development foundation in 1976.

The early history of FUCODES was troubled. In 1978 FUCODES received a $500,000 USAID grant for an ambitious rural credit program. The grant represented a 300 percent increase in its funding, but FUCODES was not able to develop the capacity needed to manage this amount of money. In 1981, most loan repayments were uncollectible, and USAID and PACT/SOLIDARIOS grants and funds from thirty local companies were suspended. As a result, FUCODES went into crisis. By 1982, the staff was reduced from twenty-eight to five, and FUCODES was subsequently reorganized with a more coherent policy and operating procedures. A year later, national and international funding was reestablished.

Between 1977 and 1979 FUCODES convened a general assembly that elected the board of directors. The organization had an executive director and four operating departments: administration, fund-raising, promotion and business development, and credit and training. After the reorganization, the general assembly included members of the contributing business firms, and the board of directors was composed of twelve elected members who were to serve on a voluntary basis and be responsible for setting policy. Four committees composed of board members and senior administrative personnel were set up: an executive committee, a credit committee, a public-relations and fund-raising committee, and an oversight committee. The credit committee is responsible for reviewing all loan requests. The executive director is responsible for day-to-day decisions and is assisted by four fieldworkers, four administrative and accounting personnel, and two support personnel.

The evolution of the credit program illustrates the dilemma of poverty reach versus sound financial management. Before its reorganization, FUCODES began working in rural areas, with agricultural projects and very poor beneficiaries organized in groups. It tried to foster a spirit of cooperation using highly subsidized credit as a tool to gradually reach financial viability. After the reorganization, FUCODES moved toward the urban sectors, with small manufacturing projects and beneficiaries serviced individually. It now functions very much like a bank, providing credit at nearly commercial rates. Thus, in the first years, FUCODES was a more socially oriented organization, concerned with the longer-term potential viability of its clients and with the organizational issues of the poorest. After the reorganization, FUCODES became a more successful economic venture. Like the Fundación Mexicana de Desarrollo Rural (FMDR), FUCODES services beneficiaries who have assets and a track record to assure repayment.

The Rural Credit Program

FUCODES's first operations were in the rural areas, with poor coastal laborers and fishermen in the Guanacaste region. FUCODES's emphasis was on organizing groups and promoting cooperatives.

FUCODES was born with the philosophy that its mandate was to promote groups and help them identify viable projects rather than only to provide technical, organizational, and credit assistance to already established groups. To implement this philosophy, FUCODES established the Rural Credit Program, with the rotating credit fund as its principal component.

At first, credit was provided as an incentive for group promotion. By 1979, FUCODES had provided credit to sixty-two microenterprises and had established thirty credit operations in agriculture, small industry, and artisanal and fishing sectors. The loan portfolio was worth $125,000. By 1981, however, 80 percent of the beneficiaries were in arrears on loan repayments amounting to $85,000, most of which was uncollectible. After the reorganization, the portfolio increased to $250,000 and sixty beneficiary groups in 1982, and it continued to grow to $290,000 and sixty-eight groups in 1985.

Although social promotion was to be complemented by credit in the early years, management of the credit program became the principal activity after the reorganization. FUCODES was now servicing existing groups having at least fifteen active members. In addition, the recipient groups had to be sponsored by a public or private organization that would guarantee the loan repayment. In the latter years, new rules were added: All enterprises had to be operational for at least two years; all beneficiary farmers had to own their own land; and the small businesses had to have the infrastructure necessary to operate. Technical assistance became limited to agriculture and livestock—originally the bulk of the grantees, but now only 12 percent of the portfolio. FUCODES no longer trains beneficiaries directly, but arranges courses with government agencies.

Sources of Support

In the early years, FUCODES planned to have a technical assistance network with fourteen public agencies, ten private organizations, and eight donor agencies. Since its reorganization, FUCODES has cooperated with the National Learning Institute (INA), the Technical Institute of Costa Rica (ITCR), the University of Puntarenas, and CINDE. Its ties to CINDE are especially close, and members of the two organizations and the USAID mission in Costa Rica meet regularly to plan strategies.

PACT provided financial support to set up FUCODES and make it operational. But overall, 97 percent of the portfolio has been financed by USAID or SOLIDARIOS. USAID has set the condition that only individuals may be financed through its loan portfolio. SOLIDARIOS and IDB funds may be loaned to groups.

In 1978, the IAF awarded FUCODES $15,000, a matching grant for a revolving credit fund. An amendment for $6,500 for auditing and accounting followed. The IAF grant, combined with a SOLIDARIOS loan of $30,000 and a PADF loan of $10,000, made it possible for FUCODES to capitalize its first revolving loan fund in 1978. The purpose of the IAF grant was to strengthen FUCODES as a development agency, improve managerial and operational effectiveness, expand fund operations, and obtain the support of the National Banking System.

In 1986, FUCODES sent the IAF a proposal for $50,000 for a rural enterprise revolving fund, but was turned down. Nevertheless, a grant for $10,000 was approved in 1987, so that thirteen staff members of ten Central American development organizations could attend a seminar and workshop organized by PADF Costa Rica on fund-raising techniques.

Assessment of FUCODES

Compared to other national development foundations, FUCODES's average loans are larger, credit regulations are more demanding, the number of direct beneficiaries is smaller, and a higher percentage of the portfolio is oriented toward small manufacturing enterprises. FUCODES is exceptional in that it has an operating surplus. It is well capitalized, highly liquid, well managed, and has its debt situation under control. FUCODES is still dependent on outside funds but expects to become financially self-sustaining in the near future.

FUCODES has become a well-established institution in Costa Rica. Many prominent companies are members. There were 250 affiliates by

1985. They provide some financial support but are mainly important because of their networking power. Influential businesspeople sit on the board of directors, but FUCODES does not use its political clout to lobby for its beneficiaries or to try to affect policy.

PURISCAL: Co-management of an Agricultural Supply Store

The Unión Cantonal de Asociaciones de Desarrollo de Puriscal (PURISCAL) is an example of a regional community development association promoted by the state, through the creation of the National Directorate for the Development of the Community (DINADECO) in 1967. Furthermore, it illustrates an interesting partnership with another regional agricultural service organization. Although there is complementarity in the joint program, there are also tensions between the membership organization and the more technically oriented service organization.

DINADECO began to organize community groups in the rural sector during the José Figueres administration (1970–74). The associations were used to promote local participation and capacity building. In addition, higher-level structures like unions were stressed. PURISCAL is one of fifty unions of community development associations in Costa Rica.

From their creation to the present, community associations and their unions have received support from the state—through a fixed income from a percentage of the property tax—and credit from the Popular Bank. In addition, community associations are often used to channel funds that members of congress appropriate to their constituencies while in office.

Origin of PURISCAL

In the early 1970s, a community worker from DINADECO spent six months in the Puriscal area encouraging the development of community associations. There a young, charismatic leader, greatly inspired by the new form of organization fostered by the state representative, organized his community into an association and in 1975 became its first president.

Almost all activities carried out by these associations were related to community-built infrastructure—mainly aqueducts, sewage and drainage systems, and roads. These needs were very pressing, but the farmer communities felt that their most serious problem was being overcharged by the commercial input stores. However, financing, constructing, and managing a store of their own was beyond their capabilities. Thus, a second-level organization was formed in an attempt to fulfill the need for a service that could not be obtained from the associations. The local leader mentioned above played the role of a catalyst in the creation of a union that affiliated seven associations and 700 members. By 1984, the membership had grown to twenty-six associations with a total of approximately 3,000 members.

The legal status of PURISCAL is that of a private, nonprofit community organization formed to foster the cultural and economic development of the region, according to the Law and Regulation on Community Development. The general assembly of PURISCAL, which is made up of elected representatives of the associations, elects a seven-member board of directors.

Coordinating Independent Efforts

From 1976 to 1982, while searching for the funds needed for the project, the union was mainly trying to stay alive as an organization. Its leaders had to constantly remind the members of the associations to elect representatives and participate in the general assembly meetings. The distance from association to association and from house to house in the communities made communication and dissemination of information very difficult. Keeping PURISCAL alive during the difficult fund-raising years was an achievement in itself.

In the late 1970s, the regional director of the Ministry of Agriculture tried to coordinate the independent efforts of PURISCAL, the Centro Agrícola Cantonal (CAC), and the regional cooperative (COOPEPURISCAL) to build and operate an agricultural supply store in Santiago de Puriscal. The cooperative splintered off to pursue its own goals, but PURISCAL and CAC became partners.

CAC, a regional service organization, was created in 1969 by the government as a municipal body formed by farmers and professionals. It began its activities in 1971 with a reforestation project and became an autonomous institution two years later with the objective of mediating between the different government agencies in the area. Gradually, the center developed its own technical and administrative capacity to manage projects in the entire canton. It now operates a processing plant for cattle feed, an apiculture project, an agricultural credit program, a fruit tree nursery, a warehouse, and the new agricultural supply store.

The store was set up in 1982 to be comanaged by PURISCAL and CAC. To compensate for PURISCAL's partial loss of control over store matters, farmers from its board were given director positions at CAC. The original store started with $18,000 in capital, enough to cover initial operation and inventory costs. Member associations had initially contributed $100 each for the store project. Later they managed to get a loan from the Popular Bank for $178,000 and a piece of land in the city of Puriscal from the municipality. In 1984, part of an IDB loan to CAC in the amount of $145,000 permitted the store to become fully capitalized. PURISCAL assumed legal responsibility for the repayment of the loan and had to pay 8 percent interest to CAC. CAC, in turn, paid 1 percent interest on the IDB loan.

PURISCAL was also coresponsible for managing the store. Because all members and directors were volunteers who held regular jobs and did not have the time to administer such a large venture, they decided to create a five-member administrative council. Four members were to be selected by PURISCAL and one by CAC. The administrative council members elected by PURISCAL were also the directors and administrators of CAC. Two of them held paid managerial and administrative positions and were regarded as highly skilled. The other two were important local figures that sat on CAC's board. PURISCAL thought it had made a smart move by making CAC indirectly responsible for the store. As time went by, however, PURISCAL began to realize it had lost much of its decisionmaking power to CAC.

How the Store Operates

The store operates basically as a consumer cooperative and sells products at 10 percent over wholesale price to cover operating costs, which include the transportation of agricultural inputs to the more distant associations. In the beginning, only member associations were permitted to use the store, but the store later began selling to nonmembers as well. This was possible because the primary objective was not to subsidize inputs but rather to provide fixed and stable prices for the area. The fact that commercial stores often unite to offset the cooperative impact is proof that such a strategy can be successful.

The store's goals are not only to stabilize prices in the area but also to sell at a large enough volume to become self-sustaining. In this way, CAC gains by being able to expand its services: The store will become the main distribution outlet for feed concentrates produced at CAC's new processing plant. PURISCAL also has tangible results to show to the member organizations that contributed. Thanks to an IAF grant, PURISCAL has been able to start some training programs and hire a veterinarian and an agronomist who will serve as extension workers.

The project has managed to overcome its biggest crisis to date, which occurred when the local leader was replaced by a highly trained outsider hired by the administrative council. At that point, the administrative council had come under control of CAC, as mentioned above. Thus, the store improved its administrative capabilities and increased sales, but it also lost the support of many of the local leader's followers.

IAF Involvement

The Inter-American Foundation has funded PURISCAL and two of the member associations. The grant for $33,500 in 1985 was used to purchase office equipment, hire a secretary, and buy a passenger vehicle. Initially it was thought of as a complementary grant to the store project, but it actually served to strengthen and give more leverage to the original creators of the store, who have become increasingly overshadowed by the more experienced CAC leaders. IAF's support gave PURISCAL a chance to pursue its own smaller projects, such as the training program and an agricultural information bulletin. It also made the union feel more secure and enabled it to take an independent stance when CAC became domineering and paternalistic.

IAF considers PURISCAL an effective intermediary-type organization but also understands its limitations. The IAF funded the store because it had the potential to become economically viable and benefit a large number of people. The IAF's grant also included money for PURISCAL's training projects, thus adding a social element. However, the Foundation, realizing that PURISCAL did not have the organizational capacity to channel resources to the associations, decided to fund the other grantees individually.

The Success of the Store

The joint project between PURISCAL and CAC is exemplary. The first arrangement of its sort in Costa Rica, the store has been successful and has reached economies of scale where individual efforts have been fruitless. Yet it does not replicate the government's efforts. It needs fewer staff and keeps the decisionmaking process closer to the bases. Perhaps most important, the joint project combines two different types of intermediaries with different comparative advantages: on the one hand, a somewhat elitist, highly capable and educated group of *técnicos*, originally recruited for agricultural production projects; on the other hand, a less-experienced base-group leadership initially organized for community projects.

The case illustrates the tensions and complementarities that such a collaboration can engender, especially between the community leadership inherent in PURISCAL's structure and the CAC professionals. The supply-store project further illustrates the dilemma faced by an organization when it is confronted with the economic pressure to become more inclusive and serve nonmembers as well as members.

URCOOPAPA: Moving Away from Cooperative Ideals

The Unión Regional de Cooperativas de la Provincia de Cartago (URCOOPAPA) is one of the ten second-level cooperative bodies in Costa Rica. The URCOOPAPA case is a good example of how the state and the leaders of the cooperative sector interact. It is also illustrative of the difficulties that beset an exclusive commodity-oriented marketing organization, and how these difficulties forced it to become a nonexclusive multipurpose service agency, operating along business lines.

The cooperative sector in Costa Rica is significant: It includes approximately 400 cooperatives with 200,000 members: about 25 percent of the economically active population. This sector has received a great deal of government support, particularly from the Partido de Liberación Nacional (PLN), which has created a number of autonomous cooperative support organizations. In the 1960s the cooperative movement gained momentum with the support of the Alliance for Progress. During these years, base groups began forming federations. In the 1970s the cooperative sector grew steadily. Four new second-level cooperatives were created, among them URCOOPAPA. The state has created policies that are very favorable toward the cooperative movement. These include fiscal and tax advantages, official subsidies, reduction in all freight charges, and preferential consideration in many other areas.

The Union's Difficult Origins

URCOOPAPA's origins date back to 1974–75, when a group of potato farmers from Cartago collectively attempted to solve their processing and marketing problems. The leaders of three co-ops, motivated and supported by government promoters, embarked on a regional effort to market potatoes and formed URCOOPAPA. But a consensus at the member level was never reached.

Each of the three cooperatives was at a different stage of consolidation, but all were relatively weak. Two more cooperatives joined later, but still none of the members was in a position to set up a successful potato marketing union: some were too weak financially; others did not focus on the activities required to further URCOOPAPA's operations. By 1986, the union had eight affiliates with a total of 4,500 members. It kept adding more co-ops because it hoped to become a regional power rather than a federation with a monopoly on a single product.

One of the main problems between URCOOPAPA and its members was that the delegates of the three founding co-ops divided the most important union positions among themselves and directed their attention to the second-level organization. At the same time, the base co-ops were more concerned about their immediate crises than about building up an organization that did not immediately solve their problems. By 1979, the co-ops began questioning the union's goals and criticized it for its lack of progress in meeting them. The co-ops expected the union to provide them with subsidies and low-interest loans; for its part, the union wanted financial assistance from its members.

URCOOPAPA's first activity was to conduct a study of the region's medium-and small-scale farmers. It found that the main problems were overproduction caused by lack of planning and the oligopolistic nature of the marketing structure. URCOOPAPA believed that it could eliminate the uncertainties of the present system by providing an alternative marketing channel for its members. The first step was to build storage facilities for the vegetables produced in the area. Despite a very rough beginning, the union managed to build an impressive plant and learn how to operate it effectively, eventually consolidating many important market outlets. By 1983, URCOOPAPA's presence in the area had stabilized commercial practices and improved the quality of the produce. With the introduction of trademarks and better packaging methods, URCOOPAPA has made shipping and handling easier. The storage facilities have made it possible to supply the markets in low-production seasons.

In addition to the storage plant, URCOOPAPA opened an agricultural supply store, set up a credit and training program, and developed a research project for agricultural diversification and the improvement of potato seeds.

URCOOPAPA divided its functions into organizational departments that would charge for services and were expected to become self-sufficient. The more socially oriented programs were to be subsidized by the income-generating functions. Yet it seems clear that the price for efficiency and financial soundness in this case was likely to be a loss of small-farm orientation.

URCOOPAPA's Transformation

In 1977, URCOOPAPA's leaders, deciding that they needed a manager, hired a young, ambitious engineer who soon took over the helm of the organization. A growing administrative elite began to dominate the board of directors. This came about in part because all staff were also members of the union. Thus they had the double status of member and paid employee. As members they could also participate at the director level and head the different ad hoc committees and councils. In addition, they could become members of the administrative council, which hires and re-elects the manager.

In 1983, INFOCOOP (the national government entity supervising co-ops) gave URCOOPAPA authorization to deal with individual members directly, abandoning its exclusively second-level status. In 1984, the Law of Cooperative Associations was amended to allow the creation of a hybrid cooperative: one that functioned as both a first- and a second-level entity. In 1986, the board of directors of the National Production Council (CNP) agreed to provide URCOOPAPA with $835,000 through the purchase of shares. The state, in turn, provided the CNP with the necessary backup resources to place the federation on a sound financial footing. In exchange, the CNP was given one seat in the cooperative's administrative council. URCOOPAPA was now transformed into the Cooperativa Cogestionaria Agro-Industrial de Servicios Multiples de Cartago, (HORTICOOP).

After an initial period of experimentation with potato processing, HORTICOOP decided that its future was not in the storage and marketing of potatoes alone but in expansion and diversification of services. The union realized that unless it could secure national and/or international funds indefinitely, it would have to become more efficient to survive. Decentralization of administration, diversification of services, and an upgrading of staff were seen as partial solutions to past inefficiencies and financial crises.

Power struggles were an important factor in making a second-level cooperative "scale down" into a first-level one. A few influential farmers requested decisionmaking capabilities proportional to their financial contributions. In response, the manager and top personnel decided to transform the union into a first-level comanaged cooperative. The co-ops decided to stay on as members, even though they could no longer control the general assembly.

In the general assembly, all farmer members and workers had one vote, but each co-op had only one representative. In 1986, the ratio of co-ops and farmers on the administrative council—formerly four to three— became three to one and included two additional worker representatives. Three subcommittees were created. Today all are headed by top administrative personnel who are paid staff as well as affiliates of the cooperative. The struggles at the operational level were smoothed out by giving all the directors and chiefs of the departments the same status.

URCOOPAPA's original sections and departments were transformed into four divisions in 1984. During the transformation a fifth division was added, so although the organization scaled down in level, it nevertheless expanded its activities and was restructured in such a way that a tremendous future growth was possible.

A Second Chance

Without the heavy debts, the cooperative had a second chance to succeed. In November 1985, when management was planning the transformation, it was decided that the five divisions had to aim at financial self-sufficiency. The question now became which functions could realistically be self-sufficient, and which had to remain subsidized because of their social importance?

The changes in the organizational structure illustrate the efforts of one organization to rethink and reorganize its operations, so that the new cooperative could become economically viable.

Success in Attracting Funds

URCOOPAPA was highly resourceful in attracting funding. Its political contacts gained it access to money channeled directly from the state in the form of grants and loans from INFOCOOP, the State Bank, the Centro Agrícola Cantonal, the Law of Financial Equilibrium, the Tax Law on Cement, and the National Production Board, which agreed to absorb URCOOPAPA's debts as it reorganized. It received technical assistance from many institutions, including the Ministry of Agriculture, and many autonomous public agencies.

Both URCOOPAPA and HORTICOOP also received private funds, both through "intermediary" private organizations and international donors. The Association for the Development of the Small Entrepreneur (ADEPE), for example, made funds available for the supervised credit projects. FUCODES, the Potato Seed Association, and the Biological Services of Costa Rica supplied assistance. USAID provided grants for the seed and diversification project and for a study on the feasibility of exporting perishables and a loan for marketing and agroindustry feasibility studies.

In 1980, the IAF gave URCOOPAPA its first grant for $3,210 as part of a preliminary investigation to enable some officials of the union to visit modern processing and storage facilities in the United States. The second grant for $300,730 was to provide working capital for the new potato storage and packaging facility. In addition, the grant was used to purchase new potato-cleaning equipment that brushed rather than washed the vegetables. The purpose was to obtain a product that could be stored longer. In 1983, a third grant, in the amount of $2,225, was used to send the manager to another training course.

This case illustrates the close relations between the state and the cooperative sector in Costa Rica. It is also an example of the financial problems most co-op federations have. Most important, this case shows how a weak base, with little capacity to strengthen the federation, led URCOOPAPA to move away from an intermediary status toward a hybrid form in which both base co-ops and individual members are served.

13

Profiles from Chile

Country Context

The contextual framework for understanding contemporary nongovernmental organizations (NGOs) in Chile is the traumatic events of the 1970s: first, the attempts of the Allende regime to take Chile down the road to socialism, followed by the ferocious military coup and the repressive dictatorship that lasted for sixteen years. In the rural sector, the agrarian reforms begun under the administration of Eduardo Frei, but much intensified during the Salvador Allende years, have created new forms of rural organizations and also a state apparatus for campesino mobilization and support to the bases. Most of this structure was dismantled, and the remaining peasant-based groups were constantly harassed during the Augusto Pinochet years. Yet the movement provided some of the conditions leading to the emergence of new kinds of civic developmental institutions.

First, a vast array of informal grassroots organizations initially focused on providing daily subsistence, including such basic needs as food, health care, housing, and later on employment and small-scale productive endeavors. These grassroots associations served rural and urban poor people as a buffer against the hardships that accompanied the junta's radical restructuring of the Chilean economy.

Second, all this grassroots activity gave rise to, but also was made possible by, a support structure of newly organized grassroots support organizations (GSOs), often sponsored by church authorities. The Catholic church in Chile has played a key role in launching intermediary organizations to support human rights and grassroots survival groups. It has also served as an umbrella over other NGOs by protecting and legitimizing them during the years of persecution, when all organizing was suspect. Chilean intellectuals and socially committed professionals displaced from government and university positions gravitated to the new NGOs, whose social-service work was made possible by a host of European and North American donors anxious to channel poverty aid through nongovernmental intermediaries.

236

The Chilean NGO universe is especially rich in research and social-advocacy centers. It is significant that many middle- and upper-class intellectuals and academics became directly involved in grassroots action programs of a practical nature. Writes Brian Loveman (1991):

> The military regime's repressive policies and emphasis upon reducing the role of the public sector had the unintended consequence of spawning a panoply of nongovernmental organizations which provided employment and income for displaced professionals and political appointments of the regime. . . . These NGOs came to occupy a unique place in Chilean political life, in Chilean society and in the Chilean economy. (p. 10, 13)

In the rural scene, as in Peru, NGO activity in Chile is enmeshed in the aftermath of the agrarian reforms of the 1960s and early 1970s. It is notable that rural organization of peasants and farm laborers in Chile was not permitted before 1960—a symptom of Chilean dualism in which a modern urban industrial sector, with all the civic and workplace-related institutions in place, coexisted with a backward, semifeudal rural sector.

The agrarian reforms, though partial and incomplete, put an end to the *hacienda*-based rural land system. A large number of new farmer organizations were created for the beneficiaries of new land rights, but also for other smallholders and rural workers. The collectively managed large ex-estates or *asentamientos* were dismantled (before they could prove their viability), but many other types of rural organizations survived, albeit in a reduced form. Among these were the farmers' cooperatives, some representing and serving the remaining reform enterprises, but most working with groups of individual small family farmers. One of the largest cooperative organizations is CAMPOCOOP, a multitiered membership support organization (MSO), and one of the smallest is SADECSA, both described below. The latter is a very interesting membership association made up of several *sociedades agrícolas*, another type of base group among land-reform beneficiaries.

The significance of these member-managed MSOs goes much beyond their role achieved in the survival strategies of the 1980s or as holding operations for the remnants of organized peasantry. The privatization and open-market orientation of the economic policies pursued under the military government achieved a remarkable transformation of Chilean agriculture, which has become a prime exporter of off-season fruits and vegetables to Northern markets. But this process has sidelined peasant-based farming and rendered smallholder competition with large agroindustrial complexes virtually impossible. The only way family farms can make it commercially is by forging cooperative links both in the supply of production technology and in marketing, so that they are able to acquire economies of scale and negotiating power.

Another type of GSO that is creatively supporting survival strategies among the rural and urban poor is CET. This organization promotes such things as urban gardens and low-input organic farming. It is not clear what the role of this type of GSO will be when the pressure to secure minimum livelihood based on self-help recedes. It is likely that CET and other such GSOs will join the ranks of the new wave of environmentalist NGOs to devise ecologically sustainable natural resource management systems.

A major intellectual current among Chilean NGOs is popular education, especially in organizations affiliated with the church. This concept includes elements of literacy, adult education, and vocational education, but also embodies the Freirean idea of mobilization through social awareness. The best known and largest of such Chilean GSOs in this field is CIDE, described below. In a way, CIDE is unlike other organizations profiled here, not only because of its subject matter but also because CIDE is mainly a generator and disseminator of educational methodologies for other NGOs and institutions.

As the 1990s began, the context in which Chilean NGOs had been operating was drastically shifting. In the coming decade NGOs will have to redefine their roles in relation to the state as well as their links to their base clientele and to external donors. GSOs in particular will have to consolidate and find new niches in Chilean society.

CAMPOCOOP: A Holding Operation for Chilean Cooperatives

The Confederación Nacional de Cooperativas Campesinas (CAMPOCOOP) is a large, third-level, national confederation of small-farm cooperatives in Chile. Its primary objective is to strengthen base cooperatives by rehabilitating and improving their administrative and technical capacities. The uniqueness of this cooperative organization can be traced to its difficult and checkered history, stemming largely from the sharp reversal suffered by the Chilean campesino sector after 1973. When the organization faced near bankruptcy and dissolution in 1982, campesino leaders took control and began the process of rebuilding it from the bottom up. At present, the confederation works through a network of seven regional-based federations to reach the seventy base cooperatives. At its peak in 1973, the confederation had nearly 80,000 members. Today it struggles to support about 7,000.

Membership Control

CAMPOCOOP is a genuine campesino organization, led and controlled by elected representatives who are delegates of the constituent co-ops.

The federations bring together cooperative members in the region to explore areas of mutual cooperation, formulate plans and projects, air grievances, conduct leadership and administrative training courses, and extend services and assistance to base cooperatives (credit, production planning, and purchase or renovation of equipment).

Members of the base cooperatives are former land-reform beneficiaries who were organized by the state—during the administrations of Eduardo Frei and Salvador Allende—into *asentamientos* or large production units. These were intended to be managed by their members. In 1969, CAMPOCOOP was formed to facilitate the channeling of state resources and technical assistance to both independent small farmers and farmers working collectively. Although few of the remaining cooperatives engage in collective production today, members do collectively purchase inputs and arrange for processing and marketing.

In 1981, CAMPOCOOP went through a serious financial crisis from which it emerged as a leaner, more competent, and much more democratic organization. Now technicians and other professionals work as employees and, unlike in the past, have only advisory roles in policymaking and planning.

Reactivating Regional Federations

Because most of the base cooperatives and regional federations remain severely decapitalized, organizationally weak, and susceptible to internal conflict stemming from past failures, CAMPOCOOP focuses on reactivating the regional federations—the key service units in the system. Because the federations exhibit different levels of strength, internal cohesion, productivity, financial indebtedness, and resource ownership, assistance is scaled and tailored to the needs and capacities of each.

In a strategic move to reinforce the already functioning cooperatives and to strengthen the cooperative structure, CAMPOCOOP launched a special technical and managerial support program for the regionally based federations. They have responded positively to the support program. However, there is still much work to be done in order to build the local institutional capacity of their organizations.

CAMPOCOOP's experience in reactivating intermediary organizations at this level points to a number of important prescriptions:

- Undertake an initial profile of the socioeconomic situation of small farmers in the region (present activities, potential productive activities, and specific needs and/or obstacles).
- Implement flexible programs. Each federation must be reactivated at its own pace with activities that are appropriate to its needs.
- Provide incentives or specific services to accompany the

federation during the reorganization process and to meet critical needs (credit, legal assistance, and negotiation with banks and public authorities).

- Provide timely and meaningful support (human, material, and financial), especially if the organization is troubled by extreme indebtedness, personality conflicts, leadership crises, or mismanagement.

CAMPOCOOP has chosen to focus on a few areas and pursue them intensively rather than expand to a number of areas because of its past experience, limited resources, and firm belief that the membership must control the organization. Both the leaders and technicians expressed the sentiment that it is better to have a decentralized organization in which the regional entities supervise activities and facilitate coordination among cooperatives and service or state organizations than to create a large bureaucratic body that becomes detached from its base. The goal is to generate conditions so that the federations will be able to provide important services and functions.

Recognizing the need to provide more than managerial assistance and leadership training at the regional level, CAMPOCOOP initiated a small program of rotating credit funds for the federations of Curicó and Concepción in 1983 and 1984. The programs and approaches differed in each instance, but the federations' ability to provide their members with valuable credit, albeit in small amounts, helped to rebuild and strengthen the federations themselves. The fund continues to rotate (remain capitalized) because the borrowers' interest rate is small and there is a low rate of arrearage.

The credit program met the more immediate needs of the members and prepared them for eventual commercial transactions with banks.

Trial of a Marketing Scheme

CAMPOCOOP once sponsored a unique marketing scheme that advocated an inward, information-based system of buying and selling among campesino cooperatives throughout Chile. The project centered around the regional federation FECOSUR, which was to design a marketing and transportation system for rural cooperatives that would benefit all the regional federations. The first stage focused on asking each of the federations to help collect information about local prices, product availability, and warehousing and transportation arrangements.

Despite the initial enthusiasm of the member cooperatives and the willingness of donors to wait for the administrative structure to be set up, the marketing project became mired in problems. First interrupted by an administrative reorganization at the confederation level and later frustrated by the lack of baseline group commitment, CAMPOCOOP leaders concluded that the general environment was not favorable and that member cooperatives were not yet ready to assume the responsibilities of an integrated marketing system.

In retrospect, it appears that the federations and cooperatives were not yet capable of the commitment needed to make a marketing scheme successful. There was little individual obligation or loyalty to stick with the joint marketing system if small farmers could obtain even a few cents more by selling individually.

The need for a marketing system that is controlled by small producers is clear, but in Chile the external forces that discourage and disrupt these collaborative ventures are strong. Because CAMPOCOOP is not in a situation to influence government policy or to control and impose its will on the baseline organizations, it can only continue to educate, prod, and encourage its members to look beyond short-run gains.

The marketing scheme experiment reinforced the confederation's emphasis on training and the need to develop a critical awareness among the campesinos of the benefits of working together.

Banking on the Future

CAMPOCOOP is a special kind of intermediary organization because it is truly membership controlled. It had to rebuild its internal structure and ideology from the ground up. External factors obligated the organization to redefine the role of cooperativism for Chilean small farmers and its own role in serving them. Internal conditions forced the organization to reevaluate its services and methodologies and to examine the causes for its loss of contact with the base.

In its present state, CAMPOCOOP is functioning much below capacity because of limited access to material and financial resources. As in the case of other membership federations, it is hard to build a strong upper-tier organization when the base units are weak. However, CAMPOCOOP is successful as a "holding operation" for Chilean co-ops. It is likely that a future government will look more favorably on campesino organizations. Then CAMPOCOOP may be permitted to fulfill its original role. For now, CAMPOCOOP continues to work and rebuild where it can, using whatever resources are available to assist its members to defend their interests and articulate their needs.

CET: Counting on Beneficiaries to Manage Effective Technology

The Centro de Educación y Tecnología (CET) is a private, technically oriented organization whose objective is to provide low-cost, manageable food and shelter production methods for the rural and urban poor.

CET has an inward-looking strategy of development, one that attempts to reduce beneficiary dependence on outside materials and assistance and to maximize efficient use of locally available resources. CET works among a variety of clients but is most successful with landless rural town dwellers and urban unemployed women and youth. CET's main program is to promote organic gardening, which has been adopted by thousands of Chilean families. Other areas where CET is active include the design and construction of basic housing, food preparation, and social organization.

Basic Production Systems

CET has identified five basic production systems that reflect the situation of the small farmer and rural laborer in Chile:

1. *Pobladores rurales* (rural town dwellers) are peasants living in rural towns or in the rural periphery. They are rural laborers, the unemployed, or workers for government programs. Plots of land are very small, between 100 and 500 square meters per family. CET's productive system for this group centers on the "intensive family garden," to which a small module for chickens, fruit trees, a solar dryer, and beehives can be added.

2. *Minifundistas* usually own parcels of land that are too small (less than a hectare) to permit a family to live off their production. These farmers often engage in temporary labor arrangements on neighboring *fundos* (large estates) to supplement their income. The system designed for this group is similar to the one for the rural town dwellers but designed for a larger plot (500 to 800 square meters). On the remaining land, crops are cultivated in sections on a six-year rotational basis, with 50 percent of the area planted and 50 percent left for natural pastures.

   Crops are diversified and production is both for family consumption and for market. The production system, which is referred to as the *huerta orgánica campesina,* also includes ten chickens, one pig, and a milk cow to be kept on a half-hectare plot. All construction is with local materials.

3. *Parceleros de la reforma agraria* (small landholders of the agrarian reform) are the smallholders who benefited from the agrarian reform and have received ten to twenty hectares of land under irrigation. Many had belonged to the government-sponsored *asentamientos,* or ex-estates, which were dissolved after 1973.

   The production unit developed for the parceleros combines home consumption and commercial production. Fruit and pine trees (and other commercially marketable trees) are included in the system. It also employs a rotation of four to six years, depending on soil conditions, and emphasizes market production so that farmers can use such income to meet family needs. (CET believes that by satisfying family food needs through their own production the *parceleros* can save money and use it to pay off the land.)

4. *Pequeños propietarios del secano* (small landholders of the unirrigated drylands) face unique, often unpredictable geographical conditions that make farming activities highly risky. The *secano* (drylands) area is characterized by poor soils and a lack of water. The soil conditions severely limit the type of agriculture that can be undertaken, and there are problems with erosion. Again, the model is based on family consumption and on the *huerta orgánica campesina* but incorporates practices that will conserve water and soil (terracing, contouring).

5. *Sociedades campesinas del secano* (cooperative holdings of the unirrigated drylands) are the *ex-asentados* (former beneficiaries and members of reform co-ops) of land reform. They have large common landholdings because of the poor soil quality and lack of irrigation. The sociedades are situated on large tracts of land from 500 to 2,000 hectares. Like the smallholders, the sociedades must pay off their land. This intensifies their need to produce for the market.

   The productive system for the *sociedades* stresses subsistence farming but includes income-generating activities, long rotations, sheep and cattle raising, improved pastures, planting of forests for commercial exploitation (rotating sections), and experimentation with different combinations of crops and trees.

CET's Most Impressive Projects

Although CET has so far channeled most of its efforts toward improving the lot of small farmers and rural town dwellers, some of its most impressive projects are in the urban *poblaciones* (neighborhoods) of Santiago and the bankrupt semi-industrial towns near Concepción.

Basically, CET's starting point—the intensive family garden—has been used to organize groups of women and youths as a mechanism to motivate and stimulate these enclave communities. The women work cooperatively to dig and plant gardens in each member's yard. The gardens are relatively new but are already producing despite the lack of local resources. The women have proven resourceful. To alleviate the chronic shortage of animal and food wastes essential to maintain the soil quality, they have devised a rotating system of teams to collect the *desechos* (greens and other discards) left by the vegetable vendors on market days.

Another important and emerging activity of CET is in basic house construction, using a combination of wood, mud, straw, and other locally available materials. Although this activity is relatively new and not yet widely diffused, CET hopes to continue experimenting with designs, low-cost materials, and collaborative agreements with local governments to give it wider appeal.

Many of CET's resources and energies are devoted to training. CET operates three training and demonstration centers in three distinct regions (one outside the Santiago metropolitan area and two others in the south). These centers have been established in areas where CET already has strong ties with communities and local organizations. Besides training "monitors," locally based volunteers who in turn teach the fundamentals of organic gardening in their communities, CET also trains and advises the staffs of other intermediary and local organizations.

An important spin-off of training other private social-action organizations has been the formation of a group of twenty like-minded organizations called the Acuerdo de Colina. This group convenes periodically to promote the discussion of common issues and concerns and to exchange information on ongoing projects.

A Unique Methodology

CET's methodology is unique among Chilean intermediary organizations in that it focuses on the beneficiary's ability to grasp and manage an effective technology. This technology is not just for his or her own use, but to share with neighbors and family members.

Limited by a small staff and the fixed capacity of the training centers, CET relies on a system of volunteer monitors to motivate and diffuse its program to a larger audience. Like other intermediary organizations, CET has found that the monitor system is an effective and economic method of program expansion. It also adds an important element of participation, local control, and local capacity building that somewhat counterbalances the top-down aspects of the organization.

CIAL, CET's sister organization, is devoted to research issues involving organic production. CIAL acts as a coordinating center to bring together professionals, academicians, and students with links to research centers and universities that are involved in research and/or the teaching and diffusion of organic agriculture in Chile.

CET's good performance can be attributed to a number of factors: clearly defined pragmatic objectives, a well-run internal organization, carefully chosen beneficiary groups; a participatory methodology; concentration of activities around the three regional centers, and a high level of technical competence. Furthermore, CET has attained a certain degree of financial stability and has developed strong linkages to academic and research centers and to other intermediary organizations.

CIDE: Action-Oriented Popular Education Programs for the Disadvantaged

The Centro de Investigación y Desarrollo de la Educación (CIDE) is a large church-based foundation working in the area of nonformal education. As an older, well-respected organization, CIDE has aggressively pursued close working relationships with a wide range of organizations operating at all levels in Chile and throughout Latin America. These relationships are what gives CIDE so much influence in the development arena. CIDE has also successfully managed an impressive portfolio of projects funded by international donor agencies. However, in more recent years, a large number of small short-term projects appears to have contributed to the increasing bureaucratization of the organization.

Considered the leading institution of its kind in Chile, CIDE supports grassroots initiatives on various fronts. It implements community-based projects, conducts research, prepares educational materials, trains community leaders, offers evaluative assistance, and plays an influential role in shaping the methodology of social development programs in Chile. In contrast to the other profiles presented in this book, CIDE is a GSO whose function is mainly in servicing other NGOs and complementing their work.

CIDE's Early Years

CIDE was established in 1964, a period reflecting the Catholic church's increasing participation in social work programs in Chile. To carry out its objectives, the church created autonomous foundations and institutions to develop and implement social programs—always with an official board of directors that included church and lay members.

In its early years, CIDE served as a research and information-collecting body focusing on private education in Chile. During this time, CIDE began to publish its monthly journal, *Cuadernos de Educación*, which continues to be an important vehicle for disseminating research and related developments in the field of nonformal education.

In 1970, when Jesuit educator Patricio Cariola assumed the directorship of CIDE, the institution initiated a period of reorientation and change that reflected larger shifts of thinking in the field of education. CIDE remained small, but the staff became more involved in pursuing serious research. This eventually led to many staff members studying abroad in master's and doctoral programs. Also in the early 1970s, CIDE was influenced by Paulo Freire and Ivan Illich and their experimentations with adult education and liberationist ideologies, which gained widespread interest and attention in Chile.

The military coup of 1973 proved to be a catalytic event for CIDE. It forced the organization to assume an urgent, active role in representing the disadvantaged sectors of Chilean society. As the new government sought to methodically destroy the elaborate network of publicly supported social programs, CIDE formed important links with other church-based organizations, namely the Vicaría de la Solidaridad, to continue providing assistance to and programs for the urban and rural poor.

During the years 1974 to 1977, CIDE introduced a series of new educational tools such as simulation games, booklets, and dramatizations. The program took on some new directions:

- Integration of more technical materials and subjects into educational projects.
- Formation and consolidation of organizational networks (in both urban and rural areas).
- A stronger focus on the role of popular education within the broader context of social and economic development.

Research and Development

CIDE's activities are divided between research and educational support. The organization manages an extensive portfolio of development activities in nearly every region of the country, including urban-based skills programs for unemployed youth, cultural and educational activities in isolated rural communities, and a bookkeeping/management training course for small farmers and institutions.

Typically, CIDE projects complement other activities sponsored by locally based institutions, such as rural parishes, community organizations, cooperatives, and urban neighborhood associations, and with other NGOs working with base groups. CIDE staff train local monitors, or community promotors, who are then responsible for transferring the methodology and course content to the project beneficiaries. Monitors are often responsible for organizing and providing support to beneficiary groups. Seldom do CIDE project staff work directly with project beneficiaries—a more typical mode of operation among GSOs—nor does it provide assistance to the same beneficiary groups over a sustained period. Projects are seen as a point of entry to encourage the formation of popular organizations and enhance local capacity.

CIDE's research program is conducted under a separate unit. Various evaluations have pointed out that there is not enough integration between the research and action programs.

Project Benefits

The primary benefits of many CIDE action projects accrue disproportionately to the monitors. Although there is great variation from project to project, the interviews with CIDE staff, monitors, and base participants suggest this pattern of benefits.

What are the principal benefits of CIDE action projects? First, many of the project participants—especially the monitors—exhibit a heightened sense of self-confidence and self-esteem as a result of having participated in CIDE's projects. Second, CIDE projects often succeed in strengthening communication, organization, and leadership capacities. Many former monitors—and a much lower number of base participants—have continued to perform leadership roles in their communities, serving as monitors in other projects or consolidating their ties to local organizations. Many of CIDE's projects serve as vehicles through which participants become involved in broader community endeavors.

CIDE's action projects often deliver tangible benefits. Youths who take the electricity course, for example, are learning a practical skill that they use to find employment or at least use around their own houses and neighborhoods. The same can be said about the sewing course, since many of the participants intend to make clothes for themselves and their families. Further, CIDE's booklets have, from all accounts, resulted in better nutrition for the preschool children of project participants.

However, there are also some weaknesses. Interviews with former project participants indicate that the intensity of the benefits may diminish over time, although the effect seldom disappears altogether. It is also unclear to what extent CIDE's development projects achieve their more ambitious objectives. The benefits of heightened self-confidence and increased communication among project participants in rural and urban communities are important, but there is little evidence that they have been translated into broader accomplishments. It was difficult, for example, to find CIDE projects in which the participants had effectively engaged in collective action on a significant scale. This truncated chain or "spread" mechanism can be attributed in part to the limited possibilities for such activities in a highly controlled, authoritarian society. Politics clearly constrained CIDE's efforts to fully realize its development goals.

The last point is also related to the wider Chilean context. Although economic benefits (for example, increases in income, employment, production) are not central to CIDE's goals, it is hoped that over the long run the program will yield such gains. Field visits to a number of CIDE projects suggest, however, that the development sequence that begins at the psychological level seldom extends to the economic realm. There is little evidence, based on either objective indicators or participants' perceptions, that CIDE's action programs affect economic well-being. For example, participants in the skills training program for unemployed youths doubted that under present circumstances the mastery of a particular trade would result in stable employment. But even though the prospects for work are grim, they at least feel better about themselves as a result of their participation in the project. The broken sequence from popular education to economic gains has a lot to do with Chile's current economic crisis and the reduced opportunities for advancement.

Organization and Leadership

CIDE's current organizational structure can be described as hierarchical, complex, and somewhat ambiguous. The ad hoc growth and increasingly bureaucratic character of the organization is a result of CIDE's history and its tendency to assume new responsibilities and undertake new projects without anchoring them to the larger organizational objectives.

Father Patricio Cariola has served as CIDE's director for nearly sixteen years and is certainly the single most influential figure in molding and directing the organization's development. His charismatic leadership and high standards have encouraged an organizational culture based on loyalty, dedication, personal commitment, and creativity.

As CIDE has grown, it has become adept at cultivating international donor agencies and building close relationships with them. Support by many donors gives CIDE a high degree of flexibility. However, the current funding arrangements (short-term, project-specific agreements, with frequent reporting) are contributing to the administrative overload that will eventually affect project performance. There is an internal tension between living with the constant funding uncertainty and taking steps to reduce it.

There is little or no interaction between public agencies and CIDE's program areas. CIDE tried to work more closely with public school teachers, but mutual distrust and CIDE's view of itself as an "alternative" development organization have limited collaboration and transfer of methodologies. The private sector has shown little interest in the type of work CIDE conducts, diminishing the possibility that CIDE can generate more of its revenues from Chilean sources.

The competing tensions between the need to consolidate the organization and the numerous ongoing, unconnected projects that place increasing demands on the management have brought about several attempts at reorganization. CIDE believes that it must develop new institutional arrangements and procedures that will not sacrifice flexibility, creativity, and responsiveness.

Although CIDE works with different types of NGOs at different levels, it appears to be more effective in providing useful services to other support organizations, local institutions, and existing community groups than in directly organizing new groups at the community level. At the time of this field study, CIDE had had very few links with Chilean state agencies because of mutual antagonism. But this is certain to change in the future, opening up wider opportunities to affect the country's educational system.

SADECSA: Capacity Building at the Community Level

A small but dynamic organization, Sociedad de Asistencia Técnica, Comercialización y Desarrollo, Sociedades Agrícolas del Secano Ltda. (SADECSA) is a second-level association of four *sociedades agrícolas*, or small farmer societies, located in dispersed rural communities of Chile's coastal drylands.

SADECSA presents an interesting case because it is a locality-based MSO small enough to have continual personal interactions with its members. The organization performs intensive production-oriented support for its member societies, complemented by developing participatory processes and encouraging peasant expression. The organization's history also illuminates how concern with livelihood issues can spur local organization and capacity. SADECSA was formed because of an acutely felt need by the base societies to have an intermediary organization of sufficient scale to protect their land rights and to provide technical support in an extremely hostile environment.

Taking Over from CAMPOCOOP

Members of the base societies are former land-reform beneficiaries who were organized into productive *asentamientos*, or units, by the state. By and large, *asentamientos* in this region have been kept intact, despite hostile overtures by neighboring large landowners, and have maintained their joint-production mode. Agricultural production is particularly risky in this region because of poor soil conditions, erratic rainfall, and a lack of irrigation facilities.

Originally, the member societies of SADECSA were the beneficiaries of a comprehensive technical assistance project administered by CAMPOCOOP, a large cooperative federation. In 1981, when CAMPOCOOP withdrew from the project due to a severe internal crisis, the farmer societies banded together and, with the support of the project's technical director, successfully took over control of the project.

SADECSA's highly qualified technical team has transformed the once dormant societies into active productive units. Services provided by SADECSA include elaboration of each society's production plans, veterinary services, managerial and accounting services, access to purchasing of inputs and consumer goods, legal services, and a wide variety of courses ranging from home gardening to food preparation to sewing.

SADECSA's leaders expected to be able to carry out these activities without outside assistance within two years.

SADECSA's Strategies

A unique feature of SADECSA is the integration of women into the decisionmaking body. Initially only male members were elected to the general assembly, but now women have equal representation and decisionmaking responsibilities.

In the era of military government, the base communities had to struggle constantly to meet stringent administrative and financial conditions imposed to maintain their registered status as *sociedades agrícolas*. Legally, they could not increase their membership and had to remain solvent in order to keep their charter. To stabilize the precarious legal situation of societies whose charters were threatened by unreasonably tough regulations, SADECSA administered a rotating credit fund to permit those societies that needed legal assistance to contract for it. It was perhaps SADECSA's most valuable and timely service during the initial phases of the association. The strategy worked well. Each of the societies has been successful in negotiations with debtors and neighbors who were trying to encroach upon their lands. (Chile is a highly legalistic society, so that even in a very repressive situation, if one has good lawyers who can play the legal game, one can often beat the system.)

An increasing emphasis has been placed on training and diversifying production—particularly off-farm production. At the same time SADECSA embarked on a program of integrating all family members into its ongoing projects. The leadership and technical team have worked closely to formulate courses in food preparation, sewing, canning, family gardens, and small animal raising. These courses are intended for women and youth in the communities. The courses in home and family education provide women and youth with skills to improve their own family situations.

SADECSA has also been developing leaders' skills through workshops and courses. The IAF project application was formulated by representatives of the general assembly over a six-month period with the help of SADECSA's technical adviser. During the process, SADECSA's leaders were responsible for developing the project objectives, estimating the numbers of beneficiaries, preparing the budget, and so on.

These leaders have also participated in bookkeeping and tax seminars, and they offer a simplified course in order to keep staff and *cajeros* (accountant-treasurers) up-to-date about the latest reporting and tax regulations. This is particularly important, because the government can and will quickly dissolve any organization that does not keep accurate and current books.

SADECSA's Results

Although SADECSA is a relatively young organization, its activities have generated an immediate impact on members and their families. Despite numerous setbacks, including a devastating earthquake in 1985, SADECSA has managed a steady improvement in crop yields, higher-quality meat and wool, and a more rational use of member society land and water resources. Among the more concrete results are the following:

- Normalization of the land tenure situation.
- Organizational restructuring, use of improved accounting practices, and up-to-date books.
- Reorganization of production and work plans based on a rational use of each society's resources.
- Improved agricultural practices and adoption of technology.
- Joint and better marketing of products, which allows for increased profits.
- Rebates to members through SADECSA's earnings and each society's dividends.

The less visible results are still accumulating. They are related to capacity building at the community level for joint management. In SADECSA, this type of learning is easier than in larger MSOs, since the gap between base societies and their association is small.

Appendix: Rating Elements
for the Six Performance Indicators

A. Service Delivery
   1. Beneficiary Needs and Livelihood
      a. Services or products are of the type and quality that meet the needs of the beneficiaries; evidence of satisfaction
      b. Potential to enhance living levels; independent judgment of evaluators, taking into account exogenous factors
   2. Efficiency
      a. Supply of service distributed in a timely manner
      b. Share of target population actually reached by service
      c. Estimate of cost-effectiveness, where applicable and available
   3. Sustainability
      a. Position on continuum between routine replacement of public services and complementarity to public services
      b. Evidence that along with service, skill transfer or experiential learning is taking place
   4. Linkages
      a. GSO has developed linkages to financial, technical, and political resource centers
      b. GSO has achieved influence over some elements of service system that are not covered by projects

B. Poverty Reach
   1. Poverty Level
      a. Average level of beneficiaries within the income distribution spectrum (*ex ante*)
      b. Share of landless, women within beneficiary groups
   2. Benefit Distribution
      a. Relative equity of benefit distribution *within* the beneficiary groups, or relative degree of access to project benefits

C. Participation
   1. Initial Decisions
      a. Degree of beneficiary participation in project identification

and design; availability of mechanisms to facilitate such involvement

2. Implementation
   a. Opportunities for consultation or for shared decisionmaking during operation phase
3. Accountability
   a. Degree of representation of participants and leaders
   b. Members/beneficiaries have access to records, information
4. Resource Mobilization
   a. Beneficiary contributions (labor and materials) to projects
   b. Relative equity of sharing labor and other costs within group

D. Group Capacity Building
   1. Group Creation
      a. Promotion of group formation whether at the base or intermediary (membership) level
   2. Capacity Growth in Resource Management
      a. Evidence that group is learning to cooperate in effective management of common resources or collective tasks
      b. Reinforcement of system of rewards and sanctions for compliance with group norms
   3. Capacity Growth in Claim-Making
      a. Growth in ability of goal articulation, conflict resolution
      b. Leadership development to deal effectively with outside world (mobilization, bargaining)
   4. Weaning, Graduation
      a. Progress toward greater degree of independence and autonomy
      b. Progress toward acquisition of linkages to public or private services/resources after termination of projects

E. Innovation
   1. Technical
      a. Emergence of new or improved techniques that have potential for diffusion
   2. Institutional
      a. Development of more effective institutional approaches, training, extension methods, group processes of possible wider application

F. Policy Reach
   1. Horizontal Effects
      a. Evidence of reaching a significant number or "minimum mass" of beneficiaries, directly or indirectly
      b. Evidence of coalition building, networking, or cloning by the GSO

2. Regional
   a. Effects on regional economy attributable to GSO work
   b. Spillovers from exclusive clientele to wider circle
3. Vertical Influence
   a. Creation of new federative or associative structures
   b. Influence on public-sector institutions to improve quality of service
   c. Increase in public awareness of client problems and policy options
4. Macropolicy
   a. Legislative changes and other shifts in government procedures in relation to GSO's clientele
   b. Mobilization or redirection of public-sector resources more favorable to beneficiaries

Abbreviations

ACLO	Acción Cultural Loyola
ACORDE	Asociación Costarricense para el Desarrollo
ADEPE	Association for the Develpment of the Small Entrepreneur
ANAI*	Asociación de los Nuevos Alquimistas
ANTISUYO*	Asociación Civil Antisuyo
APCOB*	Ayuda para el Campesino del Oriente Boliviano
APP	Agua para el Pueblo
APRETA	Association of Small Reforesters of Talamanca
APRODESE	Asociación Pro-Desarrollo Económico
ASBANA	Asociación Bananera Nacional
ASEPADE	Asesores para el Desarrollo
CAC	Centro Agrícola Cantonal
CACH*	Centro Agrícola Cantonal de Hojancha
CAMPOCOOP*	Confederación Nacional de Cooperativas Campesinas
CAPS*	Centro de Autoformación para Promotores Sociales
CATIE	Centro Agronómico Tropical de Investigación y Enseñanza
CEDECUM*	Centro de Desarrollo para el Campesinado y del Poblador Urbano-Marginal
CENTRAL*	Central de Cooperativas Agrarias de Producción "3 de Octubre"
CET*	Centro de Educación y Tecnología
CIDE*	Centro de Investigación y Desarrollo de la Educación
CIDOB	Central de Pueblos y Comunidades Indígenas del Oriente Boliviano
CINDE	Development Initiative Coalition

255

CIPCA*	Centro de Investigación y Promoción del Campesino
CLU	Central Lanera Uruguaya
CNFR	Comisión Nacional Je Fomento Rural
CNP	National Production Council
COOPECHAYOTE	Cooperativa Agrícola Industrial de los Productores de Chayote
COOPETALAMANCA	Cooperativa de Servicios Multiples de Talamanca
CPC*	Centro Paraguayo de Cooperativistas
DAI	Development Alternatives, Inc.
DINADECO	National Directorate for the Development of the Community
EEC	European Economic Community
EL CEIBO*	Centro Regional de Cooperativas Agropecuarias e Industriales
ENCI	Empresa Nacional de Comercialización de Insumos
ESF	Emergency Social Fund
FAO	Food and Agriculture Organization
FCC	Federación de Cafeteros de Colombia
FDN*	Fundación para el Desarrollo Nacional
FEHMUC	Federación Hondureña de Mujeres Campesinas
FES	Fundación para la Educación
FETAG	Federacioes dos Trabalhadores na Agricultura
FIDENE*	Fundação de Integração, Desenvolvimento e Educação do Noroeste do Estado
FINCA	Foundation for International Community Assistance
FMDR*	Fundación Mexicana de Desarrollo Rural
FOV*	Federación de Organizaciones Voluntarias
FUCODES*	Fundación Costarricense de Desarrollo
FUNCOL*	Fundación para las Comunidades Colombianas
FUNDAEC	Fundación para la Aplicación y la Enseñanza de la Ciencias
FUNDE*	Fundación Nicaragüense de Desarrollo
GONGO	governmental/nongovernmental organization
GSO	grassroots support organization
HORTICOOP	Cooperativa Cogestionaria Agro-Industrial de Servicios Multiples de Cartago
IAF	Inter-American Foundation

IDB	Inter-American Development Bank
IIDI	Institute for International Development, Inc.
ILO	International Labour Organization
INA	National Learning Institute
INCAE	Instituto Centro-Americano de Administración de Empresas
INDES*	Instituto de Desarrollo Social y Promoción Humana
IPRU*	Instituto de Promoción Económico-Social del Uruguay
ISO	intermediary support organization
ITCR	Technical Institute of Costa Rica
IVS	International Voluntary Services, Inc.
JAPDEVA	Junta de Administración Portuaria de Desarrollo Económico de la Vertiente Atlántica
MDR	Movimiento para o Desenvolvimento Regional
MSO	membership support organization
NAISA	New Alchemy Institute S.A.
NBS	National Banking System
NDF	national development foundation
NGDO	nongovernmental development organization
NGO	nongovernmental organization
OEF	Overseas Education Fund
ORD*	Organization for Rural Development
OTA	Office of Technology Assessment
PACT	Private Agencies Collaborating Together
PADF	Pan American Development Foundation
PAIT	Programa de Apoyo al Ingreso Temporal
PEM	Programa de Empleo de Emergencia
PISCES	Program of Investment in the Small Capital Enterprise Sector
PLN	Partido de Liberación Nacional
PO	people's organization
PROTERRA*	Instituto Tecnológico Agrario Proterra
PSC	public service contractor
PURISCAL*	Unión Cantonal de Asociaciónes de Desarrollo de Puriscal
PVO	private voluntary organization
SADECSA*	Sociedad de Asistencia Técnica, Comercialización y Desarrollo, Sociedades Agrícolas del Secano Ltda.
SIF	Social Investment Fund
SINAMOS	Sistema Nacional de Movilización Social

SOLIDARIOS	Council of American Development Foundations
UELC	Unión of Ejidos Lázaro Cárdenas
UNDP	United Nations Development Programme
UNIDAD*	Unidad de Educación para el Desarrollo de Chimborazo
UNO*	União Nordestina de Assistência a Pequeñas Organizações
URCOOPAPA*	Unión Regional de Cooperativas de la Provincia de Cartago
USAID	U.S. Agency for International Development
USEMI*	Unión de Seglares Misioneros
VO	voluntary organization
WINBAM	Windward Islands Banana Growers' Association

*One of the thirty NGOs in the study sample.

Bibliography

Aguirre, Francisco. 1991. "Complementaridades y Tensiones en las Relaciones del Estado en el Desarollo Agrícola: Una Trayectoría." Paper presented in a workshop on Technology Generation and Diffusion, December, Santa Cruz, Bolivia.

Alberti, Giorgio, and Enrique Mayer, eds. 1974. *Reciprocidad e Intercambio en los Andes Peruanos*. Lima: Instituto de Estudios Peruanos.

Alliband, Terry. 1983. *Catalysts of Development: Voluntary Agencies in India*. West Hartford, CT: Kumarian Press.

Annis, Sheldon. 1987. "Can Small-Scale Development Be a Large-Scale Policy? The Case of Latin America." *World Development* 15 (Suppl.):129–134.

Annis, Sheldon, and Peter Hakim, eds. 1988. *Direct to the Poor: Grassroots Development in Latin America*. Boulder, CO: Lynne Rienner.

Arbab, Farzam. 1988. *Non-Governmental Organizations: Report of a Learning Project*. Reflections on Organizations for Development Document. Bogotá: Centro Latinamericano de Educación y Technología Rural (CELATER)/PACT.

Ashe, Jeffrey. 1985. *The PISCES II Experience: Local Efforts in Micro-enterprise Development. Vol. 1.* Washington, DC: U.S. Agency for International Development.

Avina, Jeffrey M., and Alan R. Lessik, with Arelis Gomez, John Butler, and Denise Humphreys. 1990. *Evaluating the Impact of the Inter-American Foundation*. Rosslyn, VA: Inter-American Foundation.

Ayres, Robert L. 1985. *Banking on the Poor*. Cambridge, MA: MIT Press.

Bebbington, Anthony. 1988. "Sustainability and Resilience East of the Andes: Some Implications of Farmer Knowledge and Economic Crisis for the Design and Monitoring of Agricultural Strategies." Manuscript, Centro Internacional de Papa (CIP), Lima.

Bebbington, Anthony. 1990a. "NGO-State Relationships in Latin American Agricultural Development: An Area Awaiting Innovative Strategies." Unpublished paper, Centre of Latin American Studies, Cambridge University, Cambridge, England.

Bebbington, Anthony. 1990b. "Peasant, Institutions and Technological Change in the Andes." Paper presented at the annual meeting of the Association of American Geographers, Toronto, Canada, April 1990.

Blayney, Robert G., and Diane B. Bendahmane. 1988. The *Inter-American Foundation and the Small and Micro-Enterprise Sector*. Rosslyn, VA: Inter-American Foundation.

Bowden, Peter. 1990. "NGOs in Asia: Issues in Development." *Public Administration and Development* 10:141–152.

Brana-Shute, Gary, et al. 1985. "Final Evaluation Report, Organization for Rural Development (ORD)." Manuscript from the files of the Inter-American Foundation, Rosslyn, VA.

Bray, David Barton 1991. "'Defiance' and the Search for Sustainable Small Farmer Organizations: A Paraguayan Case Study and a Research Agenda." *Human Organization* 50 (2):125–35.

Breslin, Patrick. 1987. *Development and Dignity: Grassroots Development and the Inter-American Foundation*. Rosslyn, VA: Inter-American Foundation.

Brown, David L., and David C. Korten. 1989. *Understanding Voluntary Organizations: Guidelines for Donors*. Public Sector Management and Private Sector Development Working Paper, Country Economics Development Department, World Bank, Washington, DC.

Buijs, Dieke. 1982. "The Participation Process: When It Starts." In *Participation of the Poor in Development*, edited by Benno Galjart and Dieke Buijs, 50–71. Leiden, Netherlands: Institute of Cultural and Social Studies, University of Leiden.

Carroll, Thomas F., and Helga Baitenmann. 1987. "Organizing Through Technology: A Case from Costa Rica." *Grassroots Development* 11(2):12–20.

Carroll, Thomas F., Helga Baitenmann, and Denise Humphreys. 1987. "A Typology of Grassroots Support Organizations." Manuscript prepared for the Inter-American Foundation, Rosslyn, VA.

Carroll, Thomas, Denise Humphreys, and Martin J. Scurrah. 1989. "Organizaciones de Apoyo a Grupes de Base en el Peru: Una Radiografía." *Socialismo y Participación* (Lima) 50:37–51.

Carroll, Thomas F., and John D. Montgomery. 1987. *Supporting Grassroots Organizations*. Cambridge, MA: Lincoln Institute of Land Policy.

Catholic Relief Services (CRS)/SED. 1991. "Inter-PVO Working Session, Village Banking." Working session paper, Baltimore, MD.

Centro de Investigación y Promoción del Campesinado (CIPCA). 1987. "Evaluación Conjunta de la Institución: Informe Final de la Misión Evaluadora." Manuscript, Piura, Peru.

Chambers, Robert. 1983. *Rural Development: Putting the Last First*. London: Longman.

de Janvry, Alain. 1983. "Perspectives for Inter-American Foundation Programs in Chilean Agriculture." Report prepared for the Inter-American Foundation, Rosslyn, VA.

de Janvry, Alain, Robin Marsh, David Runsten, Elizabeth Sadoulet, and Carol Zabin. 1988. *Rural Development in Latin America: An Evaluation and a Proposal*. Monograph prepared for the Inter-American Institute for Agricultural Cooperation (IICA). Berkeley, CA: University of California, Giannini Hall.

Development Alternatives, Inc. (DAI), and Cornell University. 1985. *Private Voluntary Organizations and Institutional Development: Lessons from International Voluntary Services, Inc., and the Institute of International Development, Inc.* Washington, DC: Authors.

Devres, Inc. 1988. *Synthesis of AID Evaluation Reports: FY 1985 and FY 1986*. USAID Evaluation Occasional Paper No. 16. Washington, DC: U.S. Agency for International Development.

Diskin, Martin, Steven Sanderson, and William Thiesenhusen. 1987. *Business and Development: A Workable Partnership*. Rosslyn, VA: Inter-American Foundation.

Douglas, David. 1990. "In the Vessel's Wake: The U.N. Water Decade and Its Legacy." *Grassroots Development* 14(2):2–11.

Drabek, Anne Gordon. 1987. "Development Alternatives: The Challenge for NGOs: An Overview of the Issues." *World Development* 15 (Suppl.):ix–xv.

Edgecomb, Elaine, and James Cawley. 1991. "The Process of Institutional Development: Assisting Small Enterprise Institutions to Become More Effective." GEMINI Working Paper No. 15, Bethesda, MD.

Esman, Milton J., and John D. Montgomery. 1980. "The Administration of Human

Development." In *Implementing Human Development*, edited by Peter T. Knight (World Bank Working Paper, No. 403). Washington, DC: World Bank.

Esman, Milton, and Norman Uphoff. 1984. *Local Organizations: Intermediaries in Rural Development*. Ithaca, NY: Cornell University Press.

Evans, Sara, and Harold Boyte. 1986. *Free Spaces*. New York: Harper and Row.

Faller, Rudolf. 1984. *Informe de Evaluación de los Proyectos del BID para Crédito Agropecuario*. Washington, DC: Inter-American Development Bank.

Farbman, Michael, ed. 1981. *The PISCES Studies: Assisting the Smallest Economic Activities of the Urban Poor*. Washington, DC: U.S. Agency for International Development.

Ferrin, Cynthia L. 1983. "When the Price Is Right: Cooperative Marketing in Uruguay." *Grassroots Development* 7(2):39–42.

Ferrin, Cynthia L. 1989. *The Small Farmer Sector in Uruguay: A Partnership in Development Cooperation*. Rosslyn, VA: Inter-American Foundation.

Figueroa, Adolfo. 1986. *Productividad y Educacion en la Agricultura Campesina de American Latina*. Rio de Janeiro: Programa ECIEL.

Finsterbusch, Kurt, and Warren A. Van Wicklin III. 1987. "The Contribution of Beneficiary Participation to Development Project Effectiveness." *Public Administration and Development* 7:1–23.

Fite, Richard W. 1987. "A Critical Analysis of Selected Inter-American Foundation Projects in Peru." Paper prepared for Prof. T. F. Carroll, Kennedy School of Government, Harvard University.

Flora, Cornelia Butler, and Jan L. Flora 1985. "Community Stores in Rural Colombia: Organizing the Means of Consumption." *Grassroots Development* 9(1): 16–25.

Fonseca, César, and Enrique Mayer. 1988. *Comunidad y Producción en la Agricultura Andina*. Lima: FOMCIENCIAS.

Foster, George M. 1973. *Traditional Societies and Technological Change*. New York: Harper and Row.

Fox, Jonathan. 1989. "Grassroots Organizations vs. the Iron Law of Oligarchy: Reflections from the Mexican Peasant Movement." Manuscript, Massachusetts Institute of Technology, Cambridge, MA.

Fox, Jonathan, and Luis Hernandez. 1989. "Offsetting the Iron Law of Oligarchy: The Ebb and Flow of Leadership Accountability in a Regional Peasant Organization." *Grassroots Development* 13(2):8–15.

Frantz, Telmo Rudi. 1987. "The Role Of NGO's in the Strengthening of Civic Society." *World Development* 15 (Suppl.):121–27.

Freire, Paulo. 1970. *The Pedagogy of the Oppressed*. New York: Herder and Herder.

Friedmann, John, and Mauricio Salguero. 1987. "The Political Economy of Survival and Collective Self-Empowerment in Latin America: A Framework and Agenda for Research." Manuscript, University of California at Los Angeles.

Galjart, Benno. 1982. "Project Groups and Higher Level Associations." In *Participation of the Poor in Development*, edited by Benno Galjart and Dieke Buijs. Leiden, Netherlands: Institute of Culture and Social Studies, University of Leiden.

Garilao, Ernesto D. 1987. "Indigenous NGOs as Strategic Institutions: Managing the Relationship with Governments and Resource Agencies." *World Development* 15 (Suppl.):113–20.

Gaude, J., et al. 1987. "Rural Development and Labour-Intensive Schemes, Impact Studies of Some Pilot Programmes." *International Labour Review* 126(4) (July–August):203–219.

Gilleland, Lynn. 1988. "IAF-Funded Agricultural Marketing Projects." Draft report prepared for the Inter-American Foundation, Rosslyn, VA.

Gomez, Sergio. 1982. "Programas de Apoyo al Sector Campesino en Chile."

Working Paper No. 157. Santiago, Chile: Facultad Latinamericana de Ciencias Sociales.

Gomez, Sergio. 1989. "Nuevas Formas de Desarollo Rural en Chile: Analisis de los ONGs." In *Una Puerta Que Se Abre: Los Organizmos No Gubernamentales en la Cooperacion al Desarollo,* edited by Rodrigo Egaña and José Antonio Abalos, 139–72. Santiago, Chile: Taller de Cooperacion al Desarollo.

Goodell, Grace. 1985. "Paternalism, Patronage and Potlatch: The Dynamics of Giving and Being Given To." *Current Anthropology* 26(2):247–66.

Gorman, Robert F., ed. 1984. *Private Voluntary Organizations as Agents of Development.* Boulder, CO: Westview Press.

Gow, David D., et al. 1979. *Local Organizations and Rural Development: A Comparative Reappraisal.* Washington, DC: Development Alternatives, Inc.

Grijpstra, Bouwe. 1982. "Approaches to Initiating and Supervising Groups for Rural Development." *Rural Development Participation Review* 3(2):1–7.

Guggenheim, Scott, and Maritta Koch-Weser. 1991. "Participation for Sustainable Development." Draft report, NGO—World Bank Committee Meeting, 21–22 October 1991, Suraj Kund, India.

Hayami, Yujiro, and Vernon W. Ruttan. 1985. *Agricultural Development: An International Perspective.* Baltimore, MD: Johns Hopkins University Press.

Healy, Kevin. 1988. "A Recipe for Sweet Success: Consensus and Self-Reliance in the Alto Beni." *Grassroots Development* 12:32–40.

Hellinger, Douglas, et al. 1983. "Building Local Capacity for Sustainable Development." A.T. International Working Paper, Washington, DC.

Hirsch, Silvia Maria. 1988. "APCOB, CIDOB and the Capitana of Izozog: A Case of Grassroots Development in Bolivia." Paper prepared for the Inter-American Foundation from the author's doctoral research.

Hirschman, Albert O. 1984. *Getting Ahead Collectively: Grassroots Development in Latin America.* New York: Pergamon Press.

Hoff, Karla, and Joseph E. Stiglitz. 1990. "Imperfect Information and Rural Credit Markets: Puzzles and Policy Perspectives." *World Bank Economic Review* 4(3):235–50.

Holdcroft, Lane. 1978. *The Rise and Fall of Community Development in Developing Countries 1950–65.* Paper prepared for USAID, Office of Rural Development Administration, Michigan State University, East Lansing, MI.

Holt, Sharon. 1991. *Village Banking: A Cross-Country Study of a Community-Based Lending Methodology* (GEMINI Working Paper No. 25). Bethesda, MD: Growth with Equity through Microenterprise Investments and Institutions.

Honadle, George. 1981. *Fishing for Sustainability: The Role of Capacity Building in Development Administration.* Washington, DC: Development Alternatives, Inc.

Honadle, George. 1982. "Structural Aspects of Capacity Building, or Who Gets the Fish?" *Rural Development Participation Review* (Cornell University) 3, no. 3 (Spring) (special supplement on integrated rural development).

Honadle, George, and Jerry VanSant. 1985. *Implementation for Sustainability: Lessons from Integrated Rural Development.* West Hartford, CT: Kumarian Press.

Hornsby, Anne. 1989a. "Building 'Healthy' Organizations: Some Thoughts on Organizational Consulting for Economic Development." Paper prepared for the Inter-American Foundation Mid-term Conference of Doctoral Fellows, Quito, Ecuador.

Hornsby, Anne. 1989b. "Discussion Memo No. 2: On Social Utility." Paper prepared for the Inter-American Foundation Mid-term Conference of Doctoral Fellows, Quito, Ecuador.

Huffman, Sandra L. 1981. *A Review of the Inter-American Foundation's Support for Health Activities.* Rossyln, VA: Inter-American Foundation.

Humphreys, Denise. 1989. Private communication with the author.

Humphreys, Denise, Thomas Carroll, and Martin Scurrah. 1988. "Grassroots Development Organizations in Peru." Manuscript prepared for the Inter-American Foundation, Rosslyn, VA.

Inter-American Foundation. 1976. *They Know How . . . An Experiment in Development Assistance.* Rosslyn, VA: Inter-American Foundation.

Inter-American Foundation. 1985. "Memorandum on Reflections on a Foundation Learning Exercise on Intermediary Organizations." Internal memorandum, 25 March.

Johnston, Bruce F., and W. C. Clark. 1982. *Redesigning Rural Development.* Baltimore: Johns Hopkins University Press.

Jourdan, Catherine M. 1988. "Poverty Alleviation in Selected Rural Development Projects." M.A. dissertation, Graduate School of Arts & Sciences, George Washington University, Washington, DC.

Kilby, Peter, and David D'Zmura. 1985. *Searching for Benefits.* Special Study No. 28. Washington, DC: U.S. Agency for International Development.

Korten, David C. 1980. "Community Organizations and Rural Development: A Learning Process Approach." *Public Administration Review* 4(5):480–511 (September-October).

Korten, David C. 1987b. "Third Generation NGO Strategies: A Key to People-Centered Development." *World Development* 15 (Suppl.):145–60.

Korten, David C. 1990. *Getting to the 21st Century: Voluntary Action and the Global Agenda.* West Hartford, CT: Kumarian Press.

Lacroix, Richard L. J. 1985. *Integrated Rural Development in Latin America.* World Bank Staff Working Paper No. 716. Washington, DC: World Bank.

Ladim, Leilah. 1987. "Non-Governmental Organizations in Latin America." *World Development* 15 (Suppl.):29–38.

La Forgia, Gerard M. 1985. *Local Organizations for Rural Health in Panama: Community Participation, Bureaucratic Reorientation and Political Will.* Ithaca, NY: Rural Development Committee, Cornell University.

LaForgia, Gerard M. 1987. "Health Committee Federations in Panama." Report to the Inter-American Foundation, Rosslyn, VA.

Lassen, Cheryl A. 1989. "Evaluating the Impact of INCAE Management Training Programs for Grassroots Development Organizations." Manuscript from the files of the Inter-American Foundation, Rosslyn, VA.

Lehmann, David, ed. 1982. *Ecology and Exchange in the Andes.* Cambridge: Cambridge University Press.

Lehmann, David. 1990. *Democracy and Development in Latin America: Economics, Politics and Religion in the Post-War Period.* Philadelphia: Temple University Press.

Leonard, David K. 1982a. "Analyzing the Organizational Requirements for Serving the Rural Poor." In *Institutions of Rural Development for the Poor,* edited by David K. Leonard and Dale Rogers Marshall, 1–39. Berkeley, CA: Institute of International Studies, University of California.

Leonard, David K. 1982b. "Choosing among Forms of Decentralization and Linkage." In *Institutions of Rural Development for the Poor,* edited by David K. Leonard and Dale Rogers Marshall, 193–226. Berkeley, CA: Institute of International Studies, University of California.

Liebenson, Paul M. 1984. "Legal Services Projects of the Inter-American Foundation." Unpublished paper.

Loveman, Brian. 1991. "Private Development Organizations and International Cooperation: Chile 1973–1990." Article prepared for the Inter-American Foundation, Rosslyn, VA.

Lurie, Carol Ann. 1986. "Private Voluntary Organizations: The Participation Paradox." Master's thesis, Department of Urban Studies and Planning, Massachusetts Institute of Technology, Cambridge, MA.

Mahaffie, John B. 1987. "Grassroots Development in St. Vincent: The Organization for Rural Development." Paper for Economics 233, George Washington University, Washington, DC.

Mann, Charles K., Merilee S. Grindle, and Parker Shipton. 1990. *Seeking Solutions: Framework and Cases for Small Enterprise Development Programs.* West Hartford, CT: Kumarian Press.

Marsh, Robin. 1991. "The Importance of Risk in Technology and Diffusion: The Case of Small Maize Producers in Mexico." Paper prepared for the XVI Conference of the Latin American Studies Association, Washington, DC.

Martens, Bertin. 1989. *Economic Development That Lasts: Labour-Intensive Irrigation Projects in Nepal and the United Republic of Tanzania.* Geneva: International Labour Office (ILO).

Martin, Patricia A. 1983. *Community Participation in Primary Health Care.* Washington, DC: American Public Health Association.

Martinez-Nogeira, Roberto. 1984. "El Desarrollo de Instituciones Para la Participación y el Cambio Social: El Instituto de Desarrollo Social y Promoción Humana de Argentina y el Instituto de Promoción Economico-Social de Uruguay." Paper prepared for the Inter-American Foundation, Rosslyn, VA.

Martinez-Nogeira, Roberto. 1987. "Life Cycle and Learning in Grassroots Development Organizations." *World Development* 15 (Suppl.):169–77.

Maybury-Lewis, Biorn. 1987. "Federations in the Brazilian Rural Workers Movement: A Case Study of the Federation of Agricultural Workers in Rio Grande do Sul." Paper prepared for the Inter-American Foundation's research on grassroots support organizations, Rio de Janeiro, Brazil.

Meehan, Eugene J., with Charles Reilly and Thomas Ramey. 1978. *In Partnership with People: An Alternative Development Strategy.* Rosslyn, VA: Inter-American Foundation.

Midgley, James. 1986. *Community Participation, Social Development and the State.* London and NY: Methuen.

Montgomery, John D. 1988. *Bureaucrats and People: Grassroots Participation in Third World Development.* Baltimore: Johns Hopkins University Press.

Moser, C. O. N. 1989. "Community Participation in Urban Projects in the Third World." In *Progress in Planning,* vol. 32, part 2. Oxford: Pergamon Press.

Murray, Gerald F. 1984. "Pastures, Charrales and Wood lots: Returning the Wood Tree to Costa Rican Cattle Country." Paper submitted to Inter-American Foundation.

Murray, Gerald F. 1985. "Promotores, Patrullas and Cash Flows: An Analysis of Credit Projects in Rural Guatemala." Paper presented to the Inter-American Foundation, Rosslyn, VA.

North, Douglas C. 1990. *Institutions, Institutional Change and Economic Performance.* New York: Cambridge University Press.

Office of Technology Assessment (OTA). 1988. *Grassroots Development: The African Development Foundation.* Washington, DC: OTA.

Organization for Economic Cooperation and Development (OECD). 1989. *Development Cooperation in the 1990s.* Report by Joseph C. Wheeler, Chairman of the Development Assistance Committee, Paris.

Otero, María. 1986. *The Solidarity Group Concept: Its Characteristics and Significance for Urban Informal Sector Activities.* New York: Private Agencies Collaborating Together (PACT).

Padrón, Mario C. 1982. *NGOs and Grassroots Development: Limits and Possibilities.* The Hague, Netherlands: Institute of Social Studies.

Padrón, Mario C. 1986. "Los Centros de Promoción y la Cooperación Internacional al Desarrollo en América Latina." Paper presented at Europe-Latin

America: Political Relations and Development Cooperation, International Seminar, Buenos Aires, Argentina.

Padrón, Mario C. 1987. "Non-governmental Development Organizations: From Development Aid to Development Cooperation." *World Development* 15 (Suppl.):69–77.

Pastore, José. 1988. *A Fundação Interamericana No Brasil (1983–87): Esta Valendo a Pena?* São Paulo: Inter-American Foundation.

Paul, Samuel. 1982. *Management of Development Programs: The Lessons from Success.* Boulder, CO: Westview Press.

Paul, Samuel. 1987. *Community Participation in Development Projects: The World Bank Experience.* World Bank Discussion Paper No. 6, Washington, DC.

Paul, Samuel. 1988. *Governments and Grassroots Organizations: From Co-existence to Collaboration.* Washington, DC: World Bank.

Perraton, H., et al. 1983. "Basic Education and Agricultural Extension: Costs, Effects and Alternatives." Staff Working Paper, World Bank, Washington, DC.

Peterson, Stephen B. 1982. "Alternative Local Organizations Supporting the Agricultural Development of the Poor." In *Institutions of Rural Development for the Poor,* edited by David Leonard and Dale Rogers Marshall, 125–50. Berkeley, CA: University of California Press.

Pezullo, Susan, 1988. "Curdled Milk: A Mexican Dairy Project Gone Sour." *Grassroots Development* 12(3):2–9.

Private Agencies Collaborating Together (PACT). 1989. *Trends in PVO Partnership: The Umbrella Project Experience in Central America.* New York: PACT.

Private Agencies Collaborating Together (PACT). 1990. *Steps Toward a Social Investment Fund.* New York: PACT.

Putnam, Robert D. 1992. "Governance and the Civic Community." Paper presented at the International Conference on Culture and Development in Africa, 2–3 April, Washington, D.C.

Rahnema, Majid. 1985. "NGO's: Sifting the Wheat from the Chaff." *Development: Seeds of Change* (Journal of the Society for International Development) 3:68–71.

Reichert, Josh. 1985. "Process Evaluation of CO-321, Centro de Cooperación al Indigena (CECOIN)." Memo, the Inter-American Foundation, Rosslyn, VA, December.

Reilly, Charles. 1985. "Who Learns What When How? Development Agencies and Project Monitoring." In *Social Impact Analysis and Development Planning in the Third World,* edited by William Denman and Scott Whiteford, 32–49. Denver, CO: Westview Press.

Ricca, Caryl. 1987. "Culture and Development: IAF Funding of Artisan Groups in Latin America and the Caribbean." Unpublished paper, George Washington University, Washington, DC.

Ritchey-Vance, Marion. 1991. *The Art of Association: NGOs and Civil Society in Colombia,* Country Focus Series No. 2. Rosslyn, VA: Inter-American Foundation.

Salmen, Lawrence F. 1990. "Institutional Dimensions of Poverty Reduction." Working paper WPS 411, Country Economics Department, World Bank, Washington, D.C., May.

Salmen, Lawrence F., and A. Paige Eaves. 1989. "Between Public and Private: A Review of Non-Governmental Organization Involvement in World Bank Projects." Policy, planning and research working paper WPS 305, World Bank, Washington, DC.

Sanyal, Bishwapriya. 1991. "Antagonistic Cooperation: A Case Study of Nongovernmental Organizations, Government and Donor Relationships in Income-Generating Projects in Bangladesh." *World Development* 19 (10): 1367–79.

Scurrah, Martin. 1987. Personal communication with the author.

Shifter, Michael. 1984. "Centro de Investigación y Desarrollo de la Educación (CIDE): Finding a Niche." report, Inter-American Foundation.

Smith, Brian H. 1983. "U.S.-Canadian Non-Profit Organizations as Transnational Insitutions." Yale University Program on Non-Profit Organizations Working Paper No. 70, New Haven, CT.

Smith, Brian H. 1987. "An Agenda of Future Tasks for International and Indigenous NGO's: A View from the North." *World Development* 15 (Suppl.): 87–93.

Smith, Brian H. 1990. *More Than Altruism: The Politics of Private Foreign Aid.* Princeton, NJ: Princeton University Press.

Society for Participatory Research in Asia. 1990. "Strengthening the Grassroots: Nature and Role of Support Organizations." Report prepared by L. David Brown and Rajesh Tandon, New Delhi, India.

Spaulding, Thomas. 1982. "Grassroots Support Organizations in Rural Development: A Review of Four Organizations Funded by the Inter-American Foundation." Unpublished paper, George Washington University, Washington, DC.

Stone, Linda. 1989. "Cultural Crossroads of Community Participation in Development: A Case from Nepal." *Human Organization* 48(3):206–13.

Tendler, Judith. 1981. *Rural Credit and Foundation Style.* Rosslyn, VA: Inter-American Foundation.

Tendler, Judith. 1982a. "Rural Projects through Urban Eyes." World Bank Staff Working Paper No. 532. Washington, DC: World Bank.

Tendler, Judith. 1982b. "Turning Private Voluntary Organizations into Development Agencies: Questions for Evaluation." Program evaluation discussion paper no. 12. Washington, DC: U.S. Agency for International Development.

Tendler, Judith. 1983a. *Ventures in the Informal Sector and How They Worked Out in Brazil.* Evaluation Special Studies No. 12. Washington, DC: U.S. Agency for International Development.

Tendler, Judith. 1983b. *What to Think about Cooperatives: A Guide from Bolivia.* Rosslyn, VA: Inter-American Foundation.

Tendler, Judith. 1988. "Northeast Brazil Rural Development Evaluation: First Impressions." Draft prepared for the World Bank, Cambridge, MA.

Tendler, Judith. 1989. "What Ever Happened to Poverty Alleviation?" *World Development* 17(7):1033–44.

Tendler, Judith, John Hatch, and Merilee Grindle. 1984. *Captive Donors and Captive Clients: A Nicaraguan Saga.* Rosslyn, VA: Inter-American Foundation.

Toth, Csanad, and James T. Cotter. 1978. "Learning from Failure." *International Development Review/Focus* 3:27–32.

Turner, Bertha, ed. 1988. *Building Community: A Third World Casebook from HABITAT International Coalition.* London: HABITAT International Coalition.

Uphoff, Norman. 1987. *Local Institutional Development: An Analytical Sourcebook with Cases.* West Hartford, CT: Kumarian Press.

Uphoff, Norman. 1989a. "Approaches to Community Participation in Agriculture and Rural Development." In *Readings in Community Participation,* vol. II, 417–498. Washington, DC: Economic Development Institute, World Bank.

Uphoff, Norman. 1989b. "Drawing on Social Energy in Project Implementation: Results of a Learning Process Approach to Improving Irrigation Management in Sri Lanka." *Sri Lanka Journal of Development Administration* 6(2): 103–37.

Uphoff, Norman. 1992. *Learning from Gal Oya: Possibilities for Participatory Development and Post-Newtonian Social Science.* Ithaca, NY: Cornell University Press.

Uphoff, Norman, John M. Cohen, and Arthur Goldsmith. 1979. "Feasibility and Application of Rural Development Participation: A State of the Art Paper." *Rural Development Committee Monograph Series*. Ithaca, NY: Cornell University.

van der Heijden, Hendrik. 1985. *Development Impact on Effectiveness of Non-Governmental Organizations: The Record of Progress in Rural Development*. Paris: Organization for Economic Cooperation and Development (OECD) Development Center.

van Dusseldorp, D. B. W. M. 1981. "Participation in Planned Development Influenced by Governments of Developing Countries at Local Level in Rural Areas." In *Essays in Rural Sociology in Honor of R. A. J. Van Lier*, 25–88. Wageningen, Netherlands: Department of Rural Sociology of the Tropics and Subtropics, Agricultural University, Wageningen.

VanSant, Jerry. 1986. "The Role of International and Host Country NGOs as Intermediaries in Rural Development." Paper, Development Alternatives, Inc., Washington, DC.

Wasserstrom, Robert. 1985. *Grassroots Development in Latin America and the Caribbean: Oral Histories of Social Change*. New York: Praeger.

Weber, Ron. 1991. "Agua Para el Pueblo: The Experience of the Foundation." *Grassroots Development* 14(2):8–10.

Weintraub, Sidney, Peter Szanton, and William P. Stedman, Jr. 1984. "The Inter-American Foundation Report of the Evaluation Group." Paper, Austin, TX.

Wenner, Mark. 1989. "Assessing Screening Mechanisms and Institutional Viability: A Case Study of a Costa Rican Group Lending Scheme." Paper prepared for the Inter-American Foundation's Mid-year Conference of Doctoral Fellows, Quito, Ecuador.

Wolfe, Alan. 1991. "Three Paths to Development: Market, State, and Civil Society." Paper presented at a meeting on Development, International Cooperation and the NGOs, 6–9 March 1991, Rio de Janeiro, Brazil.

World Bank, Operations Evaluation Department. 1985. *Sustainability of Projects: First Reviews of Experiences*. OED Report No. 5718. Washington, DC: World Bank.

World Bank, Operations Evaluation Department. 1987. *World Bank Experience with Rural Development 1965–1986*. OED Report No. 6883. Washington, DC: World Bank.

Yudelman, Sally W. 1987. *Hopeful Openings: A Study of Five Women's Development Organizations in Latin America and the Caribbean*. West Hartford, CT: Kumarian Press.

Zalaquette, José. 1981. "Informe de Evaluación de la Fundación Comunidades Colombianas (FUNCOL)." Manuscript in the files of the Inter-American Foundation, Rosslyn, VA.

Index